# An Ancient Land
## Genesis Of An Archaeologist

David Price Williams

*Paperback:* ISBN 978-1-913802-50-9
*Hardback:* ISBN 978-1-913802-49-3
*eBook:* ISBN 978-1-913802-51-6

*Book design by: Ian Sharman*

FRONT COVER PICTURE:
*View over Jerusalem from the Mount of Olives (© DPW)*

BACK COVER PICTURE
*Entrance to the Church of the Holy Sepulchre, Jerusalem (© DPW)*

www.markosia.com

First Edition

This is for my *indlulamitsi,*
my very own giraffe.

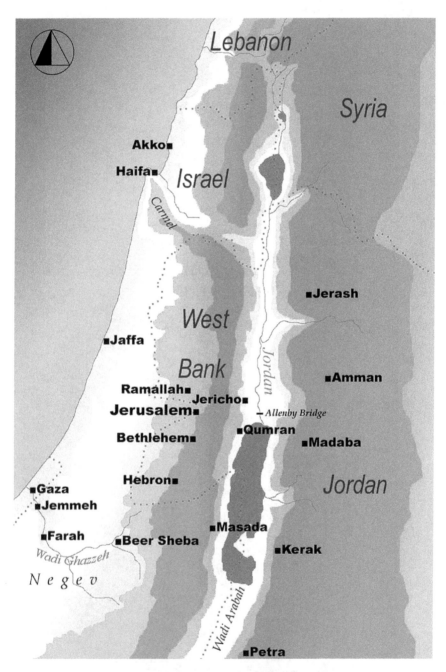

*Map of the Holy Land (© DPW 2020)*

# CONTENTS

# SOME FORETHOUGHTS AND THANKS

This account recalls my time in the Middle East, from 1970 to 1975. Before I travelled there I thought I knew everything about that part of the world; at least, I knew everything about what it was like at the time of Nebuchadnezzar or Xerxes or Caesar Augustus. I knew its ancient peoples and their histories, their kings and their councillors, their cities and their sieges. I knew what languages they spoke, and the various dialects they used and in what kind of script they wrote. I could read everything they'd ever written - in the original tongues. I could even have spoken with them if they'd been alive today. But they weren't. They'd all been dead for more than two thousand years. By comparison, about the present peoples of the area, and about their recent past, I knew less than nothing - absolutely zero. I didn't know who they were or where they'd come from, or when. None of that had ever interested me. All that was about to change with my first visit to the Levant, and especially to Jerusalem; I was about to experience the region as it was in the here and now, red in tooth and claw!

There are many people I would like to thank for my new life - friends and colleagues, people who affected me peripherally and those who were at the centre of my encounters. There were people like Bill Melson and Alan Linden, Victor E. Krantz Jr. and Chip Vincent, Desmond Collins, Carolyn Grigson and Peggy Nuttall, Paul and Mary Slawson and Tony West. There was Peter Parr, my tutor who nurtured me through my PhD, Peter Dorrell and 'Peter' Grimes (W. F. Grimes) the Director of the Institute of Archaeology who gave me much encouragement. There were some of my students, like Jonathan Tubb and Robin Duckworth. Then there were the people with whom I worked closely like Juliet Prior and Rita Gardiner, scientists who were instrumental in changing my thinking on the nature of recent earth history - what came to be the crux of my research as it unfolded. And there were all my friends in East Jerusalem and Bethlehem, people like Sami ed-Dhib and Raji Khoury. At the top of my list I have to thank my closest friend Louis Hattem and his wife Nura. Louis helped me immeasurably, always smiling, always positive. He truly was like a brother to me.

I must also thank my loyal proofreaders too, Eleanor Klepies, Rebecca Davies and especially Lynn Gunter, who have tirelessly sought to keep my writing in check and my spelling as close to correct as they could.

But I reserve my ultimate thanks for my lovely wife Sue who entered into this whole escapade one way and came out of it totally differently. To her I give my heartfelt gratitude for what has been, and still is, more than forty-five years of support, affection and love! I wrote 'An Ancient Land' at the instigation of our daughter Alice, who incidentally may even have been conceived there, and of our son Dave. They wanted to know what on earth I'd been doing in the Middle East and why I have retained such strong loyalties to some of the people I encountered there.

As with my other memoires, I have heard voices from those times, speaking clearly to me out of the mist as though they're just over my shoulder, as though I'm still sitting at the leopard-skin bar in the Ritz Hotel in Ibn Khaldoun Street, or travelling down the hot tarmac on the road to Jericho. My memory of events has not diminished with the years, and, if anything, my imagination is livelier than ever, perhaps too lively sometimes, so please excuse any glaring errors, exaggerations or omissions. I've told it as I saw it. Maybe someone else would have felt it and seen it quite differently. But it was a highly formative time for me, in my thinking, and dare I say, in my life.

When my time there was over, I knew that for me nothing would ever be the same again. At times it was wonderful and exciting, frustrating and pioneering, as well as both deeply disheartening and incredibly exhilarating by turns. I wouldn't have missed it for the world. But I'll never go back. I knew at the time that they were golden days for me there, especially in Jerusalem, but once it was over, I knew it was over for good. Remembering what that great philosopher Heraclitus of Ephesus once said, 'No man can bathe in the same river twice!' I had to admit to myself that life had to move on and with the completion of this remembrance I know that chapter is closed.

*Kew, December 2020*

CHAPTER ONE
# GAZA TRIP

*In the GAZA-RAFAH area the Armistice Demarcation Line*
*shall be as delineated in paragraph 2.B (i) of the Memorandum*
*of 13 November 1948 on the implementation of the Security*
*Council resolution.*
Armistice agreement between Egypt and Israel,
23 February 1949

One morning in the autumn of 1969 I was pottering about the Institute of Archaeology in Gordon Square WC1 alternately drinking coffee and languidly drawing illustrations for someone or other's forthcoming excavation publication, when a disembodied voice called idly from the next room.

"David, there's a chap coming this afternoon from Washington, from the Smithsonian. I think you ought to meet him."

This was Peter, my tutor, speaking. I discovered that he was referring to an archaeologist, a certain Dr. Gus van Beek by name, who was Curator of Old World Archaeology in the National Museum of Natural History, Smithsonian Institution, in Washington DC, an august body indeed. I found out on further enquiry that Dr. van Beek was a Middle Eastern archaeologist who had worked at the famous excavations in Jericho in the 1950s directed by the even more famous Dame Kathleen Kenyon (it was automatically assumed that anyone who had worked at Jericho under Kay Kenyon was to be revered as a person of supreme training). Following from this van Beek had then become well-known in his own right by excavating sites in South Arabia, styled at that time as 'The Aden Protectorate', in particular a pre-Islamic site named Hajar bin Humaid. Because of this he was one of the very few archaeologists who also had access to the archaeology of Saudi Arabia, a rare and significant honour.

Anyway, Dr. van Beek – 'call me Gus' – duly turned up that afternoon in Room 209 and I was introduced to him.

"Say, David, I'm about to excavate a new site near Gaza. Well, it isn't new actually, it was first excavated in the 1920s by your friend Flinders Petrie, and you have some of the material from that excavation here at the Institute I believe. It's Tell Jemmeh. You know the site David? Well I need a field surveyor and Peter recommended you. We can't get good field surveyors in the US. It's really an awfully important position. Of course, we'd pay you. Well, what do you say?"

I forbore to tell him that I'd learnt my field surveying skills from Lonnie, a native of New York City, but there we are. I was newly returned from my first overseas assignment, at Knidos in south western Turkey, and news of my apparent success there must already have reached these hallowed halls of WC1.

I temporised.

"Well, I had expected to go back to Knidos in Turkey where I was this year. That's an awfully important site too and …"

"And, David, we'd pay for your airfare, and, and a weekly stipend,' he continued, unabated. 'It's such an awfully important job! I'm sure you'd love it. It's going to be really great. And you'd be a great asset to the dig, you know."

Never mind how 'awfully important' the job was, I suddenly thought, or that I'd be a great asset; it was a paid position, actually paid, and as usual I was totally skint. In an instant, that fact left no contest as far as I was concerned.

"Well, I'd have to …"

"Great, David! I knew you'd do it. I'll send you a letter confirming all the arrangements, the flight details, salary, things like that. It'll be great, just great!"

And with that Gus was gone.

"Tell me about Tell Jemmeh," I asked Peter when he'd left, "And what's the stuff he referred to that we have here?"

I spent the next few days finding out what I could about Tell Jemmeh and 'my friend' Flinders Petrie. William Matthew Flinders Petrie, who had in truth died before I was born, was considered to be just about the father of Middle Eastern archaeology, especially in the Nile Valley and the Holy Land. He was extremely well-known to everyone that was anyone in the subject and had published enormous amounts on Egyptology and his excavations in Egypt and in adjacent Palestine. He was so famous in fact that he could be said to have created the science of archaeology single handed.

And from his various later excavations in Palestine in the 1920s he had accumulated a considerable collection of pottery and small finds belonging to the last two millennia BC which he had donated to University College London and these had then had been further donated to the present Institute of Archaeology upon its creation as a research institute in 1957 to form the basis of a reference collection. Among that material were cabinets of pottery from Tell Jemmeh, largely made up of non-descript groove-decorated grey ware bowls belonging to sometime in the Iron Age. I'd never really paid them much attention before, but we had cupboards-full of it.

As for Flinders Petrie himself, it turns out that he had been the grandson of the famous navigator Matthew Flinders, the man who had surveyed and named Australia. Surveying very much ran in the young Flinders' veins too it seems, and it is said that he had calibrated his own theodolite while yet a young man, indeed an amazing feat. I knew people at the Institute who had known Petrie, or who certainly knew of him, and one point that kept recurring was that he was naturally extremely numerate. He apparently had a party trick of being able to multiply huge numbers together in his head, as though moving a mental cursor on the slide rule in his mind's eye, he said. His interest in Egypt was initially stimulated by the quack science of 'pyramidology', a belief in the mystical properties of the dimensions of the Great Pyramid at Giza, and it was that which had attracted him to travel to Cairo in 1880 to measure the pyramid's exact proportions, something which he did with supreme accuracy and which had never previously been achieved.

But he soon forsook this bizarre pursuit, going on instead to excavate numerous sites up and down the Nile Valley, and with his highly methodical approach he was able to transform the study of Egyptology from a practice peopled by romantics and dilettantti into a thoroughly responsible and recorded science. Amongst many other approaches, he invented a corpus of pottery types, assigning a number and letter to each shape and decoration of vessel he dug up. With this corpus, he was able to record all his classification of forms as he discovered them, which allowed him to write the report of each season's excavations on the steamer on his way home to Britain, where it was immediately published upon his arrival, an astonishing achievement. His name was appended to a bibliography with over a thousand entries.

In the late 1920s, Petrie fell out with the British authorities in Egypt which caused him to relocated his researches to southern Palestine, then under a British Mandate, Palestine having been ceded to Britain by the League of Nations as part of the notorious Sykes Picot agreement, a Franco/British plan to dismember the Ottoman Empire at the end of the First World War. He was already in his mid-seventies. The story has it that in late 1927 he travelled by train from Cairo to Gaza and immediately started to dig the sites along the Wadi Ghazzeh, the southern border of Ancient Palestine with Egypt. He identified three great tells here, Ajjul, Jemmeh and Farah. These were the huge mounds of the ruins of Bronze and Iron Age cities which had been alternately the southern defensive cities of the people of Palestine or the northward positions of Egyptian expansion into the Levant. Tell Jemmeh was the middle one of these, a few kilometres southeast of Gaza City and its orange groves, on the edge of the Negev Desert.

Several senior members of the Institute had actually worked with Petrie as young students in 1928 when he had excavated Tell Ajjul, the ancient site of Gaza itself, just up the road from Jemmeh, and dig stories were rife if a little alarming. Petrie, it seems, was known for his extreme asceticism and thought nothing of the privations of the deserts where he was working. Apparently he had a fearsome wife named Hilda who ran the commissariat on his excavations with a rod of iron.

"We only ever had pilchards and bully beef, bully beef and pilchards, to eat, all tinned of course, and never ending," I was told. "What we didn't finish at one meal would turn up at the next. That's all there was for months on end!" And speaking of the hardships they had to endure, "She was a harridan, his wife, a real hard case! Those sites in Palestine are covered, and I mean literally plastered, in bits of broken pottery – smashed up storage jars, amphora handles, endless bits of bowls and jugs – everywhere. Well, we had been excavating in Gaza for a few days when I happened to ask Lady Petrie (Flinders had been knighted by then) what we should do, since the toilet paper had run out. 'Oh' she had replied, 'You can use pot-sherds, that's what Flinders and I do!' and turning on her heel she walked off! It was terrible."

I wondered whether that was the kind of thing that Gus had in mind for our own excavations or were our rear ends to be spared the abrading effects of ancient earthenware? No matter. In due course details of his proposed excavation were sent by Gus from Washington and I was appointed field surveyor of the new Smithsonian expedition. I learnt that this was to be a very formal organisation, and I noted that my 'plane ticket, when it arrived, had been paid for by the US Government, no less. Did that mean I was a US employee I wondered? My salary had been set at $100 a week to be paid in the celebrated green backs of that country, and all my other expenses would be taken care of, I was assured. $100 a week! This was a considerable amount of money for a starving PhD student – the dollar was then about 2:1 so it represented some £50, times the twelve weeks for which the dig was scheduled, making it £600 in total. With few personal outgoings to take care of I reckoned that was quite a haul.

I looked at the airline ticket I'd been sent. It was from London via Athens to Tell Aviv on TWA, their daily 'round the world clockwise' flight. It was only when I saw the destination 'Tell Aviv' that a small qualm entered into my calculation. Tell Aviv was the main airport for the state of Israel. Wouldn't that cause a problem for Gus in relation to his burgeoning work in South Arabia, I wondered? The face of the whole Arab world was implacably set against

Israel, which had only been established just over twenty years previously in the turmoil at the end of the Second World War, and it was perceived by everyone in the region to be the pariah of the Middle East. That much I knew. Still, with the US Government behind the excavation what could possibly go amiss, I thought. And anyway, I had studied the ancient world of Palestine and its archaic languages extensively. The ancient and the modern shouldn't be allowed to impinge on one another; that was my response.

Thus equipped with the invincible armour of ignorance I boarded the famous Trans World Flight Number 001 and flew across Europe to Athens and then on across the Mediterranean to the Levant. It was during this second part of the flight that the 'plane actually flew over the southern tip of Turkey and looking through the left hand window I wistfully saw the Knidos peninsula passing below us from something like 30,000 feet.

Later that afternoon we arrived at Lod Airport outside Tell Aviv and upon disembarking were confronted by total chaos, an unrestricted and bawling bedlam, with everyone pushing and shouting to get through immigration, to find their luggage, to get through customs, to exit the building itself, to find a cab and to leave the airport. Fists were waved, fingers were pointed and faces contorted into accusing grimaces. It seems that nothing was too small that it couldn't be argued about. The officials were surly, the passengers were universally ill-tempered and the net result was certainly unpleasant. This was my first experience of Israel and its inhabitants, and it was to be the first of many similar encounters. From whatever country these people had originally come, they were not too fulsome about their appreciation of their fellow travellers.

Notwithstanding this bruising introduction I found a cab and handing the scrap of paper with my destination to the driver we drove off at high speed on the road south. It was to be an uneventful journey of some two hours. The scenery became less and less green as we approached the edge of the Negev, a huge semi-arid region which led south to the Egyptian border. The sun set and we travelled the last part of the way in the dark, so I had no idea where I was when we arrived at a high wire fence and a gateway guarded by a watch tower manned by heavily armed soldiers, with arc lights illuminating the perimeter. It looked a bit like a prison camp left over from the war. This was Kibbutz Re'im, which was where the expedition was to be billeted, so with some trepidation I handed my passport and letter of appointment to the officious gate guard and we were ushered through.

I discovered that Gus had rented a portion of the kibbutz to house the staff and the volunteers who were to do the digging on the excavation, a few of whom came out to greet me. They were Americans who had been studying archaeology with Gus in Washington, mainly young people the same age as myself or younger and they were really friendly, the antithesis of the cantankerous bunch I had met when I had first de-planed. I breathed a sigh of relief as Gus strode through the mêlée and welcomed me to the expedition. I was shown to my quarters, a room in a hut with a veranda and a shower which I was to share with three other men, set in a garden of pepper trees. I had arrived.

Next morning we drove to the site. It was only now I discovered that Tell Jemmeh was not only vaguely in the general vicinity of Gaza, it was right on the edge of the Gaza Strip, a Palestinian Arab enclave which had been deliberately left outside the borders of Israel in 1949. It had been under Egyptian control until 1967 since which time it had been occupied by the Israelis and as a result was in constant political turmoil and not to put too fine a point on it, its inhabitants were considered to be singularly antagonistic to the new Jewish state. The border was only about three kilometres or so away across the desert, and the people who had settled the local kibbutz were paranoid about possible incursions by insurgents from the huge and fractious population there, imagining that they themselves would all be summarily murdered in their beds or blown up in the fields around about any and every day of the week. As a result, the perimeter fence was constantly and heavily patrolled and there were security barriers everywhere where we were staying.

Also, although the archaeological site itself was only a few hundred metres away, it was in the direction of the Strip. The last part of the road that led to it was a dirt track along which the settlers feared land mines could have been planted at any time during the hours of darkness. With this in mind it had to be swept each morning at dawn by an army bomb disposal unit even before we could approach the excavations. It was all a bit alarming, though I took some comfort, albeit academic, from the parallel that Tell Jemmeh had probably also been of important military significance way back in the Iron Age three thousand years ago and here it was, still showing the same characteristics. This offered a continuity of sorts. But thinking this through again, it didn't really help. We were here on someone else's active military front line in the real world of today, and that didn't have the advantage of being sometime way in the distant past where I could think about it dispassionately and without apprehension. Pushing such despondencies temporarily to the back of my mind, I got out of the vehicle and looked up at the tell. It was huge – thirty metres high and three hundred metres in diameter, all man-made. This was the 'heap of ruins' that we had come to dissect.

Tells are a familiar feature of the Middle Eastern landscape. Flat topped and steep sided these mounds are a phenomenon which characterises the archaeological evidence for the civilizations that have risen and fallen in this part of the world, from Egypt to Mesopotamia and from Arabia to Persia. They were built, layer by layer, period by period, by the lives and toil of the cultures of the past; they are made up of the remains of the alleyways and streets, the city walls and temples, the palaces and forts, and the houses and hovels of the countless thousands of people who over the millennia have lived there. And the magic ingredient that drew these disparate peoples together, from an archaeological perspective at least, the glue that united them all and welded them forever to this one city, this one tell, even if they themselves perceived that generation by generation they were very different from one another, as they well might have been, is one very simple substance – mud. The Middle East abounds in dwellings made of simple sun-dried mud bricks. Before the recent advent of concrete, mud brick was the building material of choice, a perfectly acceptable and a very flexible medium, with the added advantage of the interior of such buildings being warm in winter and cool in summer.

Neolithic people at the very initiation of village life ten thousand years ago had used mud bricks. Buildings from the beginning of the Bronze Age some five thousand years ago were built of them on a grand scale, and they were still using them to build palaces in the Iron Age about three thousand years ago. Through the endless years of ancient history the people here had erected mud brick structures, plastering the walls with mud, making their floors with mud and covering their timber and brushwood roofs with mud. And when the cities burned down as they were wont to do because the roofs so frequently caught fire, the debris from the mud bricks remained. The inhabitants stoically flattened them out and built the next city in the same way as the last, one on top of another. They made the bricks near water off the site and then carried the newly-dried bricks to the top of the remains of the previous city to build their new walls - again, and again, and again. Unwaveringly, these mud brick cities were built on the same site, for hundreds and sometimes thousands of years.

Eventually, the height of the mound of ruins grew so elevated above the landscape and held such a commanding view of the surrounding countryside that it made the site even more desirable, being even more defensible, so that the next inhabitants were wont to surrounded the summit of their mound with even more walls, and towers, and gatehouses, all of course also built of mud brick, all carried from below the site, which only added even more to the accumulation of the occupation layers, until the tell reached gargantuan proportions, a 'mound of many cities' as one archaeologist called it. And here was Tell Jemmeh, the local example of that same phenomenon.

Petrie thought that it had been the site of the Biblical city of Gerar, where according to the Book of Genesis Abraham and Isaac had each passed his wife off as his sister, leading to endless complications involving Gerar's Philistine king, Abimelek. But that's another story! Gerar or no, I spent the morning looking around the tell and evaluating how it was to be surveyed. There was no mistaking Petrie's excavation. He had managed to remove a huge portion in the centre of the mound in just a few months in 1927/8. It had eroded considerably in the intervening forty or so years, but there was still quite a large proportion of the site untouched. Gus pointed out where he would like his trenches to be laid out in four metre squares with metre-wide baulks, which I duly did, setting them at 45 degrees to the edge of the tell to ensure that any walls that may be discovered were likely to cross the trenches at an angle rather than being parallel to the sides, an important consideration for the evaluation of the stratigraphy of the site, the way in which the layer-cake of different strata were to be dissected and understood. And with that the new excavations of Tell Jemmeh began. During that first week I also laid out base lines, sub stations and survey points and triangulated the whole tell and its surroundings as a preliminary to producing a contour survey of the mound, which was to be my main task.

The Americans I was with were on the whole a congenial group of people, but that first week I naturally gravitated towards one person in particular, the photographic expert rejoicing in the name of Victor E. Krantz Junior. Vic was the expedition photographer, a senior staff member who actually was employed by the Department of Photography at the Smithsonian, so he knew Gus, and more importantly, he knew about the way in which the expedition had been put together - the details, the gossip, the personalities involved and so on. He spoke with an attractively slow American drawl and we got on well together from the very beginning, helped in no small part by our mutual love of gin. We had both brought a couple of bottles of the noble juniper-flavoured elixir with us to relieve the boredom of the evening hours, he to mix martinis and me to fix gin and tonics. It was a partnership made in heaven, and I was to learn a lot too from Vic about what was going on with the dig that was not seen on the surface, as well as more importantly how to mix the perfect dry martini.

It was on one evening that first week, gins in hand on the veranda of our billet, that he suggested to me that I accompany him up to Jerusalem for a little recreation on the forthcoming weekend, when we would have two full days off. He'd arrived a few days early from Washington and had already spent time enjoying himself there before coming to the dig. He knew of a good hotel, he said, near the Old City, and he'd like to go back there and meet the new friends he'd made. We could get a lift to the nearest local town and a bus up to the Holy City. I agreed with alacrity. I needed to buy more tonic for my nightly rounds of G &T anyway. So it was, after work stopped at midday on that Friday that we showered off the dust and set out on our jaunt. On the bus up to Jerusalem I swear we met the same cantankerous people I had seen in the airport when I first arrived, but being full of the spirit of adventure I ignored them and after an hour or two drove into Jerusalem bus station.

"Where's the hotel?" I asked Vic.

"Well, David, it's certainly not in this part of the city. This is the Israeli part. We want the Arab part."

And with that, he hailed a cab and we bundled in.

"Hotel Ritz!" he said, and the driver, with a wince or two, sped across the city through the dividing line between the two parts of Jerusalem and into the Arab streets of Al Quds, the 'Holy One'. In a side street near the Old City we drew up outside the Hotel Ritz, not quite as grand as the one in London or Paris perhaps, but an attractive modern building in Ibn Khaldoun Street. We were greeted by a doorman and helped out. In a trice I was standing in the cool of the reception area being welcomed by the chap behind the desk. I did not know it then, of course, but the Ritz was to become the centre of my alternate universe and the chap behind the desk, one Louis by name, was to become one of the firmest friends I have ever made. Some years later he was to arrange something for me which led to the most important event in my whole life, before or since, and which was to change my existence absolutely and totally; but that of course was still in the future.

On that first afternoon, however, I took my room key and on Vic's suggestion, we repaired to the bar for a late afternoon libation. We toasted our arrival in the Holy City, appreciating the comfortable surroundings and the leopard-skin stools and after a suitable time we ordered a refill. Replete with a juniper-favoured bonhomie we retired to our rooms for a pre-cocktail snooze before taking another shower and then fulfilling another engagement at the leopard-skin bar – it wasn't real leopard-skin, you understand, but after a week suffering the privations of the desert anything felt like an improvement. Thinking about it now, five decades later, I was to spend many a happy hour at that bar over the years to come, sampling the various bottles of liquors on display which, like the widow of Zarephath's barrel of meal and cruse of oil, 'wasted not neither did they fail!'

Thus it was in a gin-induced state of euphoria that Vic and I sauntered through the lobby of the Ritz Hotel and out into Ibn Khaldoun Street in search of a night's entertainment, or at least dinner, which we found in the upper rooms of the Golden Chicken Restaurant around the corner – 'Arab dishes a specialty'. By comparison to the very restricted diet of the dig, it was culinary nirvana. This was my first experience of Arab meze – hummus, tahini salad, baba ganoush, tabbouleh, olives and fiery green chilli peppers all eaten with *khoubiz* , Arab flat bread, and washed down with liberal helpings of Latrun Red, a wine lovingly made by the Trappist monks of the Latrun Monastery, a 19th century holy pile outside Jerusalem. They may have sworn an oath of silence, these monks, but the wine spoke volumes on their behalf about the bright sunshine and balmy days of the Mediterranean. In case we had missed any of its nuances, we ordered another bottle with the *mousakhan*, Palestinian grilled chicken on a bed of red onions favoured with a liberal sprinkling of the spice sumaq. And throwing caution to the winds, we accepted an 'on the house' glass of arak with our Arabic coffee to end the evening. I don't know if the Latrun monks had found it yet, but I felt that we had a glimpse of paradise that evening, and in an alcoholic haze, we retired to the hotel, to bed and to a well-earned sleep, with the promise of the Old City in the morning.

CHAPTER TWO
# THE HOLY CITY

*Jerusalem the golden,*
*with milk and honey blest,*
*beneath thy contemplation*
*sink heart and voice oppressed:*
*I know not, oh, I know not,*
*what joys await us there;*
*what radiancy of glory,*
*what bliss beyond compare!*
St Bernard of Cluny, 1145

What an extraordinary vision Jerusalem has presented to the world over the centuries, indeed over the millennia, representing as it does the epicentre of three of the world's great religions. The capital of Solomon's kingdom in Old Testament times, it was the site of the Temple on Mount Zion, focus of the most passionate Jewish aspirations, where the Ark of the Covenant, the very throne of God, had been kept. It was the city where Christianity had begun, where Jesus of Nazareth had arrived from Galilee at the end of his ministry and where he had been crucified at Calvary by the Romans under pressure from the Sanhedrin and subsequently had risen from the dead. And it was Al Quds, the Sacred One, the first place towards which, according to the beginning of the Quran, a Muslim should face in prayer, before that became changed to Mecca, and it was the place where Muhammad miraculously travelled by night and ascended into heaven, making it the third most holy place in Islam.

For a city that is at once so consecrated, so revered, and so divinely inspiring to so many people it ought to be a place of supreme peace and profound piety, one of overwhelming devoutness and hallowed prayer. But alas this is not the case, nor it seems was it ever such. It has been fought over, argued about and tossed to and fro by the storms of history with such ferocity that even today it bears the scars of thousands of years of strife, a strife which is still being perpetuated. Blood has flowed along its streets, since the time it was first built by the Jebusites in the Bronze Age right up to the present, when it was occupied by Israeli forces at the end of the Six Day War in 1967, a mere three years before my first visit. From the era of the ancient Israelites, or the time of the Assyrian King Sennacherib, or the Babylonians during the reign of

Nebuchadnezzar, from the Persian King Cyrus and the Hellenes at the time of Antiochus Epiphanes, or the Roman Empire under Hadrian, or the epoch of the Byzantine Emperor Justinian, the Umayyad Caliphs, the Crusader Kings from Baldwin I onwards, the Ottomans under Suleiman the Magnificent right up to the days of the British Mandate and into contemporary times, Jerusalem has been a perpetual target for over-weaning political ambition and intense religious bigotry. And yet, as I walked into the Old City that morning, for me its very stones exuded a clear, calm and spiritual message which transcended the centuries; for the first time in my life I felt I was walking on hallowed ground.

I had been infused with the essence of Jerusalem from my childhood. You could say that it had been woven into the very fabric of my being. I have read all the Biblical references to it, I've sung hymns about it, and I've listened to sermons in English and in Welsh extolling its quintessential and aspirational beauty, and its remarkable sacredness. In Welsh it's known as Caersalem, the Fortress of Salem, a name so revered that many chapels the length and breadth of Wales are named for it. Indeed the psalmist could have been speaking for any of the three faiths when he wrote 'If I forget thee O Jerusalem, let my right hand forget her cunning; let my tongue cleave to the roof of my mouth if I prefer not Jerusalem above my chief joy'. And now, here I was entering into the very heart of this sacred city, centre of the spiritual cosmos. After breakfast on that Saturday Vic and I walked down to the Damascus Gate, called more picturesquely in Arabic 'Bab al Amud', the Gate of the Column - apparently in Roman times Hadrian had erected a column just here. For the first time I saw the impressive defences built by Sultan Suleiman the Magnificent in 1537. They were still intact and standing to full battlement height.

But the thing which struck me most as I first entered through that ancient portal were the blocks which made up the paving of the gate and of the streets inside; they were so polished by the passage of human traffic over the centuries that they shone in the daylight, even in shadow. This was also my first experience of a Mediæval souk, the market city which has been a feature throughout the cities of Arabia from Cairo to Damascus and from Aleppo to Baghdad and beyond. Millions of feet have for a thousand years or more passed this way, going to and from the religious shrines, or engaged in the making and mending, or in the buying and selling of every commodity the Orient has to offer from saffron to saucepans. The air was heavy with the aroma of spices and sweetmeats, of vine leaves and vegetables. It was an atmosphere which was at the same time exciting and yet exotic to the senses; it spoke of great age and more especially of the great traditions with which the Arab world is shot through. But above all, Jerusalem is a place of great sanctity and prayerfulness, and it was that which really has set Jerusalem apart from any other exalted city of the Middle East – its holy places – and that is what we had come to see.

*  *  *

The one place which dominates the Old City, the Temple Mount, is the real personification of Jerusalem and the focal point of the city, revered by all three Faiths of the Book. After suffering the most turbulent of histories, it is today the nucleus of belief for hundreds of millions. This is where Solomon built the first Israelite temple, three thousand years ago, probably on the site of an even earlier Canaanite sanctuary dating back to the pre-literate Bronze Age. Reading between the lines of the Book of Kings, the scale and luxury of Solomon's temple and its associated buildings were his attempt to emulate the extravagance of a tenth century BC oriental despot, importing gold and expensive Lebanese cedar from Hiram, King of Tyre. It was a life-style it seems he could ill afford and he was forced to forfeit twenty cities in Galilee in payment for his profligacy, which apparently didn't please Hiram one bit. That temple was destroyed by Nebuchadnezzar in 587 or 586 BC when, according to the Old Testament, 'every worst woe befell the city, which drank the cup of God's fury to the dregs.' The people who survived the subsequent onslaught were taken to Mesopotamia into captivity, where apparently 'by the waters of Babylon, they sat down and wept and hung their harps on the trees'.

After being replaced by another temple in the Persian period, the Jewish temple was completely rebuilt by Herod, the Roman client king of Judea, at the end of the first century BC. Herod was not really a Judean. He was actually born into an Idumean family from beyond the borders of southern Judah and his mother it seems was a Nabatean Arab. As such, he was the ideal puppet for the Romans, more or less a local potentate who paid lip-service to Judaism but who was sufficiently removed from the power of the priests and the strict orthodoxy of the Pharisees that he was able to wield sway over them. The vast temple he built was his way of ingratiating himself against the censures of the local populace, but in case of rebellion he still built himself a number of strongly-made fortresses nearby to act as bolt holes.

The temple constructed by Herod was literally an overwhelming edifice. Built in the Roman style with vast and heavy masonry, it stood on a huge, rectangular, purpose-built platform which encased one complete hillside within the city, covering all the remains of previous religious shrines that were there. On the north side he erected the fortress known as the Antonia, named after his Roman patron, Mark Anthony, where he billeted his army in case of any immediate local crisis. After Herod's death, when the city fell under the direct rule of a Roman prefect, the best known of which of course was Pontius Pilate, the fortress was transformed into the Praetorium, the barracks for the Praetorian Guard, giving them direct access onto the Temple Mount in order to quell any religious disturbance which could easily lead to political unrest. This was what it was like in Jesus' day, when the local inhabitants by all accounts found themselves in a desperately uneasy relationship with their Roman masters.

The constantly simmering turbulence eventually broke out into open revolt in 66 AD, ostensibly over taxation, although religious intolerance was never far from the heart of matters. The Emperor Nero appointed an army general, Vespasian, to crush the insurrection. Vespasian and his son Titus, along with three legions, the X Fretensis, V Macedonica and the XV Apollinaris, defeated most of the rebels in Judea and finally began a prolonged siege of Jerusalem. Those trying to escape the city were crucified, as many as five hundred a day by some accounts, until eventually the besiegers finally broke in through the walls in 70 AD, massacring many of the remaining inhabitants. The defences of the city were destroyed as well as the Temple and other buildings. The city was then put to the torch and most of the survivors sold into slavery. Although the uprising continued to flicker on in the Judean Wilderness, the last of the rebels were eventually overcome at their final stronghold, Masada.

It is the remains of Herod's temple, or rather, not the actual temple but the western revetment of the platform on which it was built, that constitutes what is known today as the Wailing Wall, revered by Jews all over the world as the site of the Temple of Jehovah, and where they pray with great fervency, facing the wall and pushing religious messages into cracks in the masonry. It's ironic that it should be this piece of wall, since the whole edifice had been built by Herod in a cynical ploy to placate the Jews and to keep them in their place; I imagine he would be smiling in his tomb if he knew. With the reawakening of the Zionist movement at the beginning of the 20th century, even this fragment of broken wall has become a source of friction between the Jewish community and the Muslim religious leadership, who are worried that the wall is being used to further Jewish nationalistic claims to the Temple Mount and thus to Jerusalem as a whole. Outbreaks of violence at the foot of the wall have become commonplace. *Plus ça change!*

During the time of the Emperor Hadrian some sixty years after the Jewish War of 66 AD, the population again broke out into feverish rebellion against the Roman régime. This was too much for the administration in Rome, and in 135 AD Hadrian had the city totally demolished, its inhabitants slaughtered and its monuments erased once and for all. It's thought that more than half a million people were killed in this uprising. He built a new city in a Roman style on top of the obliterated ruins and he gave it a new name, calling it after his patronymic, Aelia Capitolina. Forbidding Jews ever to return, he commanded that a pagan temple be built to Capitoline Jupiter on the site of Herod's shrine, and as such the city continued for two hundred years until the Roman Empire itself collapsed and the eastern portion of the empire, the Greek speaking half, was transformed by Constantine into the New Rome, the Byzantine Empire, with its new capital at Constantinople and its newly permitted religion, Christianity, now approved by the royal house. So it was that in about 325 AD Jerusalem officially became a focus for the worship of Christ. Helena, Constantine's mother, made a pilgrimage to the Holy City in search of the sites associated with Christ's life and more importantly with his death and resurrection. The discovery of the location of Golgotha, the place of the crucifixion, became her overwhelming objective. But amongst many other searches for the holy places of Christianity, she is said to have built a small church on the Temple Mount, the Church of St. Cyrus and St. John. It was soon enlarged and called 'Hagia Sophia', the Church of Holy Wisdom, but it must be said that the location of Solomon's temple was never to take on the importance for the Christian faith that it had for the Jews, nor that it was to assume for the third religion of Jerusalem, Islam, which was yet to come. The Christians had other areas of the Old City in mind.

Palestine was seized by the Muslims in 637 AD and Jerusalem was to be of great significance to the new conquerors. According to the Quran they believed that the Temple Mount was the place where Abraham had been about to sacrifice Ishmael when God intervened. Of course if you happen to be Jewish, it was Isaac that nearly was done to death not Ishmael, but that's a small detail in the overall scheme of things.

Even more significantly for the Arabs, the Temple Mount was the place to where Muhammad had made his famous Night Journey, and from where he then ascended to heaven and into the presence of Allah, accompanied by the Angel Gabriel. In the centre of the mount is an upstanding rock, where, according to some believers, you can actually see the hoof-print of the horse that translated Muhammad into paradise, the so-called Foundation Stone.

The location was established as the focal point of the Islamic miracle of this night journey by Caliph Omar ibn al Khattab, a companion of the Prophet, and indeed the Islamic building here is sometimes referred to as the Mosque of Omar. But the Qubbat As-Sakhrah, the Dome of the Rock, was actually constructed by a later successor, the Umayyad Caliph Abd al Malik, in 691 AD on top of the rock in question. It has been renovated many times since but it retains much of its original character. And today it is this shrine which forms the most notable feature of the Jerusalem skyline, the one which always features in the pictures of the Holy City, a most colourful octagonal building with the dramatic golden dome (see front cover).

But the Muslims also built the Masjid al-Aqsa on top of Herod's Platform, al Aqsa Mosque, the Farthest Mosque, referring again to Muhammad's Night Journey. The combination of the Farthest Mosque and the Dome of the Rock together make for Muslims the Haram ash-Sharif, the Noble Sanctuary, which has become the third most sacred place for Muslims world-wide. And this was one of the places which the Crusaders targeted some four hundred years after the Muslim conquest when they besieged Jerusalem in 1099 AD. On the 15 July of that year, the Crusaders, who had spent some three fractious and troublesome years crossing Europe and Anatolia to reach Jerusalem, broke into the Holy City after a prolonged siege. The resulting massacre was apparently awful to behold. Nearly the whole population, Saracens, Jews and possibly even Christians, were brutally put to the sword and many were deliberately mutilated. The story of the carnage wrought by these Knights of the Cross and their belligerent army has seared itself into the collective memory of Muslims to this very day. And with the butchery came limitless rapine and plunder, until the streets of the city were said to be ankle deep in blood and gore and the Crusaders had sated themselves. It was only then that they turned instead to the devotion which they remembered had been their original aim. Whatever savagery the inhabitants endured that day, Jerusalem had become Christian, and after a short while the platform of the Noble Sanctuary was to be the home to the Knights Templar, who became the most powerful of the military orders of the Crusades.

Originally known as the 'Poor Fellow-Soldiers of Jesus Christ and the Temple of Solomon', but thankfully more commonly known as the Knights of the Temple, they took the name because they had been given a part of the al Aqsa Mosque as their residence, which had been quickly converted by the Crusaders into a palace, and thus they identified their headquarters with the Temple of Solomon. They used the palace to store their equipment and built stables in the basement where, according to one visiting German monk, they kept up to ten thousand horses. They also built a small chapel at the side, which by all accounts was used from time to time by Muslims as well. But in less than one hundred years, on 2 October 1187, Jerusalem was recaptured by Saladin the Ayyubid, at which time the Haram was re-consecrated as a Muslim sanctuary. The cross which the Crusaders had erected on top of the Dome of the Rock was replaced by a golden crescent, and a wooden screen was placed around the rock below. In this fashion it has remained in Islamic hands ever since.

There was one nervous moment during the First World War when the past suddenly leapt up to confront the future. It concerned the British campaign to oust the Ottoman Turks from Palestine. The British Prime Minister Lloyd George and his Cabinet hatched a plan to roll up the Turkish Empire, beginning with Palestine, and in May 1917 Field Marshal Edmund Allenby was appointed as the commander of British Expeditionary Force in Egypt prior to his invasion of the Ottoman Empire. This was the same campaign with which Lawrence of Arabia was involved, in his case beginning from the deserts of the Arabian Peninsula. That same October Allenby marched northwards and after a series of battles he finally arrived at the gates of the Old City in December, fulfilling Lloyd George's demands that he should be in Jerusalem by Christmas. According to T. E. Lawrence, who was there at the time, he persuaded Allenby to dismount from his cavalry horse and walk rather than ride into the city, lest the Arabs, specifically the Muslims, perceived that Allenby, known affectionately as 'the Bull', was, with the defiance and considered arrogance of a conqueror, emulating the Crusaders by riding in on a charger. The famous photograph which captured the scene at the time shows Allenby marching purposefully with his aides through the Jaffa Gate, one of Suleiman's original entrances into the city, wearing a pair of riding jodhpurs having indeed just left his horse outside. In his proclamation of martial law later the same day, he made it clear that 'every sacred building, monument, holy spot, or shrine of whatsoever form of the three religions will be maintained and protected according to the existing customs and beliefs to those whose faith they are sacred.' The Islamic shrines were safe once more, at least for the time being.

But the strength of feeling which the Platform has evoked throughout its history is still very much in evidence today and if anything even more violent emotions have surfaced, in particular between today's Jews and Muslims, and even between Jews and their fellow Jews. Following the occupation of

Arab East Jerusalem by the Israelis in1967, a number of fanatically obsessed Zionists advocated the immediate use of high explosives to blow up the Dome of the Rock and bulldoze the whole place flat again as a prelude to building a new Jewish temple here. Astonishingly they were supported in this insane endeavour by cohorts of half-crazed evangelical Christians, particularly in the USA, who fervently supposed that this would constitute a preamble to Armageddon, the end of the world, leading to the 'Second Coming' of Christ and to the Last Judgment, when according to some traditions the righteous dead will be resurrected and together with the righteous living will be glorified and taken to heaven. There are still people to this very day who actually believe this foolishness to be the case. In fact, on 21 August, 1969, a fire broke out inside al-Aqsa Mosque that more or less gutted the south-eastern wing of the sacred building. Initially the Arabs blamed the Israelis for the fire, thinking that they wanted to destroy the Muslim holy places, and the Israelis blamed the Arabs, declaring somewhat irrationally that they had started the blaze so as to provoke further hostility. However, it turns out that the conflagration was started by neither side, but by an evangelical Australian Christian instead. He was one of the characters who thought that by burning down al-Aqsa Mosque he would hasten the destruction of the Haram which would instigate the 'Second Coming'. Not unnaturally he was later committed to a lunatic asylum.

From a historical standpoint, some Israeli archaeologists, if one can so dignify them with the title, when they had gained access to the Wailing Wall in 1967, began tunnelling into the Temple Mount in the hope of finding the remains of Solomon's original building which they felt would have been a major religious and, I suppose, a politically significant coup. After some considerable unpleasantness, this was stopped. Thankfully these same people have shown no signs as yet of trying to tackle the top of the Platform itself. I would suggest that the instant any infidel trowel or crow bar were to breach the paving stones of the Haram, let alone its holy shrines, it would precipitate an immediate and nasty attack of jihad, a holy war, and the end of the world would then indeed be nigh!

Paradoxically, as it turns out, some more orthodox Jews maintain that according to their interpretation of Jewish law it is strictly forbidden for any person at all in any way to enter into or onto the Temple Mount, particularly if they happen to be Jewish. Ostensibly this is for fear of treading on the place where, during the time of Solomon, the Ark of the Covenant was kept, in the place that the Old Testament calls the 'Qodesh haQodashim', the Holy of

Holies of the Temple. In that they believe this to be God's dwelling place on earth there was every chance you would be unconsciously walking over God himself, which if true would of course in their eyes constitute a most heinous religious offence. So they had settled for conducting their characteristic head-banging and bobbing up and down in a narrow section of the western retaining wall on the outside of the Temple Mount. But following the 1967 occupation even they thought nothing of bulldozing flat a sizable part of the Arab quarter of the Mediæval city to expose more of this external wall of Herod's Platform. However, nothing loathe, the even more Ultra-Orthodox Jews among them who have currently appointed themselves the custodians of the Wailing Wall have instigated continuous and vehement disputes with less fanatical, more liberal Jewish worshippers, throwing chairs and other missiles at them in an attempt to forbid them from even approaching certain parts of this external Wall. All this theology might appear to be in the realm of Loony Tunes to most people, but it's apparently very real to others, and potentially, as you can imagine, highly explosive.

Well, with all the history and unpleasantness that the Platform has witnessed, Vic and I wanted to see what it was all about and so after entering through the Damascus Gate we set off walking into the Old City. We slowly threaded our way through the labyrinth of the Mediæval souk in the shade of its ancient walls and narrow streets, alive with vitality and industry and perfumed with the myriad fragrances of Araby. We passed shops selling colourful bolts of cloth, passed butchers' shops with joints of goat and lamb hanging up, passed the Palestinian women from the surrounding villages wearing their traditional long black dresses with embroidered bodices, who had spread blankets in the street on which they had piled aubergines, green peppers, grapes, olives, vine leaves and bunches of parsley and coriander.

They sold these literally by the stone, on a steel-yard with a limestone cobble they brought with them acting as a weight. We also passed shops offering gaudily-coloured sweets and others selling sugary pastries. The alleys were a press of humanity. Donkeys piled with impossibly high loads roped in boxes trotted up and down goaded on by Arab boys in their ankle length shirts and knitted skull caps jostling lazily with tourists stopping to take photographs. Grizzled old men in galabiehs sat on stools drinking coffee from miniscule handless cups, some smoking a shisha, a water pipe. The shops were like kiosks, open to the street, one filled with piles of hazelnuts, walnuts and pistachios, another with various ground spices mounded into polychrome conical heaps in plastic washing-up bowls, another had old fashioned ladies' knickers stacked in bundles in front of it, and there was even one which displayed garishly-tasselled belly-dancer's outfits. Up and down these stepped alleys porters toiled, bent double, carrying heavy loads of all kinds on their backs roped to frames secured by leather belts passed over their foreheads. It was like nothing I'd ever seen before, full of animation and clamour and the cries of the shop keepers selling their wares.

We made our way under the shaded awnings of the quieter parts of the souk until we arrived at a tiny security gate and passing through it we emerged suddenly from the deep shadow of the city into the full brightness of the Haram ash-Sharif, with its vast open pavements dappled here and there with a few cypress trees. By comparison to the souk it was impressively wide and spacious. And there before us in the centre stood the Dome of the Rock, the Qubbat As-Sakhrah itself, vibrant in the morning light, its ethereal gilded dome reflecting the golden rays of the sun which glinted too off the blue and white tiles of its walls. It was a most beautiful sight, truly inspiring, such a vista that has greeted pilgrims here for almost a millennium and a half and speaking of all the majesty of heaven, of the brilliant artistry of the Mediæval Islamic world and of the perpetuity of belief. I was rendered speechless in respectful admiration by the sight. We walked around the Platform in the full glare of the midday sun, passed shaded fountains where a few men were sitting and talking quietly between prayer times, and we passed in front of al Aqsa mosque with its silver dome, less striking than the Dome of the Rock but nevertheless a magnificent oriental pile. I truly felt I was in another world.

That evening, gin in hand, and sitting on the balcony of my room at the Ritz as the sun was setting over the Holy City, I heard the voice of the muezzin echoing up from the Platform, invoking the faithful to the last prayer of the day. I thought of all the drama that the Platform had experienced over its long history, all the worship and adoration it had inspired, and all the hopes and prayers it had engendered. And as I sipped my G & T in the cool of the twilight, I recalled the beginning of the muezzin's cry; *'Allahu akbar'* – 'God is Great!' Yes, I thought, I suppose that's probably quite true.

CHAPTER THREE
# THE ENTRY OF THE QUEEN OF SHEBA

*And King Solomon gave unto the Queen of Sheba all her*
*desire, whatsoever she asked, beside that which Solomon gave*
*her of his royal bounty.*
First Book of Kings 10:13

Back at the dig things were moving painfully slowly. Gus, an expert in excavating mud brick, didn't want to miss the slightest nuance in the topmost levels of the site. The eight squares that he had opened were each supervised by a trained archaeologist, each of whom was on the whole adhering to Gus's snail's pace, none of them being at all familiar with the mud genre. Petrie had taken only six months to investigate a huge part of the site. At the rate Gus was going it would take six years, or maybe even sixteen years, to get anywhere near the same result.

While in Washington, Gus taught courses on Near Eastern archaeology through the Smithsonian Associates Program, a sort of extra-mural teaching, and the work force responsible for the scraping and brushing at Jemmeh, the American volunteers that he had brought with him, were all his students. They were totally untrained in any kind of archaeology and were constantly asking questions about what they were doing. For one of the trench supervisors this became wearingly monotonous.

"They keep on asking me, every five minutes, 'Is this a stone, is this a bone, is this a sherd, is this a turd?' It gets boring, you know."

But gradually, ever so gradually, the levels in the trenches began to go down. It was not inspiring stuff though - broken mud brick, mud brick debris, mud brick pits, mud brick slump and mud brick wash. There was a certain sense of sameness about the site as day followed day. Each working morning began shortly after the sun had risen and as soon as the access road had been swept for explosive devices. But from the moment digging started, the site quickly became engulfed in a fine dust as the scrapings from each trench were further sieved to recover any fragments the diggers had missed, and with a wisp of wind and with copious perspiration the workers themselves were quickly turned to a powdery taupe which blended with the very remains they were excavating.

Some respite was provided from the daily tedium by a break for breakfast when the whole crew came down from the top of the tell and sat on the ground under a grove of young eucalyptus trees. Breakfast had been brought by truck from Re'im and was the same as the locals ate – cucumbers and tomatoes with additional tomatoes and cucumbers, uninspiring insipid yogurt and maybe some days a hard-boiled egg and bread. That was it, with water to drink; not the gastronomic experience one might have hoped for.

At the end of the working morning we were all transported back to the kibbutz where a similar repast awaited us for lunch. Technically the afternoons were free, but those of us who constituted the 'staff' were expected to return to the tell and work again for another couple of hours until sundown, after which we would again be driven back to the gulag, as we came to call it. Supper, taken in the communal canteen, was invariably a deeply disappointing combination of yet more cucumbers and tomatoes and maybe some chicken, or more accurately, chicken spare parts. This kibbutz specialised in rearing battery hens kept for the production of frozen chickens which presumably they sold to local distributors to sell on to the stores in the bigger towns. But what we got to eat were the clapped out, deformed, rejected, end of the line, 'didn't make the grade' birds, or worse, the giblets left over from the processing, of which there must have been vast amounts. We often had concoctions apparently made from body parts of no known ornithological provenance – parts of the innards of birds that anatomically I for one certainly couldn't recognise, try as I might.

The food, such as it was, was cooked by all the kibbutz members in turn. Most had originally come as peasant settlers from Morocco and Algeria, or from the Yemen, and their knowledge of how to cook anything was at best minimal and more often than not totally lacking. The problem was exacerbated by a change of shift during any given day, when the first group would plan the menu for the evening, for example, spiced chicken innards, but they were followed later in the day by a group who preferred to use the giblets in some totally different way, and frequently the chicken bits arrived at the table having been cooked twice, in two different ways, by which time they were barely edible. There was a soup that I well remember that they produced on several occasions on a Friday as a lunch-time special which was particularly gruesome. It arrived in an aluminium bowl in the centre of the table, and someone sitting nearby doled out spoonfuls of it to the others round about. As the level of the soup fell in the bowl, the constituent parts of the soup revealed themselves, the main component being chicken feet - not chicken legs, but chicken claws - which arose slowly out of the remaining liquid like the arm of the Lady of the Lake. It soon became obvious that the idealism of some of the inhabitants for this commune-like existence was being sorely tested every day of the week, especially by the victuals. The dream of living the perfect egalitarian life on a collective farm was stalling because of the very things they were farming. Many found it difficult to maintain a civil approach to their fellow inmates under such inauspicious conditions, which they had to endure day in and day out.

One of our volunteers, slightly misquoting that famous 1918 Broadway jump and stomp number, summed it up perfectly:

'How ya goin to keep 'em down on the farm, now that they've seen the farm?'

We all felt for them in their sullenness.

\* \* \*

I was finding out more about Gus. He originally came from a rather strict religious upbringing in Tulsa, Oklahoma, and had obtained a divinity degree from a theological seminary in Chicago where he had studied to become a Presbyterian minister. He had then become involved with Johns Hopkins University, and it was there that he had met William Foxwell Albright, the eminent biblical archaeologist and Semitics scholar who became his mentor and it was under his influence that Gus had completed a doctorate in Middle Eastern archaeology. Gus had brought with him to the Jemmeh expedition his second wife Colyn (he'd divorced the first), and two of their three teenage sons. Colyn was a lovely lady and she and I talked a lot in the evenings about the excavations with which she and Gus had been involved in South Arabia. As we talked, I began to put two and two together, and the combination of Oklahoma, William Foxwell Albright and archaeology in South Arabia jogged something in my memory. May I digress to tell the tale?

When I had first arrived at the Institute of Archaeology in London in 1966, four years before I had come to Jemmeh, I had made a good friend there, Mohammad Abdul Wahed, who as it turned out was slated to be the next Director of Antiquities for the Government of Aden in South Arabia, soon to become South Yemen. We were having coffee together one morning when he suddenly announced, out of the blue:

"David, you've just got to come with me to the Dorchester Hotel in Mayfair this afternoon. I've got to meet this man there and I need some support."

He then told me the story about the truly extraordinary millionaire and gun-toting antiquarian Wendell Phillips, who, it transpired, was the man we were due to see. Wendell Phillips was first and foremost an oil magnate, but he was also a bizarre character. He'd made a vast fortune through owning oil concessions in the Sultanate of Oman. It was said that Wendell owned more oil concessions that John Paul Getty, then considered to be among the wealthiest people on the planet. Wendell himself had come from very humble beginnings in California, brought up in a staunchly fundamentalist Southern Baptist family and indeed he had for a time been a preacher for that cause. Quite how he'd acquired his vast fortune of concessions I never fully discovered, but with it he set out to explore the ancient civilizations of South Arabia, in particular those associated with the legendary Queen of Sheba. Perhaps he was trying to prove the literal truth of the Bible; who knows? Anyway, with his amassed fortune he was able to buy Biblical scholars whenever and wherever he wanted, and one of those had been William Foxwell Albright, the celebrated American academic and Near Eastern archaeologist. In the early 1950s Wendell had identified and then got permission from the local Imam to excavate the Moon Temple at the capital of the ancient Kingdom of Sheba, Marib, but no sooner had he uncovered it than local unrest, never far from the surface among those lawless tribesmen, forced him and his whole expedition to flee for their lives.

Now, fifteen years later, he was proposing to return to South Yemen and therefore he naturally enough sought the support of the new Director Designate of Antiquities, my friend Mohammad Abdul Wahed, whom he had somehow discovered was studying in London at the time. So, to the Dorchester that afternoon we went, Mohammad and I. The idea was that Mohammad would purport to speak poor English (he actually spoke it perfectly) and that he had brought me along to 'translate' Wendell's propositions into Arabic to slow the whole conversation down and allow Mohammad to place a little distance between himself and the great man. When we arrived, Wendell was already waiting in the lobby. He was a handsome character, and greeted us very fulsomely.

"Hiya Moohammed, how ya doing. This is who? David? Well hiya David, good to see ya! Let's sit down and have some tea."

And with that he guided us into a corner of the lobby where there were some tables and chairs and the tea was duly ordered.

I noted that as he spoke, he punctuated every few sentences of his conversation with phrases like "Of course, when I first started out, y' know, I was selling newspapers on the streets of Chicago at a few cents a time ..." It seemed to mean a great deal to him that he had risen from obscurity to be the man he was today by the strength of his own efforts. But he soon got to the nub of his proposition.

"Now, Moohammed, if I'm gonna invest two million dollars in this here new archaeological expedition in your part of the world, I'm gonna need guarantees, know what I mean?"

Mohammad turned to me and said in Arabic,

"WHAT? How much did he say? Two million dollars? That'll be American I take it?" The amount Wendell was suggesting was worth a small fortune in the 1960s.

"Listen Mohammad", I said, aside, "I'll bet there are people in South Arabia who would sell their own mother to get their hands on just a tiny fraction of that. I'd be very careful. This guy could be really dangerous!"

And so the conversation went on. Wendell strode forward with his extraordinary proposals, and Mohammad stepped back deftly at every twist and turn. In the end they agreed that the whole thing should be put in writing.

"Say, talking of writing, I'm writing a new biography," informed Wendell, seamlessly moving the conversation on.

"Oh, who of?" I countered.

"Jesus Christ," he said, without wavering. "You wanna see?"

And with that he ushered us into a lift and up to the fourth floor, where he seemed to have commandeered all the rooms. All the doors were open and banks of secretaries were typing away in various parts of adjoining suites.

"This is my research team," he announced. "The book's gonna be finished soon. You seen my other books David? This is my newest one, 'Unknown Oman'. It's just come out. Here, have a copy!"

And with that he picked up a book from a pile against the wall, and inscribed the fly leaf in a bold hand 'To David with fond alohas from Wendell'. I have it to this day.

"Well, Moohammed, you just gotta come to dinner tonight. I'm gonna announce my engagement. I'm gonna get married."

So saying he pulled out a bulging folder of pictures from his pocket and flicked through them. They were all of a rather young, shy-looking oriental girl, Shirley Au, whom he said he'd met in Honolulu. The photos showed her in various stages of undress. She had apparently come to his attention as a Hawaiian hula dancer. But before we could ask any more, he snapped the folder shut and the afternoon audience with the great man - Baptist preacher, oil tycoon, archaeological adventurer, biographer of Jesus Christ, economic adviser to the Sultan of Oman (as it said on his card) and soon to be husband of the Hawaiian hula queen - came to an abrupt end.

I never did find out if he ever ran his expedition to South Yemen. But Mohammad did go to dinner that night and found himself sitting next to

Shirley, the bride to be. He told me the next day that he couldn't resist asking her what her family thought when she told them she was to marry such an extraordinarily wealthy man, the like of which I am sure none of them could ever have imagined.

"Oh," she had replied innocently, "my mother warned me about men like Wendell!"

Lowell Thomas, the journalist who'd made T. E. Lawrence's name, later seems to have called Wendell 'the American Lawrence of Arabia'. I also know that it's said that some years later Wendell and his Arabian experiences provided the model for Steven Spielberg's character 'Indiana Jones', but that's another story.

*  *  *

I related my experiences with Wendell to Colyn and amazingly I discovered that she herself knew him very well. They shared an interest in the archaeology of South Arabia and her husband of course had also known William Foxwell Albright, one of the academics Wendell had bought.

"You know how he got to know these professors, don't you David?" she related. "During the war Wendell was in the US navy, and when the fleet docked in a particular city, while most of the seamen would be off to find the red-light district, he would go to the nearest university and talk to the academicians there, and because communications were so bad they'd always ask him to give their greetings to their colleagues in the States when he got back there. Some months later when he was in the US he'd find the relevant professor and say 'Hi, I bring you filial greetings from Professor so and so'. He collected them, like stamps. It was amazing. By the end of the war he was acquainted with everyone."

She obviously knew him well. And she continued with her narrative.

"He was in the habit of buying celebrities, Wendell was. I've seen pictures of him for example with his arm around Charles Lindbergh, the well-known aviator, as well as photos of him with various Middle Eastern sheikhs. But I'm not sure he ever married his hula dancer, you know. Sunshine was very upset about him doing that!"

"Who?" I asked, puzzled.

"Sunshine; Sunshine Phillips, that's his mother. She had a big influence on him."

And after that, Colyn and I got on famously. She was in the process of publishing the material from the excavations of Hajar bin Humaid, the site that she'd been excavating with Gus in South Arabia. After a while, she sighed and declared that it was a great pity that 'Gussie' had decided to excavate in Israel. She was sure that it would put an end to the brilliant future they'd been planning in Arabia. When I asked her what had changed his mind, she hesitated for a while, and then said, somewhat wistfully:

"Oh, Ora. It was Ora. She is the one who persuaded him. That's why he's here, you know. It was all her doing."

And from that moment it quickly became apparent that all was not well in the van Beek ménage, three sons and a brilliant forthcoming career in South Arabian archaeology notwithstanding.

The mention of Ora, Ora Pilch as she was then, threw something of a spanner in the finely balanced expedition works. Ora was a highly extrovert, somewhat persuasive and dramatic young Israeli modern dance-teacher who had turned up to Gus's lectures in Old World Archaeology in Washington the previous winter. After a few weeks she had approached her esteemed tutor and suggested that with his background and experience he shouldn't be wasting his time excavating in the Empty Quarter of Arabia or wherever it was, but in the Holy Land, and more especially in Israel, where all the historical events he was describing had really taken place. Gus was apparently at first flattered by the attentions of this extraordinary lady and her terpsichorean achievements in the Land of Judah and after a suitable time, like a few weeks, he became mesmerized by her suggestion.

Not to put too fine a point on it, without another thought he changed his tack from South Arabia to the Promised Land and with the enormous budgets he could command at the Smithsonian he made representations to the Israeli Department of Antiquities, who persuaded him to invest in a new expedition to Tell Jemmeh. And that's how he had got here, so Vic told me anyway. And to complicate matters more, he had brought Ora with him as one of the volunteers, to assist him with his liaison with the locals he said. But there was more to it than that, as we all gradually became aware. By the time the expedition had begun, Gus had obviously become totally absorbed by his pirouetting pupil and her highly passionate personality. Just like Wendell a few years before, Gus's Oklahoma upbringing and preacher-man background had eventually led him to succumb to his very own danseuse, an unnervingly close parallel, I thought.

But Colyn was naturally not at all amused by the attention her husband was paying to Ora, notwithstanding the fact that Ora had also brought with her some of her own extended tribe – she and her current husband had had four children in quick succession, one or two of which had accompanied her to Jemmeh. On several occasions Colyn unburdened herself to me.

"I don't understand what he's up to", she objected bitterly. "This forward young woman is just the kind of thing that Gussie has railed against all the years I've known him. He has always said that women like that, you know, are immoral, full of sin, and should be avoided like the plague. I don't understand what he's doing paying her any attention at all?"

And one could imagine a fire and brimstone van Beek in his younger days preaching damnation upon all loose women, à la Sodom and Gomorrah. I got the impression that Colyn would be happy to cast Ora in the persona of Jezebel, the biblical widow of King Ahab, who had painted her face and adorned her hair before being thrown down from the window. At any event the whole affair represented an interesting distraction for everyone on the expedition crew, and conversations quickly grew up speculating on the exact relationship between them all. It certainly helped to alleviate the boredom in the long summer evenings before bedtime.

As for Vic, he told me privately that Gus's philandering had not gone down too well in the Smithsonian either. The authorities there were less concerned about any issues of moral turpitude that might be involved but they were severely questioning the fact that as a result of his recent infatuation he was giving up his pre-eminent position in South Arabia. To the academic world, and especially to his colleagues at the museum, this was far more significant, far more damaging. Also, there was the secondary issue of where they should be directing any public funds that might be involved.

"He got called in, you know, by the Director, who told him 'Listen, Gus, with all this shit flying around, you're being stabbed in the back, and you're being stabbed in the front, and man, well, you're like bleeding to death.'"

"And that's why I'm here, you know, to try to represent the Smithsonian in the middle of all this mess. Quite what I am supposed to do to make it any better I don't know, but that was the compromise that Gus made with the Director when this whole thing blew up, that he would have another member of the museum staff along to keep the peace, as it were. Fancy another martini?"

Thinking back over the years to those times, and to the minders that the Smithsonian sent out to preside, or otherwise, over the potential disasters of Gus's change of direction, by a strange and convoluted process it was this very aspect of the Jemmeh expedition which was eventually to set me off on the path to my own independent career as a field archaeologist. Naturally I didn't know that at the time, and it would be another year or two until it became obvious, but I suppose that with the outcome I now know, I should be grateful for Gus's indiscretions since they indirectly contributed to what I would do after Jemmeh. But this will appear in the memoire later. At the time I accepted Vic's offer for another of his specials and passed him my empty glass.

*  *  *

I have to say that Vic probably made the best dry martini east of the Sahara. To me he was the martini king, though I must confess I'd never tried one before I'd met him. There were a number of rules you had to follow, he told me seriously. Primarily the gin should go into the shaker first, after the ice of course, followed by the Italian white vermouth; it must be Italian vermouth too, no foreign substitutes would do.

Now, the amount of the vermouth was of paramount concern. Ideally, it should only be a small amount, say less than 20% of the whole, and even better results could be achieved by just swilling the neat gin around in an empty vermouth bottle to give it just a tad of flavour.

"If you want it any drier," he said with a twinkle, "Why, you just put the gin in the shaker with the ice and point the whole caboose towards Italy."

But that was a bit too perfectionist for our needs. To finish, you had to pour the resulting mixture out of the shaker with style, lifting the container up and down as you poured, and then you delicately slid the olive onto a cocktail stick and thence into the finished product. I have to say that the resulting experience was astonishing, and as there were no cocktail bars anywhere nearby to make comparisons, I had to agree with his diagnosis. Vic's dry martinis made your lips go numb!

A final ingestion of the juniperous fluid led inevitably to bed. Before retiring to my sack I was wont to lave myself with oil of citronella which was said to be a sure-fire way of keeping the mosquitoes from biting in the night. The only thing was it did give off a fairly heady aroma which tended to fill the room.

"Christ!" one of my room-mates exploded the first time I used it, "You smell like a fucking Christmas candle!"

I had to agree, but then I fell into a deep sleep unaffected as the rest of the inmates were by the visitations of the blood-sucking little insects. I slept well throughout every night I was there, though whether it was the application of the citronella oil or the sub-cutaneous tides of the gin I will never know. I kept up with both the whole time just in case.

CHAPTER FOUR
# SEPULCHRAL FISTICUFFS

*How I long for the New Jerusalem,*
*Just to see my Saviour´s face.*
*All my heart is in Jerusalem*
*My home, my resting place*
*I´ve heard that the streets are paved with gold*
*And the light there never fades;*
*I´ve heard of treasures to behold*
*That words could not explain*
TaRanda Greene 2012 : modern gospel music

As each weekend approached at Jemmeh, my spirits rose above the dust and dirt of the dig and Jerusalem beckoned. What a very fortunate country this is, I thought. Islam keeps Friday as the holy moment in the week; the Jews have their holy day, Shabbat, on a Saturday; and Christianity has chosen Sunday for its day of rest. There is nowhere else in the whole world where you can legitimately celebrate a three day weekend, every weekend of the year. In that the three religions are similarly inspired, there is probably some deep-seated, calendrically-computed cock-up hidden in the theological paperwork somewhere, but who cares. Whatever scribal miscalculation or mathematical blunder may have taken place, I made the most of every extended weekend while I was at Jemmeh by leaving as soon as was humanly possible at the end of the Friday morning shift and disappearing to the Holy City as fast as I could to convene for Friday evening prayers at the leopard-skin bar of the Ritz, 'Thank God I'm back' being the invariable text of the day. I soon got to know all the dramatis personae at the hotel and I was always welcomed with open arms.

Amazingly in the whole six seasons I was to spend in the Holy Land, whenever I went up to Jerusalem, which I did with never-failing zeal, I stayed nowhere else. It became a home from home for me, in the end more literally than I could ever possibly have imagined. The hotel was owned by a family of Christian Arabs who also had hotel interests in Amman, Jordan and in the Lebanon, in Beirut, and it was managed on the family's behalf by Abe Salami, a rather fiery but very respected hotelier. But the man I got to know well, and who became my very close personal friend and confidant, was Louis Hattem, who acted as a sort of under-manager and general factotum at the hotel and more often than not was on the reception desk. Louis lived in the Old City with his wife Nura and their three children, Mazi, Mary and the youngest, Hattem. And it was Louis who introduced me to the sacred Christian sites of the Old City. His own family had originally come from Damascus but Louis had lived all his life in Jerusalem and knew it like no other.

\* \* \*

The overwhelming focus for Christians, for the best part of two thousand years, has been the reputed place where Jesus was crucified and where he had been buried, and by extension where he also rose from the dead. This is the place that the Empress Helena, Constantine's mother, having been converted to Christianity, is said to have uncovered in 326 AD at the time she made her first pilgrimage to Jerusalem. When Hadrian had razed the original city to the ground at the beginning of the second century, he had used this quarter to build a temple to Aphrodite, but Helena was said to have seen through the mirage. One early writer says:

"When the empress beheld the place where the Saviour suffered, she immediately ordered the idolatrous temple to be destroyed, and the very earth on which it stood to be removed. When the tomb, which had been so long concealed, was discovered, three crosses were seen buried near the Lord's sepulchre. All held it as certain that one of these crosses was that of our Lord Jesus Christ and that the other two were those of the thieves who were crucified with Him."

I suppose you could say that Helena was one of the first, and certainly the most successful, Biblical archaeologist of all time, assuming of course that these early descriptions of her exertions are correct. But she didn't leave it at that either. Having checked which of the three was the true cross by having some passing woman heal herself of an incurable illness by touching it, she sent fragments of this cross, along with some of the nails which were conveniently found close by, back to Constantinople. From there they have at various times found their way around the nefarious ecclesiastical establishments of greater Europe. Although as a slightly choleric John Calvin pointed out some twelve hundred years later:

"There is no abbey so poor as not to have a specimen (of the Cross). In brief, if all the pieces that could be found were collected together, they would make a sizeable ship-load!"

Whatever the truth of the matter, a church was built by Constantine on the spot that his mum had identified, and this included, it was said, both the rock of Golgotha, the 'Place of the Skull', where the cross had stood, as well as a tomb originally belonging, according to the Gospels, to Joseph of Arimathea. This is alleged to be the very tomb in which the body of the crucified Jesus was laid, and from which three days later He rose again from the dead. These elements were incorporated into the new church. Now, such is the importance of the location that as the centuries progressed and Jerusalem changed hands between Christians and Muslims, and as antagonisms ebbed and flowed, the church was pulled down, put back up again, pulled down again and then re-erected a number of times, so that the building that now stands on the spot is a mishmash of styles, ages, designs, titles and chapels. Actually, the most imposing part of the current building, at least from the outside, is the huge dome erected over the tomb, but this only dates from 1870, after a previous dome had collapsed in a fire.

To gain entry to the present church, you have to walk across an open courtyard and through one small single doorway (see back cover), the only way in, a feature which has itself been the cause of some hairy incidents in the past when alternating groups of panicking pilgrims have trampled each other to death in the narrow ingress. Still, putting a positive gloss on things, I suppose if you were going to go it's as auspicious place as any to leave for the next world. Passing through this single entry you can then experience the whole panoramic confusion of the interior, at the centre of which is the *Kouvouklion*, 'the cubicle', a sort of tiny church within a church, which is said to be built over the very tomb of Jesus, or at least what remains of that tomb, since the limestone has been quarried back all round it to leave it as an upstanding bench. This is the most holy part of the whole edifice, and if the church and its component parts have witnessed their disputes and arguments over the centuries, this, the most sacred and revered of rocks, has paradoxically suffered the most. It has been bickered about so many times and quarrelled over with such vehemence it's a wonder it's still there.

The first thing you notice about the *Kouvouklion* is the queue of people trying to get into it – it can only hold about a dozen people at a time. Pilgrims line up to get their holy fix which in due course they will do, but as they wait they are pushed and shoved about by the officiating priests whose job seems to be to keep them in line. When their turn finally comes, they have to bend down almost double under a tiny doorway before they can enter into the very presence of, well, a slab of rock really, which they find decorated with religious icons and endless hanging lamps and candles in one huge chaotic muddle, looking something like an artistic and holy 'dog's breakfast'.

When I went in to catch a glimpse of the sacred stone, which incidentally you can't actually see because it is now totally encased in marble in an attempt to make it even more spiritually alluring, there was a priest inside the doorway whose clear objective as far as I could ascertain was to make himself as disagreeable as possible to visitors in order to discourage them from spending any time at all inside his tiny kiosk. He was in charge of candles, and as each pilgrim came in with a candle they'd bought in the main body of the church, he was supposed to tell them where to place their candle as they said a personal prayer to the Almighty and in certain cases where to kneel down to kiss the stone itself, or rather the marble covering the stone. After a few seconds the priest shooed the whole group out of the opposite doorway and the moment they'd left he grabbed all the candles and blew them out ready for re-sale to the next party of gullible worshippers. It was all desperately dispassionate and uninspiring, I thought, but then again I suppose I've never been one for myth and ritual.

There are lots of chapels and altars inside the rest of the church, one even dedicated to the Empress Helena herself which was built in Crusader times in a sort of cellar. It contains a chair said to be the very one in which the Empress sat while supervising the excavation of the True Cross, but quite how this has survived the extremes of destruction to which the whole building has been subjected is not vouchsafed to visiting pilgrims. This chapel is held sacred by the Armenian Church, as are two others, the Chapel of Saint Vartan, named for some obscure Armenian soldier of the fifth century who fought in an even more obscure war against the Persians, and the Armenian Chapel of the Division of the Robes, presumably referring to the lottery which took place over Christ's clothing at the time of the Crucifixion.

Meanwhile, on the other side of the church is the Greek Orthodox Catholicon, said to be the main altar of the church - if you happen to be Greek Orthodox that is - along with another two Greek Orthodox chapels, the Chapel of Saint Longinus, the Roman soldier who is said to have pierced Jesus' side with a spear, though quite why he achieved canonization I'm not quite sure, and the Chapel of Derision, which is where I assume it is believed Jesus was mocked by the soldiers. Further round are an additional three chapels also claimed by the Greek Orthodox Church. The first is the Chapel of Saint James the Just, who was amongst other things supposed to be Jesus' brother, the Chapel of Saint John the Baptist, though quite what he is doing here is something of a mystery, and the Chapel of the Forty Martyrs of Sebaste, commemorating some other abstruse group of Roman soldiers who were killed for confessing their Christianity in something like 320 AD.

Two other chapels are held sacred by a third Christian group, the Roman Catholic Church, and administered on their behalf by the Franciscan Order - the Chapel of Mary Magdalene which is said to be where she was confronted by Jesus after the resurrection, and the Chapel of the Apparition, where Jesus' mother met him, also after the Resurrection.

If you think that's complicated, you should see what happens next. The three denominations, the Greek Orthodox, the Armenians and the Roman Catholics, are the dominant three churches which hold sway in the building as a whole. But there are some lesser players who also have minor areas within the Church, like the Coptic Orthodox, the Ethiopians and the Syrian Orthodox churches; but that's about it. The whole of the rest of Christendom has absolutely no say in what happens inside the building at all – none of the Protestant denominations like the Church of England nor the Non-Conformists like the Lutherans, Calvinistic Methodists, Congregationalists, Presbyterians, Baptists, the Seventh Day Adventists, Plymouth Brethren, the Church of Christ and the Latter Day Saints and on and on as far left as you can go to the happy clappers and beyond - none of them gets a look in. The whole edifice of the Church of the Holy Sepulchre and the events that take place inside are orchestrated solely by the big three. Even the Copts, possibly one of the earliest Christian sects in existence, actually have to camp on the roof of the building, being excluded from remaining inside the main structure for any length of time.

You would think, wouldn't you, that in such a consecrated location, in such a sacred place, and with all the brickbats, with all the slings and the arrows of outrageous fortune which are forever being hurled at the Christian Church worldwide – kidnappings, murders, accusations of gross sexual misconduct, church burnings and general mayhem - by everyone from Islamic Jihadis to half-crazed nihilists and other demented soldiers of the Antichrist - that the various sects would actually huddle together for warmth, or at least they would support each other in a spirit of brotherly love, not to mention, in such a seminal place, an atmosphere of common Christian fellowship, but not a bit of it. Even among big three, the Greek Orthodox, the Roman Catholics and the Armenians – in fact especially among this trinity - there is an unrelenting and a bitter hostility which apparently stretches back for a millennium or more, back to the days of the warring popes and self-interested patriarchs of Mediæval times. Today it still manifests itself with such ill-disguised malevolence that it frequently breaks out into internecine warfare - literally. Monks, priests and other accompanying servants of

God arrayed in full religious regalia and armed with their respective holy trappings actually set about one another physically, the one group attempting to wallop the other senseless because they have left a door open, somehow disrespecting the other's sect, or moved a chair out of the sunlight into the other's space. If it weren't so tragic, it would really be side-splittingly funny to see these pious combatants brawling in the candle light. It happens all the time apparently, and the police have to be called in to restore order while the injured acolytes are hauled off to hospital to be bandaged up. It seems to me that in the vehemence of the fracas for domination over who owns what of the sanctified real estate, they have long since forgotten what the Church of the Holy Sepulchre has been built there to commemorate, namely the suffering and sacrifice of Our Lord for the salvation of humanity.

In an attempt to lessen the incidence of these ludicrous imbroglios, an uneasy status quo has had to be agreed, not that it is by any means always adhered to, which says that nothing, absolutely nothing, can be removed, re-positioned, redecorated or restored in those areas of the building which are in common use in case somebody else takes offense. This has meant that most of the interior of the Church is in an escalating state of disrepair owning to lack of maintenance, but such unwavering dilapidation does keep the peace, at least some of the time. One utterly foolish example of the use of the status quo is that at some point in the dim and distant past someone put a ladder up to one of the windows under the rotunda, the lantern underneath the dome, presumably to mend something, and afterwards they forgot to take it down again. No-one can remember who had done it, when, or more importantly, exactly why this was. But what is important is that being in a public area, even though it's on the outside of the building, the ladder cannot now be moved, so it's still there to this day, after hundreds of years, just above the entrance door. It's known as the 'immovable ladder', and as the name suggests, it doesn't get moved.

And if these idiocies weren't enough, there are various liturgical happenings of an even more alarming nature which are conducted by the followers of the various divisions of Christianity. Take the Greek Orthodox Church, for example. They hold a very special service in the Church every year on their version of the end of Easter Saturday when they annually relive what they call the 'Miracle of the Holy Fire', an event which seems to have been going on for at least the last thousand years, though how it first originated is anyone's guess. During this Paschal ceremony the Patriarch and his followers perambulate a few times around the *Kouvouklion*, which you remember covers the sepulchre. The Patriarch then enters the narrow doorway alone where it is firmly believed that simultaneously a fire from heaven is wondrously ignited on top of the stone of the tomb itself. From this miraculous holy flame, he lights his own candle and stepping outside into the body of the church offers the light to the first person who is waiting. Whoever this character may be, you can bet your life that he has paid a great deal of money to the Patriarch to be the primary receiver of the flame, and as such he becomes the first to light his candle from the one offered to him, as it is firmly believed that when it leaves the little building in the middle of the Church the 'Holy Fire' is at its most pure. From his candle, all the others are lit as quickly as possible by the thousands of members of the congregation who have been standing around in the dark waiting, and they in turn light the candles of those in the courtyard outside so that the holy flame can be enjoyed by everyone. It's then even flown by 'plane to the various orthodox countries like Greece, Romania, Bulgaria and Serbia. You can just imagine the perilous chaos which can ensue in the stygian gloom inside the church before the flame is lit, followed by the frantic scramble to obtain the light for oneself. The pandemonium and commotion this whole performance engenders has over the centuries caused endless people to be burnt, scorched, physically disfigured and even crushed to death. It's clear to any sane observer that the event is totally lacking reason, and more particularly, it's demonstrably dangerous too. But they never learn, and every year brings yet another opportunity for accidental self-immolation to the thousands of followers who turn up to witness the phenomenon.

But not everyone who professes Christianity believes that the 'Holy Fire' is such a miraculous event. Some people have accused the Patriarch of taking phosphorous with him into the sepulchre and lighting his own candle from that. The historian Edward Gibbon, in his magnum opus about declining and falling, describes the Miracle of the Holy Fire as a 'pious fraud', but then, being a self-confessed admirer of ancient Rome, he always set his face implacably against anything Greek. Another great Christian commentator, General Charles 'Chinese' Gordon, went even further. He maintained that the original Holy Sepulchre was nowhere near the present church but was to be found outside the Damascus Gate, just behind what is now the pizza parlour on Sultan Suleiman Road. This he maintained was a far better example of a first century AD burial chamber, with the advantage of a stone doorway as well, and in any case, he felt, the rocky outcrop into which this tomb is cut looked from some angles, if you squinted a little, somewhat like a skull and therefore had more right to be called 'Golgotha'. For many of the people denied a presence inside the Church of the Holy Sepulchre, his notion is considered the right one – the 'Garden Tomb' as it is now called.

\* \* \*

Less disputatious, but by no means less controversial, is the so-called Via Dolorosa, 'The Way of Sorrows', said to be the route along which Jesus carried his cross from the point where he was condemned by Pontius Pilate to the place where he was crucified. Accepting for the moment the latter to be the present location at the Church of the Holy Sepulchre, the most accepted starting point of the Via Dolorosa is normally considered to be just to the north of the Temple Mount and for me, for a time anyway, this was the one and only place where you could conceivably make any real archaeological connection with the story of Jesus as related in the Gospels. The focal point is part of a Roman pavement exposed in the cellar underneath what today is the Convent of the Little Sisters of Zion and this was said to be the actual place where Pilate passed judgment upon Jesus. In the Gospel of John (19:13) it is reported that 'Pilate sat down in the judgment seat in a place that is called The Pavement', and there he allowed the clamouring Jewish hierarchy to prevail to the extent that Jesus was then taken away and crucified. The location seemed to be very plausible, as 'The Pavement' could well have been the courtyard of the Antonia Fortress, barracks of the Praetorian Guard. It's certainly Roman in date, and in the right place for it.

As an aside, I've always had a soft spot for Pontius Pilate. He must have thought he was doing so well, his career prospects under the Emperor Tiberius set fair in the foreign service of Rome. "Got a nice new job for you, Pontius old chap, but there's some good news and some bad news. The good news is that you'll have the rank of Procurator. The bad news is that I'm afraid the job's in Judea" (which was reckoned to be one of the most fractious places in the Empire, so much so that the procurator had to live not in the capital, Jerusalem, but at Caesarea on the coast so that he could make a quick get-away in case of insurrection against Roman rule).

The Gospel says Pilate took his seat on 'The Pavement', which in Greek is the *Lithostratos*. Here in the Little Sisters Covent is what purported to be that very *Lithostratos*. You can walk down stairs and onto what is clearly Roman paving and here you could imagine the scene unfolding, the slightly off-hand Pilate relaxing in his chair, the chief priests and elders baying for Jesus' blood, making a real threat, so the writer of John says, by saying to Pilate, "if you let this man go you are no friend of Caesar's". I'm sure Pilate knew that this could only mean that they would create merry hell in the Province if they didn't get their way and that his career as procurator would be in deep trouble, in which case the hapless Pontius would in no uncertain terms be for the diplomatic bum's rush. I always felt that standing on the ancient stones of this floor was a real and perhaps only link to the Gospel story, if one wanted one, that is. And to add to the verisimilitude, in the road outside was part of a Roman triple archway. Admittedly only part of the middle arch is now visible, the two side arches having being incorporated into the houses on either side of the narrow street, but it is still known by its traditional name, the Ecce Homo Arch, the Arch of 'Behold the Man', the very words Pilate had used before he sent Jesus to his fate. And that's also one of the reasons why this might well have been the traditional start to the Via Dolorosa. The Catholics have built three churches here to celebrate the fact, so it must be true, mustn't it?

Well, not entirely. Imagine my disappointment when some twerp of a Catholic priest maintained, during the time I was there, that Jesus had not been tried by Pilate in the Antonia at all, but at King Herod's palace, which was in a totally different part of the city. This priest had made a careful study of the Antonia, and the Pavement in the cellar of the Little Sisters, he said, didn't belonged to it at all, but to one of the forums built by the Emperor Hadrian for his new city Aelia Capitolina, which would have been later, a hundred years after Jesus had been and gone. What a let-down! And as for Pilate, well for his pains he went on to receive one of the worst and most vilifying reputations of anyone in the Roman Empire thanks to what he must have thought of at the time as a rather trifling affair, crucifixions in his day being so commonplace. However, maybe he can take some small comfort from the fact that for some perverse reason he was later canonised by the Ethiopian Orthodox Church, so at least in Addis Ababa he is Saint Pontius. That must count for something.

Whatever the truth about the location of the point of its commencement, let's go back to the Via Dolorosa. We are now really in the area of myth and tradition. Various quasi-significant locations are pointed out along the route of the cross where prayers may be said, including the places of the Three Falls, or to some, it should be Seven Falls, which are supposed to places where Jesus stumbled under the weight of the cross. None of these is mentioned in the Gospels. Neither is the incident commemorated at the Fourth Station, the encounter with Mary, Jesus' mother. Nor is the Sixth Station, the encounter with Saint Veronica, where Veronica was said to wipe Jesus' face and where an imprint of his face miraculously transferred itself onto her veil. By the way, there are a number of Catholic churches in Spain, Italy and Austria, and even one in Russia, who all claim that they can verify that story because they actually own the one true and genuine imprinted material, known commonly as the 'Holy Face', but alas the whole thing is likely to be a Mediæval confection anyway. The only station on the Via Dolorosa which in any respect refers to the New Testament story is what today is the Fifth Station (or should it be the Seventh?) which commemorates Jesus' encounter with Simon of Cyrene, where Simon was compelled by the Roman soldiers to carry the cross the rest of the way to Calvary. Whatever, the Via Dolorosa eventually arrives at the Church of the Holy Sepulchre and the last few stations are actually inside the building, prone once more to the whole catastrophe of squabbling and scrapping to which we have referred above.

So, that's it - Christian Jerusalem. The Via Dolorosa, as you can imagine, sees many re-enactments by pilgrims of the events leading up to the Crucifixion, ranging from the totally bizarre, like people acting as Roman soldiers with plastic helmets on their heads which look a bit like upside down children's potties, to more serious pilgrims who take the whole journey rather more prayerfully. But for me, the very best, the most thoughtful and the most impressive Christian building in the Old City is actually very near the beginning of the Via Dolorosa though it has nothing to do with it. It's the Church of Saint Anne and it was built by Arda, the widow of the first Crusader King of Jerusalem, Baldwin 1, in 1138. The church is an almost perfect example of Romanesque architecture. The three-aisled basilica incorporates impressive cross-vaulted ceilings and pillars, a really clear, clean vertical profile and an almost totally unadorned interior, a feature so much contrast to the other cluttered Christian monuments of the city that it's refreshing in its starkness. For me it is a place of great innocence and sanctity, seldom visited by tourists. If you had to go anywhere in the Holy City to reflect on the events of the Gospel story and the origins of Christianity, this would be a good place to start.

## CHAPTER FIVE

# PERSIAN EROTICS

*A peculiar people the Persians;*
*They do have the strangest diversions.*
*They make love all day*
*In the usual way,*
*But they store up the night for perversions.*
Traditional limerick (if you happen to have an interest in
the Middle East, that is)

After a tedious few weeks of brushing through mud brick wash and waste,
something of consequence at Jemmeh was at last beginning to emerge from
the dust-filled squares at the top of the tell. And what should appear but intact
mud brick walling, not of rectangular walling but, unusually, circular walling,
the curvilinear walls of the interior of a structure which Gus immediately
informed us was a granary. How did he know that? Apparently Petrie had
excavated exactly the same feature in his dig over forty years before. The great
thing about this mud brick was that because it was an interior wall, that is,
it didn't face outwards into the weather, it had been left un-plastered, so that
should you wish to you could appreciate every course, every crack, every
joint and every feature of the bricks themselves.

As far as we were concerned, these bricks were prosaically inanimate mud
rectangles and as such they carried no special significance, laid as they were
one upon another and suggestive of nothing more surprising than, well, a
wall. But for Gus, they took on a wholly different significance. They were
'sexy', he proclaimed, 'really sexy', these mud bricks. In fact he declared
somewhat indiscriminately that all mud bricks were sexy, regardless of how
old or how large or small they were. Quite how had he arrived at this singular
appellation was difficult to ascertain, but our best efforts to decipher his
thought processes led us to conclude that he was conflating the vocabulary
of the excavation itself with his off-site, pent-up, mid-life passion for Ora,
and this in such a personal way that it was becoming a trifle embarrassing,
though some would say, intriguingly salacious too. I looked long and hard
at that granary whilst it was being cleaned. Try as I might I couldn't see the
connection between this simple yet effective method of ancient construction
and any erotic connotation or feminine wiles, wicked or otherwise. Maybe
I just didn't have enough imagination, I told myself. Sexy or not, the mud

brick was a whole lot more attractive to photograph, as Vic told me, than endless backfilled pits of rubble - you have to understand that we enjoyed only limited opportunity for excitement at the tell.

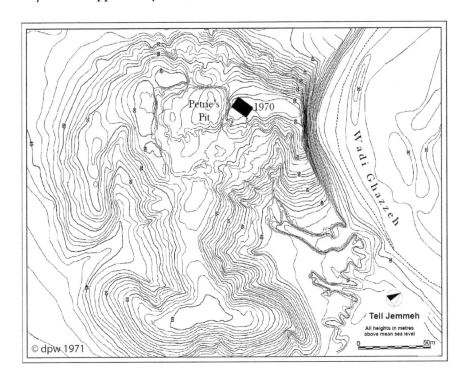

*Tacheometric survey of Tell Jemmeh (© DPW 1971)*

I was doing my own thing too with the topographic survey which by now was starting to take shape. I was using the method that Lonnie had shown me at Knidos, namely tacheometry, which is a fast and effective way of finding the position and height of any point relative to any other anywhere on or off the tell using a T2 Wild tachometric theodolite and some lists of tables which involve the already computed cosine of the angle of declination or elevation – don't ask me to explain the mathematics, because I can only keep them in my head long enough to do the necessary calculations, and in any case I had a book of ready-calculated reduced levels so I didn't need to think too hard.

But what was interesting was working out the theory of errors. Some mistakes in readings were inevitable, given the optical restrictions of the instrument, and these could normally be distributed between the various angles and distances that I was dealing with. If the error was less than the width of a finely pointed pencil lead when the topographic map was eventually drawn, then it wasn't worth losing sleep over. That's what it said in *Redmond's Manual of Tacheometry*, so who was I to worry. But I did heed Lonnie's advice to me; "Keep it in figures as long as you can Dave. Figures are magic. No-one knows what you are up to with figures!" In the end I had books and books full of readings. And I did get one very positive benefit. One of the squares being excavated had turned up a survey beacon which was marked on Petrie's map of the site, and it had an absolute height above sea level, worked out no doubt by some hapless British surveyor after the First World War, so I could use that to value all the contours I was going to create. Wonderful!

\* \* \*

Gus rarely sympathised very much with the volunteers; they were his workers after all and he didn't really get involved with their welfare either, other than to feed and house them. But, on one occasion he decided that we should all have an outing to see another archaeological site. He announced it one morning at breakfast in the eucalyptus grove. He had organised that at the end of the week we would all be going on a trip to Masada, the great rock fortress overlooking the Dead Sea, to see the recent excavations there. A bus had been ordered to take the whole group, volunteers and all. Maybe he thought that seeing such a dramatic excavation would encourage his workers to more intensive mud brick brushing, who knows?

Now, coincidentally, that same week, Masada came into my line of vision from another direction. In the middle of the week we were told to expect a visit from a committee of big-wigs from the Department of Antiquities interested to see our new granary perhaps, or more likely, the story went around, checking on Gus and his permit. The group duly arrived, somewhat overdressed for the Negev, we felt, but they came during the middle of the morning and Gus, with Ora in tow, showed them around. There was lots of standing about staring glumly into excavation squares at the newly exposed walling, though I think on this occasion Gus refrained from using any suggestive descriptions of the mud brick. Then they wanted to see the other parts of the dig, and finally they came over to where I was surveying and asked a lot of seemingly elementary questions about what I was doing. Having been well-schooled by Lonnie, I kept it as technically high-brow as possible, lots of mathematical formulae, loads of figures and trigonometric diagrams, that sort of thing. One or two even wanted to peer through the theodolite, but since it was full of cross hairs and revolving dials with incomprehensible numbers on them it only strengthened my hand, namely that I was engaged upon a serious scientific pursuit. They went away suitably impressed.

It was at this point that one of their number, whom I discovered was the boss of the whole show, Moshe Dothan, the Director of Antiquities, lingered behind as the group moved off. Taking me aside, he spoke quietly about the possibility of me doing a job for him at Masada. Apparently the surveyor there had just passed away leaving the survey unfinished. Could I use my magic system, tacheometry, to make a contour survey of the summit of Masada, he asked? It would take some time, he realised, but he was very anxious to have the job done as it was a very important excavation and I would be paid handsomely for my pains. I told him I had not seen the site but that co-incidentally we were due to go there in a day or two and I would take a look at it and let him know. He passed me his card and as he departed he said I should say nothing to Gus or anyone else and then walked off to catch up with his colleagues.

Well, I thought, that was quite a turn-up. I'd only been in the country a few weeks and here I was being asked to take a look at one of their key sites.

In due time, the day of the trip dawned. There were vague strictures mentioned about climbing Masada in the heat of the day and that we should dress suitably and carry water with us, though we were also told that you could buy Coca-Cola and other soft drinks at the bottom before you went up. I conspicuously don't like Coca-Cola, so I decided to make other plans. The canteen of the place we were staying had an area near the door with two spigots for public use, the one with still water and the other with soda water, both ice cold. So at breakfast (we were having our cucumbers and tomatoes in the canteen for a change) I took along my own litre water bottle with its polystyrene insulation and decided to fill it up before the trip. The still water wasn't working that morning so I filled the bottle up with soda water and then went out to join the rest of the group.

On the bus across the Negev to the Wadi Arabah, the southern extension of the Jordan Rift Valley, there was much laughing and joking among the volunteers – they had the day off after all – and one of their number, a young, slightly overweight girl called Sharon, pointed at Vic and me and suggested that being the sort of people we were she wouldn't put it beyond us to bring our gin with us, since we seemed to live on the stuff. The story did the rounds of the bus, and one or two pointed to my insulated water bottle and insinuated that knowing me I would have it filled with gin and tonic rather than water. I smiled beatifically but said nothing. We drove down to the Dead Sea then north to Masada and arrived at the bottom of the mountain. It is very dramatic, a diamond shaped outlier of the Judean Wilderness in the middle of a rock desert with sheer cliffs over three hundred metres high. It was here that Herod the Great had built one of his bolt holes, a place to which he could escape in a hurry in case of civil unrest or worse and on the northern end of this high plateau he had built a truly remarkable gravity-defying palace. It was this we were going to visit.

The only way to the summit of this glowering mountain was by means of what is known as the Snake Path, which winds its way backwards and forwards up the side of the cliffs to the top (there was no cable car as there is today). By the time we arrived at the base of the path, it was late in the morning and the sun was beating down out of a clear, cloudless ultramarine sky. The air was still and hot. I craned my head back to look at the path; it was a long way up. The group set off, the younger ones walking with quite a will to reach the top. I adopted the technique I'd been taught in the mountains of Wales – start unhurriedly and walk with a deliberately slow step, methodically, one foot in front of the other. And up we all went. As we rose out of the valley the sun on the exposed slopes seemed to grow even stronger. The Dead Sea looked like a shimmering indigo mirror in the distance. There wasn't a tree to be seen or any other shade on the path, not even a blade of grass. It just continued back and forth inexorably upwards in the heat, higher and higher, hotter and hotter. The ones that had set out early were beginning to flag now, noticeable slowing down and stopping for rests. I just continued at the same steady pace, up and up. About half way I began to pass some of the early starters sitting on the side of the rocky pathway. They called after me to ask how my gin and tonic was lasting. Two thirds of the way up the Snake Path reached the bottom of the vertical cliffs that make the summit of the fortress so impregnable and where there were iron steps for some of the steepest parts of the climb. It was here that I found Sharon, flaked out at the bottom of a flight of stairs. She was totally exhausted. She had a couple of friends with her, but it was clear to me that she was in some distress from the heat, and more especially from dehydration. I stopped and spoke to her. She needed fluids, I told her. With that I opened my water bottle and offered it to her. The contents were still nice and cold, the polystyrene had seen to that. Her friends remembered the joke about the gin. But Sharon needed something quickly and she clutched the bottle gratefully. Now whether it was the coldness of the water, or because it was the fizz in the soda, or that Sharon was half dead with fatigue, or that she'd never tasted it before, I shall never know. But as the bottle touched her lips and she took one sip, her eyes widened in disbelief and she said incredulously:

"Oh my God, it is gin and tonic! It really, really is. David has brought his cocktails with him like I said. Can you believe it? He's a total crazy, this guy. But I mean, total!"

I took the bottle back without a word and continued my slow walk to the top, but thus was born the myth that I had indeed climbed Masada in the heat of the day in the middle of the summer keeping myself going on half a litre of Gordon's gin and Indian tonic water. I never disabused anyone of the story, and keeping my council, I simply basked in the notoriety, as it was mentioned every night of the week back at the dig whenever I was on the veranda knocking back the actual gin and tonic. Yet another mad Brit in the desert, à la Lawrence of Arabia, they said.

I reached the top of the mountain and passing through the defensive wall which had once encircled the whole area I sat down in the shade of the stub wall of a building to take stock. The crest of Masada is more or less flat for most of its compass, with prodigious views up and down the Jordan Valley. It's at the far corner of this summit that Herod had built his hide-away, the so-called Northern Palace, which in its present form dated to about 25 BC. To approach it, you have to walk around a whole series of storage magazines and in through a small gateway. Once inside the palace there is a Roman style bathhouse complete with hypocaust and flues; can you imagine, a bathhouse, at the top of this remote and craggy outcrop? It was fed by an ingenious series of cisterns and channels cut into the limestone just below the crown of the mountain.

From there access is gained to the most remarkable part of the whole palace - a series of three rooms cantilevered out over three natural rock terraces, stepping down one level below the next, and teetering right on the face of the rugged cliffs. The uppermost level was apparently mainly used for residential purposes, originally decorated with mosaic floors and wall paintings. Beyond that there was a semi-circular colonnaded terrace surrounding what the excavators considered was probably a garden. On the two lower levels there were imposing colonnaded reception halls; both had bathing facilities. The lowest reception level is the best preserved of the three. It consisted of a square room with engaged Corinthian columns all the way round forming a sort of atrium. The walls had a plastered dado that was richly painted with imitation marble frescoes. Herod had to be all kinds of an extravagant maniac to order this almost impossibly situated edifice to be built. The whole complex was virtually unassailable, which is presumably why Herod chose it in the first place.

I walked gingerly up and down the staircases of the palace and thought about the offer to survey the whole thing that had been made to me earlier in the week, and then a flash of foreboding came over me. If the last surveyor had died, what did he die of? He hadn't pitched over the side of the palace while taking his measurements and fallen to his death on the rocks a thousand metres below, had he? The vision scared the daylights out of me. I suffer from vertigo as it is, even watching people rock climbing on the television. I'd be absolutely hopeless scrambling about in a place like this. Surveying the flat, uninteresting summit was one thing. Measuring angles and distances in the palace area, where I was sure they would want most of the work done, was quite another. Even if they could arrange a series of miraculous sky hooks from which to hang, I'd be terrified out of my wits. Then and there I decided that for me Masada was a survey too far. I would have to decline the offer, payment or no.

I clambered back to the Snake Path and slowly and cautiously descended to the bottom again where I found the rest of the group drinking soft drinks in the cafeteria. Some of them hadn't even got as far as the top. They'd turned round and gone down again. I didn't blame them. I said nothing about my own self-revelation in Herod's palace, and after a few minutes we all got back on the bus and started the long drive back to Tell Jemmeh. When I was next in Jerusalem I looked up Moshe Dothan in his offices at the Rockefeller Museum, which had been a Palestine Museum until only three years before, and I told him that unfortunately I could not be spared from the essential work at Tell Jemmeh. I didn't discover anything about the previous incumbent at Masada, and discretion being the better part of valour, I sloped off back to the Ritz for a conciliatory G & T.

*   *   *

Back at Jemmeh the granary was shaping up well and was now revealed in its entirety. It was a lined circular pit about five metres across. This was just the underground part, Gus said. Above ground it would have been like a large conical sugar loaf of corbelled mud brick. There were some built like this near Aleppo in Syria and still being used, but these at Jemmeh belonged to the ancient Persian Period, the time when the Achaemenid kings ruled an empire which stretched from the Aegean coast of western Turkey right the way across central Asia and half way to China, and they did so by developing an administrative system of pure genius which they ran from their capital cities in what today is southern Iran. The Persian armies had invaded and then lost the Nile Valley several times, and off and on southern Palestine had been the southwestern border of their vast sphere of influence, until, that is, they had finally been defeated by Alexander the Great in the 320s BC who had swept through Asia Minor, down through the Levant, across the Nile Delta and then back into Mesopotamia before he destroyed their capital city at Persepolis on the other side of the Zagros Mountains and finally taken their eastern empire right the way to Afghanistan and beyond. There are still blue eyed people in Uzbekistan who reckon they are descended from this amazing Macedonian, even today, almost two and a half thousand years later!

Anyway, for a couple of hundred years before Alexander's arrival, Palestine was in Persian hands and Tell Jemmeh was from time to time right on their boundary so it was of great interest to them. Petrie had established this in the 1920s. He'd excavated what he'd called a large Persian courtyard palace here, maybe even the residence of a minor Persian governor or military official and he concluded that Jemmeh had been a fortified Persian administrative centre in the fifth century BC, either for the invasion of Egypt, or to repel any threat from Egypt. The granaries, these circular conical roofed buildings, were for storing the grain to feed the Persian armies who were billeted there. Petrie reckoned the granaries had been built just before 455 BC, a date when it was known that the Persians invaded the Delta, but Gus was all for the granaries being later, perhaps 450 or even a year or two later still. Big deal! All the scraping and brushing for the whole season had led to this earth-shattering discovery. I have to say that compared to Petrie's massive excavations, I was underwhelmed.

But there was one mildly dramatic discovery which took place just before the 1970 season came to an end. It was a small event but afforded some of us a little light relief. We had one site supervisor who was Israeli, so he said, who went by the name of Yichael Lehavy, and slightly older than the rest of us he was wont to be somewhat bumptious, proclaiming that he knew everything about the Bible and everything about the archaeology of the Holy Land. He tried to persuade us that he'd seen it all and done it all. One morning he was working on his note book at the side of his square when one of the volunteers hesitated and then picked up a small lump of unfired clay from the bottom of the trench. It looked just like a small pebble.

"Is this anything?" she asked – she was always asking the same question over and over again about any piece of pottery or stone from her trench. She handed it to him and as he cleaned it he became very animated because he recognised that on the top of the little lump there was a word scratched into the clay, but in the old Canaanite script so it looked rather spidery.

"Can't you see?" he bawled at her, more irritated than usual. "I mean, look at it properly". She took the piece back again and rubbed it a bit.

"Can't you see those marks on the surface?"

"Oh, those", she said, noticing the scratches. "I must have scraped it a bit with my trowel. So it's nothing then?"

And with that she hurled it out of the trench onto a huge pile of stones all of similar size which were the tailings which had been tipped out of the sieves over the last two months after each bucket had been searched.

"Shit! What are you doing?" he shouted. "That's a 'pym', an ancient weight. There are only a few that have ever been found. What have you just done with it?"

It was indeed extremely interesting, as he said, and he'd been right. The 'pym' was a weight equivalent to two thirds of an ancient shekel, about seven and a half grams in today's money. The word appears in the Book of Samuel but for centuries nobody knew what it meant until the first one had been discovered in about 1906, so when scholars that were translating the Old Testament in the seventeenth century had come to the word they had no idea what to make of it. It was something to do with sharpening ox goads, and they translated it in the King James' version as a 'file' - 'and they had a file to sharpen the ox goads'. But with the discovery of the little weight with the name 'pym' on it, the translation changed to 'and they charged a pym to sharpen the ox goads'. Finding another of these little weights would be an interesting addition to our knowledge of everyday life in ancient Palestine. But it had been thrown onto the discard heap, along with thousands upon thousands of little pieces just like it. It took Yichael four days sorting through the whole pile to find it again, much to our amusement.

However the next incident wasn't such a laughing matter. I remember that for a while Yichael shared a room with three others of us and from time to time he was wont to mew in his sleep, nothing too dramatic, just a periodic quiet high-pitched wailing sound. We took no notice of it at first until one night it became very persistent, rising and falling in a rather more alarming way and loud enough to wake us all up. After a minute or two, I'd had enough and leaping out of bed (I slept in the top bunk) I went over to his cot and said:

"Yichael, what the hell's the matter with you? You are waking us all up!" He opened his eyes and looked at me with a terrified stare.

"My name isn't Yichael Lehavy", he moaned. "It's Hans-Yoachim Bauer. I was a soldier in the Haganah, the resistance movement during the end of the British Mandate, and I was in this area with a friend, another soldier, in the same wadi near Gaza on an operation against a British patrol. There was a hut on the side of the wadi and I knew it was booby trapped, but he didn't. We'd hidden in the Wadi for a short time until he decided to rush at the door of the hut. It exploded and he was blown to pieces. I keep seeing it in my dreams. Being here has brought it all back to me. I'm crying out to try to warn him, but it was too late. It's always too late."

It was a dramatic revelation. We were all momentarily stunned at his openness and honesty, which was quite unlike his normal demeanour. And he was never the same again from that point. He was much quieter, much less belligerent. The exorcism had done him a power of good, but it reminded me that Israel had been forged in blood, something about which I thought a lot after that.

CHAPTER SIX
# HOLY TOADSTOOLS!

*"They will break all my laws and all my commandments that
I commanded them. And then they will begin to quarrel with
one another."*
Dead Sea Scrolls 4Q390 Frag 2 Col1. (Qumran Cave 4
Scroll 390)

You may remember that I have already mentioned the Palestine Museum, renamed the Rockefeller, located in East Jerusalem, and it was here I discovered that some of its contents were likely to have a particular fascination for me, because the museum housed some of the original Dead Sea Scrolls. I had worked on the scrolls as part of my first degree, only in photographic facsimile admittedly, and only the scriptural scrolls, but that gave me a more than a passing interest in seeing them, and here they were on display, along with some of the material from the excavations at Khirbet Qumran near the Dead Sea, next to where they'd been found. Qumran was said by some to be the place where the scrolls had actually been written.

The scrolls were then and still are now a highly contentious issue. There have been endless scholarly discussions and continuous fierce popular disputes about them - their context, their meaning, the characters mentioned in them, and especially their relevance to the birth of Christianity, if any. They first turned up in 1947, in caves next to the Dead Sea, hence their name. But they were not the result of any systematic work by archaeologists; rather the largely accidental and fortuitous discovery by a few Bedouin Arabs, and later by the clandestine excavations of people interested in making a profit from them. They couldn't have emerged onto the stage of history at a worse time, when the political situation in Palestine was at fever pitch in the highly charged atmosphere just before the British withdrawal from the Mandate, the establishment of the State of Israel and the division of the Palestinian West Bank, in other words when everyone's attention was focused somewhere else. When they were first found, their importance, and even their authenticity, was not fully understood. To begin with they were traded through antiquities dealers and shady Christian clerics in Bethlehem and Jerusalem whose perception of what they were looking at was at best questionable and more often lacking altogether. Some of the scholars who first saw them felt that they were probably Mediæval copies of no real interest, or maybe even downright forgeries, and because of this they were not treated well. As a result, much damage was done to the scrolls and there is no doubt that parts of this whole fragile corpus were inadvertently destroyed or lost. What did become obvious after a year or two was that some people were willing to pay hard cash for them, in some cases lots of it, which in a way only made matters worse and the search for them even more frenziedly haphazard. So, what are the scrolls? The first thing to say is that they are not Mediæval copies, and certainly not forgeries. They are definitely old, dated to somewhere around the turn of the BC/AD Millennia and possibly to the beginning of the Christian era. Some think one or two may be even older. As far as their content is concerned, very briefly they are divided into two groups according to their subject matter. The first group, and the less contentious, are the scriptural scrolls, copies of all the books of the Old Testament except, for some reason, the Book of Esther. In certain cases, like the Book of the Prophet Isaiah for example, several copies of the same book were found, in part or in whole. These are the ones I had worked on, specifically Isaiah, when I was studying for my degree at Bangor. My professor thought it would be good for me to compare these very early manuscripts with the current Hebrew text of the Old Testament to see how many alternative readings or changes we could find in the manuscript transmission. The origin of the present text is perhaps a thousand years later than the scrolls and there could have been many deviations, one from the other, all of them of course being handmade copies. But I went through the facsimiles I was given anyway and found all the changes and alternatives and logged them all. Actually my professor was on the committee for the translation of the New English Bible Old Testament, which had yet to be published, and they wanted to incorporate any emendations into the footnotes of the final version. So, if you see any footnotes of Isaiah with DSS 'so-and-so', they'll have been done by me! (By the way, I think the final version of the NEBOT is a travesty; the translation is far too free and easy, but that's not my problem). But what I basically discovered was that contrary to previous scholarly opinion, in the books I examined the transmission had been amazingly accurate. Though there had been one or two changes and errors in writing, for over a millennium the texts had been copied over and over again with considerable skill. Part of one copy of the Book of Isaiah was on display in the Rockefeller Museum, so I felt a rosy glow when I saw the very scroll there in the cabinet.

That gave me an impetus to learn something about the second group of scrolls, the ones that have really caused the decades of controversy. They were found alongside the scriptural scrolls and belong to the same corpus, but they are usually called the sectarian scrolls and appear to have been written by a separatist group of religious fanatics who probably dwelt somewhere in the Judean Wilderness, maybe even next to the Dead Sea, where they had gone to live to get away from the rank and file population of the day. There are liturgical scrolls - the hymns, thanksgivings and prayers the members of the sect used in their daily worship. Then there are interpretive scrolls, books of some of the Old Testament prophets, the text of which is taken line by line and literally re-interpreted, on the basis that the messages and threats contained in the original prophesies were not meant for the time they were delivered, but for the here and now, for the time of the scrolls. As such these often contain very interesting quasi-historical and political allusions which can help pinpoint when exactly they were written and by whom.

I say 'quasi-historical' because the people writing them used special cryptographic terms for the historical figures and events they were talking about so that an outsider wouldn't understand who they meant. So for example they speak of massed armies said to be threatening the whole of Judea whom they identify as the Kittim, which strictly means 'the Cypriotes'. They can't actually have meant Cypriotes; there's no evidence of any army or threat from that direction. But the name 'Kittim' is thought to be a coded reference either for the Seleucid armies of the second century BC, during the Hellenistic period, or more probably, the Roman armies of the middle of the first century AD. Obviously, if it's the former, then clearly the texts have nothing to do with Christianity; they'd be far too early. But if it's the latter, then it's exactly the time when Christianity was being established, and if that were to be the case a whole raft of other parallels comes into play. From all the Carbon 14 dates that have been analysed from the scrolls, some of the scriptural scrolls seem to be early, but the sectarian scrolls do seem to date to the first century AD, putting them right in the frame for being the time of the first appearance of the new cult, Christianity, and this makes them more controversial than ever.

There are other sectarian scrolls too, some of which are even more interesting. These are various scrolls called Rules, like the 'Damascus Rule', the 'Community Rule' and so on, which list very specific regulations on how the members of this isolated community should behave. And there is a scroll called the 'War Scroll' or more fully, the 'War of the Sons of Light and of Darkness' which talks about the end of the world, believed to be fast approaching, a subject which is one of their constant preoccupations. And there is even a scroll made from copper, the 'Treasure Scroll', which talks about caches of buried loot in and around Jerusalem, none of which has ever been found, by the way, despite extensive searches. All these sectarian scrolls are open to endless interpretation. They make frequent mention of specific characters in the contemporary scene without actually saying who they are, and they even give them titles, like the 'Teacher of Righteousness', the 'Wicked Priest', and the 'Liar', the Spouter of Lies. All sorts of figures have been tentatively identified with these three, from Jesus of Nazareth for the Teacher to the Apostle Paul for the Liar.

So, do the scrolls refer to the beginnings of a recalcitrant Christian community, a group of converts in the desert, or to an ultra-zealot Jewish community isolated from the Jerusalem Priests and Pharisees whom they denounce as corrupt? Well, because of their cryptic ambiguity, perhaps we shall never know. What is fascinating is to see how various religious and political groups today have each embraced the scrolls and tried to hi-jack their message for themselves.

But the most interesting anecdote associated with the scrolls for me concerned someone at the Rockefeller Museum who had become associated with the scrolls soon after their original discovery. He was a Biblical scholar from Manchester University by the name of John Marco Allegro. In 1956, he had written the most popular book on their discovery, called simply 'The Dead Sea Scrolls', which was a very reasoned approach to the whole subject; his account was the first book I'd read about them. He wasn't associated with any church or faith so he told the story just as he saw it. However he later fell out with some of his Dead Sea Scrolls colleagues at the museum who thought he was over-popularising the subject. He'd brought in the TV cameras and other equipment, and they didn't want the inevitable publicity. They also believed that he was also trying to discredit Christianity, attempting to prove that the stories about Jesus were purely fictional. He responded by saying they'd cut him out because they were trying to hide some of the unpalatable truth behind the scrolls. Thereafter he was excluded from any further research in Jerusalem and he turned to other ways of re-interpreting Christianity instead.

The first year I was at Jemmeh he published what was generally considered to be a thoroughly scurrilous book called 'The Sacred Mushroom and the Cross' in which he portrayed the early Christians as a group of sex-obsessed, drug-crazed junkies high on ingesting hallucinogenic fungi, who imagined God to be the 'Sacred Penis in the Sky' – it was all very topical at the time, as you can imagine. It was also way over the top and in the end he had to resign his post at the university and retire to the Isle of Man. I once met one of his students and asked her whether he'd talked about these bizarre ideas during his everyday teaching and she said, 'Oh yes, he was always going on and on about his holy toadstools!'

* * *

I was talking to my friend Louis about all this at the Ritz one evening when he suggested:

"You ought to go and see Qumran, you know. It's just near Jericho. That's where the scrolls were found. You could go there by taxi tomorrow morning. I'll organise it for you."

And that's how I met Sami Ed-Dhib, Sami the Wolf. Sami was from Bethlehem and he owned a Peugeot estate taxi. He was a friend of Louis', and over the next few years Sami and I were to travel all over the Holy Land looking at the various archaeological sites. He had been driver to General John Glubb, 'Glubb Pasha', the legendary English army officer who led the Arab Legion in Trans-Jordan during the Second World War. Glubb Pasha had named Sami 'Abu Jamili', 'Father of the Beautiful One', because he always kept his car beautifully clean.

For my first trip, Sami turned up the next day at breakfast time and we arranged a price for the day's outing. As soon as I was ready we drove out of Jerusalem, over the Mount of Olives and down the main road that led to Jericho. I looked back from the crest of the Mount of Olives and saw the stunning profile of the Old City with the Dome of the Rock shimmering in the sunlight above Suleiman the Magnificent's walls. Once over the ridge the landscape became barren and rocky in the rain shadow of the Judean Hills. We passed through Bethany, a little Palestinian village just beyond the rise, and carried on down into the Wilderness. About half way to Jericho, Sami said we were going to take the old road and turning off the tar we drove onto a dirt track down the side of the Wadi Qelt, a deeply incised, narrow ravine which led all the way to the Jordan Valley. The track followed the course of the old Roman road, I later learned, but it was very rugged and certainly gave real sense to the parable of the Good Samaritan, the one about the man on the road from Jerusalem to Jericho who fell among thieves. Then, unexpectedly in this rock desert, just around a sharp corner we came across the dramatic sight of St George's Monastery built into the cliffs on the other side of the wadi. It just seemed to hang there on the rock wall, a Greek Orthodox monastery with white buildings and blue domes tucked into a barren fold in the limestone. It had been there since the sixth century, Sami said, though it had last been restored around about 1900.

The rock-strewn track continued downwards until we reached the edge of the mountains where the wadi opened out, and suddenly there in front of us was exposed a horizon-wide view of the broad Jordan Valley, the dark green orchards of Jericho creating a vivid oasis which was in total contrast to the austere desert all around and overlooked by the barren mountain they call the Mount of Temptation. It all formed a panorama of great theatricality and we stopped so that I could take a photograph and absorb the whole scene.

"What do you want to do right now?" asked Sami. "Go to Jericho or straight on down to Qumran?"

It was still quite early so we decided to go to Qumran first and come back to Jericho for lunch. We drove on until we gained the main road again and then turned south towards the Dead Sea. It was very strange seeing this vast body of water glistening in the sunlit haze in the middle of what was otherwise a totally arid landscape. We passed a board at the edge of the road saying that we were now '1270 feet below sea level' and drove on a kilometre or two until we saw a sign pointing right for Khirbet Qumran. We turned up onto a small rocky shelf between the sea shore and the mountains. The sun's temperature was oppressive now, hitting us like a wall of heat as I opened the door. I went over and read the notice about the site and about the excavations which had been conducted by Pere Roland de Vaux in the early 1950s. De Vaux was a French Dominican priest from the 'École Biblique et Archéologique de Jerusalem' who was also one of the scholars working on the scrolls in the Rockefeller Museum; as far as I knew he was still alive. I remembered, too, that John Allegro had done some digging here a bit later.

The site, according to de Vaux, was originally established at some date in the Iron Age, but in the condition in which he found it, it had been re-established in the second century BC, and it had later become a monastery which had housed a community of up to two hundred people whom he associated with the Essenes. The Essenes were a group mentioned by a number of contemporary historians like Pliny the Elder, the writer who perished in the eruption of Vesuvius in 79 AD, and by Josephus, a local writer who was sympathetic to the Romans. They both described the Essenes, vaguely it must be said, as a strict and separatist Jewish society living in isolation in the desert. Pliny's account actually places them next to the Dead Sea. De Vaux's interpretation of the buildings at Qumran fitted that somewhat monastic description, and he claimed he had found the refectory where they all ate and a sacred pool where they ritually bathed, fed from a complicated water system based on capturing the seasonal floods from the nearby wadi. Most importantly for de Vaux, he maintained he had discovered a scriptorium equipped with benches and desks where he reckoned they had copied and written the scrolls. Supporting his theory he found three inkwells associated with this room. For him, there was no question that Qumran was the monastery of the community of the scrolls.

When I looked at the site it was a jumble of stone walls about a foot or two high, so I couldn't really say if de Vaux had been right or wrong. But walking over to the edge of the plateau on which the complex had been built, I could see one or two of the caves in the grey marl where, a notice announced, some of the scrolls had been found. But since de Vaux's excavations, new and opposing views have been rife. Some people have said that Qumran wasn't a monastery at all, it was a Roman fort, or a winter villa, or perhaps a commercial centre servicing ships on the Dead Sea, or improbably maybe even a pottery factory. Lots of people have argued that it had nothing to do with the Essenes either, pointing out that Pliny had written that the Essenes were an all-male community but female burials had been excavated in the nearby cemetery. And others have said it was not related to the scrolls whatsoever; they had originated in Jerusalem, they argue, and were brought to the area simply to hide them during the crisis of the Roman-Jewish war of 66 AD. If you look at the various ideas and suggestions, many of them very vociferously advanced, and consider all the ferocious arguments that still surround the whole subject today, you could easily be forgiven for thinking that the interminable conferences, scholarly papers and books on the subject actually generate more heat than light and I think maybe that's in the nature of the evidence.

It's not helped by the fact that de Vaux didn't publish the excavations properly, so some of his ideas are a bit rudderless. And further, de Vaux has been accused by Jewish scholars of being violently anti-Semitic in that he did not allow them to look at the scrolls in his keeping, so much so that Israeli scholars all tend on principle to tear his ideas to shreds, and incidentally while doing so also fall out spectacularly with each other. Many are of the firm conviction that not only does Qumran have nothing at all to do with the scrolls but rather it just happens to be in the vicinity, whatever it was used for. For me that day at Qumran, such ideas all seemed very perverse, when you could actually see some of the caves where the scrolls had been found from the monastery, or whatever it was, in a vast tract of mountainous country which is otherwise totally and absolutely devoid of life. And since my first visit, evidence has stacked up in de Vaux's favour. More inkwells have been found, more than in any building of the period. Chemical analysis of the carbon inks used for the scrolls has shown that they were mixed with Dead Sea water; and the vellum on which some of the scrolls were written was made from the skins of the Nubian ibex, an animal apparently only found in the area of Qumran at the time and nowhere else in the region. No doubt the debates will continue to rage But for me, it was time for lunch, so I walked back to Sami Dhib and the Peugeot and we drove up the road back to Jericho.

\* \* \*

Now when it came to Jericho I was on much firmer ground. I remembered the first year I was at the Institute I had been given an essay to write about Jericho and told to consult two books in the Institute Library, Jericho Volumes 1 and 2. I knew everything about Jericho, I thought. I had studied its history. I knew every mention of Jericho in the Old Testament, every variation in the spelling and every alternative name for the city – *Ir HaTamarim* - the City of Palms; *Reah* - The Fragrant One; *'ariha* - and so on. Imagine my surprise when I took the volumes down from the shelf and opened them to find they were full of page after page of technical drawings of earthen-ware pots. It took me a while to realise that archaeological evidence is totally different from textual, and I became conscious that I had to change from being a linguist to becoming a proper archaeologist. But change I did, and I came to know the material from Jericho like a second skin, so it's partly thanks to the excavations here that I moved on to my new career. I was looking forward to seeing where for me it had all begun.

We drove through the streets of Jericho. It was a small town in those days, only a few thousand people, with mud-brick walled gardens full of date palms. There was evidence of water everywhere, with a substantial flow coming from springs around the town which were being used to irrigate the orange and banana groves that made the whole area so verdant. And that's why the ancient city had been built here too. It turned out to be probably the oldest urban community in the world, dating back more than twelve thousand years, to the very beginnings of human settlement anywhere on Earth. After we'd had quick shawarma for lunch, that's where we were going, to the tell of ancient Jericho, Tell es-Sultan. The tell itself covers about 14 acres near the strongest spring in the area, Ain es-Sultan, the Sultan's Spring, to the northwest of the present town.

Although it was first examined at the end of 19ᵗʰ century and again in the 1930's, it was the excavations conducted by Kathleen Kenyon in the 1950's that made the tell at Jericho famous. Kathleen Kenyon, 'Kay' as everyone knew her, was idolised at the Institute. She had been the first lecturer in Levantine archaeology there before being elevated to become Principal of St. Hugh's College, Oxford, and her techniques of excavating were legendry. Even before that, she had been a close associate of Mortimer Wheeler and had actually helped him establish the Institute of Archaeology, originally in Regent's Park, before the Second World War. Most especially, she followed his example of excavating, trying first and foremost to understand the layers of any site, the stratigraphy as it is called, in this case by cutting sections through the tell. The approach became known, to us at least, as the Wheeler-Kenyon method. Her presence at Jericho was also legendry, inspiring and encouraging her students, some apocryphally say, with a bottle of gin stuck in her back pocket. The Arabs that had working for her adored her; they called her the Great Sid – the Grande Dame. Later it was said that if you had a Jericho man working for you your dig would be done properly. And those Europeans she trained fed off her fame and brilliance, especially for excavating mud-brick. Incidentally one of those had been Gus.

The site was complicated, but Kay had worked the whole thing out, digging the great west trench right down to bedrock where she discovered the remains of the earliest settlement, the so-called Natufian, or proto-Neolithic. She also found the earliest examples of people growing domesticated wheat and barley as well as farming the earliest domesticated goats. It's this very change in the human economy, from hunting and gathering to farming, that actually begins the process leading to what we call civilization. The whole economic basis of western culture originated in places like Jericho and Kay's work was seminal in that study. Here at Tell es-Sultan she had discovered evidence of one of the most significant moments in modern human evolution - the beginnings of European civilization. But she had also excavated Jericho's later cultures too, dating to the Bronze and the Iron Ages. From the Middle Bronze Age she had discovered a remarkable series of tombs around the site. The atmosphere in the cave-like tombs in which the inhabitants had placed their multiple burials was so desiccated that even some of the organic remains had survived for almost four thousand years – fibre baskets, three-legged wooden tables and even dried fruits. It was astonishing. I knew all about these tombs because

I was studying them for my PhD and I casually looked up to see if I could detect any traces of them, but there were none to be seen.

But as I lifted my eyes from the trenches which Kay had opened, something else caught my attention. It was what looked like a huge one-story ghost town built of mudbrick located between the edge of the tell and the point where the barren mountains rose from the arid plains of the Jordan Valley. It could have been a suburb of ancient Jericho, a Bronze Age settlement perhaps, but the roofs were made of rusting corrugated iron; this was modern. I asked Sami what it was and he said quietly that it was Ain es-Sultan Refugee Camp, one of the camps to which the people of Palestine had escaped in 1948 during the war in which the new state of Israel was established. Thousands had fled the fighting and ended up in refugee camps just like this. They had come from as far away as the ancient Arab town of Jaffa on the Mediterranean coast which I had known even as a boy to be so famous for its orange orchards. More than fifty thousand people had left from there alone at that time and many of them ended up here as refugees outside Jericho. According to Sami some had still held on to the keys to their houses, hoping to return when the fighting was over, but the new Israeli Government which had seized the town did not allow them to. He told me that all those who had fled were instantly classified as absentees, their bank accounts were frozen and all their other assets, including homes and lands, were immediately confiscated without any consultation or compensation. He also said that their houses and their orchards were taken over by foreign Jewish settlers from Europe and North Africa who revelled in the quaint properties of Mediæval Jaffa which they now had expropriated as their own. Unlike the settlers, who had never been here before and who had just turned up as new immigrants, effectively as aliens in someone else's country, for the Palestinians whose families had lived there for hundreds of years and who had momently left in fear, there was to be no right of return, Sami said. They had suddenly lost everything.

I was much taken aback by Sami's story. I hadn't known anything of this history before. But his tale became even more heart-rending when he told me that in 1967, just three years before we were there, when the Israelis forcibly occupied the West Bank (including Jericho), tens of thousands of the 1948 refugees fled for a second time, this time across the river into the Kingdom of Jordan, where they are once again settled in camps but this time outside Amman. The village here at Ain as-Sultan was now all but deserted, a mute testament to an awful historical legacy. It seems that something catastrophic had taken place in Palestine at the end of the British Mandate, both during the establishment of the Jewish State, and again later with Israel's military occupation of the remainder of Palestine.

We drove back to Jerusalem in relative silence. I pondered profoundly about the tell at Jericho. In perhaps the ultimate of ironies, the very beginnings of civilised society had been discovered there 12,000 years ago, but there also was the evidence of what for modern people must have seemed like its end. Curiously, that too was exactly what the writers of the Dead Sea Scrolls just down the road had warned about two thousand years earlier - the cataclysm of the last days and of the end of time. But this was not ancient, I thought. It was a tragic result of modern history. It's a story which was to disturb me for all six years I was in the region, as it still does today, fifty years later.

CHAPTER SEVEN
# THE ASSYRIAN CAME DOWN LIKE A WOLF ON THE FOLD

*An archaeologist is the best husband a woman can have. The older she gets the more interested in her he becomes!*
Agatha Christie

I had to go back to Jemmeh for the last week of the season, but wonder of wonders, Sami offered to take me on the Sunday afternoon in his taxi, and to come and pick me up again the next Friday lunchtime. Luxury indeed! Arriving at the gulag, I was told that Gus was in a state of considerable animation. Towards the end of the previous week new mudbrick walling had been uncovered in one of the forward squares, somewhat canted over on its side admittedly, but seemingly complete. I personally hadn't noticed it as I was in such a hurry to get up to Jerusalem. The wall looked as though it might be earlier than the Persian granary, but I was informed that Gus couldn't quite make sense of it as yet. A day or two later, he was transported with excitement when a small intact open bowl was found in the mud-brick rubble surrounding the new wall. It was absolutely complete, a fine, thin, grey vessel with a carinated profile and out-turned rim. It wasn't decorated; it was just uniform dull grey. But to Gus, the little pot represented some kind of ceramic nirvana. That evening he held a seminar for the whole team and went into ecstasies about his new find. This bowl, he announced somewhat histrionically, was an extremely significant discovery, if not the most notable discovery he had ever made. Theatrically, he explained why he thought it so important. This piece of pottery was an example of Assyrian Palace Ware, he said.

"This bowl has come all the way from the Upper Tigris Valley in Mesopotamia to be with us this evening, that's in modern-day Iraq you know, an awfully long way away indeed!"

I racked my brains for any reference to Assyrians in the history of Palestine. Off-hand I could only think of Sennacherib, the Assyrian King who had invaded the Kingdom of Judah in 701 BC. Sennacherib went on to destroy the southern fortified city of Lachish. There had been a whole room at his royal palace at Nineveh decorated with reliefs which depicted just that battle. They'd been found in the 1840s and were now on display in the British Museum. There was even a famous account of it and of Sennacherib's subsequent siege of Jerusalem on a cuneiform prism, also in the BM - I'd seen it there - in which he described the event:

'King Hezekiah himself I shut up in Jerusalem, his capital city, like a bird in a cage, building towers round the city to hem him in', it read.

But as I remembered it, all did not go well for Sennacherib. The Book of Kings in the Old Testament makes a meal of what happened next. It dramatically builds the scene, with the Assyrian Military Commander, the Rab-shakeh, hurling abuse at the defenders on the walls of Jerusalem. When the city fathers asked him to speak in Aramaic instead of Hebrew, presumably so that the defenders wouldn't understand what he was saying and wouldn't be intimidated by his insults, the Rab-shakeh shouts up at them with gusto: 'I didn't come here to speak to you lot, but to these very defenders, who like you are doomed to eat their own shit and drink their own piss'. Very colourful; a lovely piece of ancient rhetoric. However, according to the Old Testament, the Angel of the Lord came down and smote the Assyrians that same night and huge numbers of them died of the plague. It's made clear that that was only what they deserved. Actually, Herodotus, the Greek historian, also talks about the same disaster in an equally colourful but slightly different way: 'In the night, a multitude of field-mice came and devoured all the quivers and bowstrings of the enemy, and ate the thongs by which they managed their shields. Next morning when they commenced their fight great multitudes fell as they had no arms with which to defend themselves'. Whether it was the plague or the field-mice, what was left of the Assyrian army limped back home to Mesopotamia while Jerusalem and the rest of Judah was spared. So what was their Palace Ware doing at Jemmeh? Intriguingly, Gus left that answer in the air, and just after that the season finished and I went back to London.

But that wasn't the end of the story for me. In fact it became even more interesting that winter. Sometime after Christmas I got a letter from Gus saying that he was going to be in London in a couple of months' time and could I meet him. On the appointed day I duly turned up at his hotel in London's West End and met Gus. He wondered if I could drive him to Oxford, or just outside Oxford anyway, to which I agreed, and we set off. We were halfway there before I asked him exactly where we were heading and Gus said we were going to see a Professor Mallowan. I had met Max Mallowan, or Sir Max Mallowan as he was now styled. I'd drawn some illustrations for a new book he'd been publishing. He was a well-known Mesopotamian archaeologist and amongst other things had recently excavated the huge Assyrian city of Nimrud in Northern Iraq. I'd even worked on some of the small finds from there as well, some of the famous Nimrud ivories, so I knew quite a lot about Max. And I recalled incidentally that he was married to the world-famous crime writer Agatha Christie. We wouldn't be seeing her, would we, I wondered?

"Sure! We're going to have lunch with her and Professor Mallowan. You're invited of course."

Well, there's a thing. After driving around a bit I found Mallowan's home, Winterbourne House, just outside Oxford. Gus rang the bell and in we went; sure enough there was Agatha. She was in her eighties by this time, a good fifteen years older than Max. I noticed that she treated Max like one of the many male characters in her novels, as though he was rather ineffectual and foppish. We all sat down to lunch – roast beef I think it was – but it was made clear that we all had to eat very quickly because their daily help, who was lurking in the background, was going to go off at one o' clock and if we hadn't finished our lunch before then the dishes wouldn't get washed up; Max seemed quite perturbed by the possibility. So, we wolfed down our beef and Yorkshire pudding in an unseemly hurry and retired to have coffee in the conservatory. I had heard from others who knew the household that they were very careful about money, despite presumably rolling in it, but trying to save an hour's wages for their maid seemed a bit tight. Anyway, as we went into the next room for coffee I noticed that there was a Ming vase in the hall, at least I thought it was Ming, and sticking out of it were two plastic roses, the ones they normally gave away free with washing powder. Amazing!

After we'd had coffee Agatha said she had something she had to do, and Max led us to his library, a long impressive room made from the hay loft of a converted stable block. The whole of the one side of the room was absolutely covered from floor to ceiling with books. The three of us sat at a table and Max asked Gus to remind him what the nature of the enquiry was? Gus mentioned Jemmeh and the Assyrian Palace Ware bowl, at which point his reasoning became clear to me. Max had excavated a great deal of the same pottery at Nimrud, his site in northern Mesopotamia. Ostensibly we were here to find out more about it. He went over to the book cases and pulled out numerous articles and books to which he wanted to refer and from then on he seemed to withdraw into his own academic world. He spoke for some time, almost as though he was speaking to himself, using the various texts he had pulled out to bolster his ideas. About half an hour later, I noticed Agatha standing in the doorway watching. Max didn't break his monologue and after a minute or two she walked slowly and somewhat imperiously down the whole length of the room, and then back again.

"Max!" she called out as she left, "It's too hot in here. I've turned the radiators off."

And with that she strode off. Another half hour passed, and then Max seemed to come to himself and it was made clear that the audience was over. I'm not sure if Gus had got what he wanted, but we were cordially wished good day and out we went, back into the minivan and back to London. That was my experience with Agatha Christie. I can't remember much else except the fabulous library. Agatha died not long afterwards and a year later Max married Barbara Parker, a lady who'd worked for him in Baghdad and some said had for years been his mistress. When I asked why she'd bothered to marry him, at his age, I was told rather wryly: "Of course she only married him for his library you know!"

\* \* \*

The 1971 season began at the end of June and we were back in the Negev. The dramatis personae had changed, the most noticeable being that Colyn was no longer there. Ora had taken her place, having seemingly supplanted her position in Gus's affections, though knowing what I knew about the way the wind had been blowing during the last season, I was not particularly surprised. But more than that, Ora was now tacitly recognised by Gus as the assistant director of the expedition, even though we all assumed she had no experience of archaeology. As the weeks passed, this was to be the cause of considerable and growing friction among the troops as she somewhat shrilly exercised her new-found position to hold forth about things of which they felt she had little or no knowledge. I was told that she also was wont to meddle with the natural ebb and flow of relationships within the staff and the volunteers, offering her tuppence worth of advice and admonition where she thought it appropriate, much to the consternation of the crew, who saw her quite frankly as an interfering nuisance.

Whether for professional or personal reasons, Gus and Ora were becoming totally absorbed with one another. Gus began to sprinkle Modern Hebrew endearments and phrases throughout his conversation. The practice tended to exasperate everybody except, presumably, Ora, upon whom it had the effect that she assumed an even greater importance. But there was a strange and singular twist to this shift in Gus's affections which was actually to my benefit. As soon as I arrived at Jemmeh that season Gus had confronted me in a rather conspiratorial way with an extraordinary suggestion. According to my contract

I was due to be paid $100 a week for my work, which of course I thought was more than acceptable. However it transpired that Gus had two budgets for his work at Jemmeh. One was a very limited amount in US dollars, from which my stipend came, but the other, which was apparently infinite, was in Israeli pounds. This I knew about from the previous season because Vic had enlightened me. The reason why the Israeli pound budget was seemingly endless was that the US Government had over the years accumulated vast amounts in aid deals whereby foreign governments were able to buy American goods with their own currency. Washington apparently had enough Polish Zloty, for example, to buy that whole country out several times over, should they want to. And they had done the same with Israel. Vic called it US Government 'funny money'. So they had an Israeli pound mountain. The currency was not convertible; you couldn't change it anywhere, and it was utterly worthless outside Israel. But since Gus was working on a US-funded project inside Israel, he was entitled to draw down apparently limitless amounts of Israeli pounds. And that was where his suggestion to me came in. Would I accept, he asked, my weekly amount in local currency rather than in green backs? He was prepared to let me have twice the amount, no! three times the amount in local – the equivalent of $300 a week! The only problem of course was that I wouldn't be able to convert it into anything useful. I'd have to spend it all in Israel. I hesitated, at which point he even upped it to four times the amount. I asked for an hour or two to think about it.

I called Louis in Jerusalem from the public phone, and he verified that the licensed money changers wouldn't touch local money under any circumstance except to sell it. Everyone, he said, was trying to get hard currency and divest themselves of Israeli pounds; it was proving extremely difficult. I explained the problem and he gave me the hint of an idea. Without explaining why, he advised me to agree to Gus's suggestion and bring the resultant cash up to Jerusalem at the weekend, so I went back to Gus and said that I would accept his offer. He asked me to sign a hurriedly typed note to that effect, which I did. He was so pleased that he handed me wads of local money, perhaps even more than I was owed. Puzzled, I let the matter rest until Friday afternoon and my next meeting with Louis who, when I got to the Ritz, suggested something so remarkable that I was quite overcome. He confirmed that there was no way that the money changers in the streets outside the hotel or in the Old City would look at local money in exchange for anything. But, he said, the Ritz had a license to change currency for its customers. I should present myself in the hotel reception at eight the following morning and he would explain the next part; I duly was there. The lobby was absolutely packed with American tourists who had just arrived from New York and they were all in the process of checking in. They were at the beginning of a ten-day religious pilgrimage to the Holy Land, and they had all been told that they needed local currency. Louis beckoned me to stand behind the desk with him and as each person asked apprehensively about where they could change money, he pointed to me and said, "Don't worry my dear, David will see to you". Out came my pile of local money and in no time at all I'd converted the whole lot back into US dollars, in ones, fives, tens and even fifty dollar bills, all four hundred plus worth, and all at the punitive hotel rate marked on a board on the counter.

"You can do that every week," he said, "but don't say anything to anyone!"

So when I went back to the dig I kept my mouth shut and every Friday took the inflated amount Gus gave me in Israeli pounds and by Saturday morning they were all converted back into dollars, hundreds and hundreds of them. I was soon rolling in it, especially since I had contrived to pay a lot of my local expenses in yet another way by a process I will describe by and by. As the American tourists would no doubt be the first tell you, happy days were here again!

*  *  *

I never discovered the purpose behind Gus's extraordinary financial jiggery-pokery. He must have wanted the US dollars for something quite different. He was perpetually to be seen sitting with Ora in a scheming huddle, oblivious to anyone else. Every few days they would vanish in their own car – they had a Renault saloon which they used – hot foot to Tell Aviv, or Herzliah or wherever, leaving early in the morning and not getting back till after dark. Sometimes they would stay out all night. Gus said they were going on important business, but he declined to say what that was. We were told to get on with the dig as normal, and occasionally I was even put in charge of the excavations. Whenever they returned they were laden with packages which immediately disappeared into their room. We all wondered what they got up to on these clandestine sorties. I could only conjecture that he needed the hard US currency for these extra-mural forays, but the meaning was never divulged to me.

A week or two later matters must have reached the ears of the wrong people. Gus called me in and spoke to me very seriously. He said that someone was arriving shortly from the Smithsonian, someone high up, someone of his own rank, to check on the expedition and to look at the accounts. He obviously didn't explain why, but he was clearly much discomforted by this development.

"You won't to tell them anything, will you?" he asked solemnly, "I mean, nothing at all OK?"

It wasn't in my interests to reveal the deal we'd made. I was doing amazingly well out of it, so, with the appropriate façade of naiveté, I agreed. I didn't want Gus knowing what I was up to either.

As the time for the Smithsonian staff member to arrive approached, the mood at the dig became more and more sombre and Gus grew more withdrawn and more nervous by the day. There were no more day trips. Gus stayed rooted to the tell and to his room. In the end you could have cut the atmosphere with a knife. Gus seemed to be in paroxysms of indecisiveness. And then the day dawned and the dreaded figure arrived, Gus's nemesis. We felt for him – we'd all been talking about it for weeks.

The man who showed up was Dr. William G. Melson, the Curator of Petrology at the Smithsonian, and equal in rank to Gus. Actually Bill was rather younger than Gus but a highly intelligent academic, and he wasted no time in telling us about himself and about why he had been sent to Jemmeh.

"I'm supposed to look at this guy's accounts. Well, let me tell you I don't care what he does with his money. That's his problem. I accepted this trip so that I could do some geology, and that's what I fully intend to do!"

Bill had amongst his other achievements been put in charge of the recent NASA programme of distributing the rock samples that had been brought back from the surface of the moon in 1969, as a result of which he was soon christened Moon-Rocks Melson. Everyone liked him. He was like a breath of fresh air, and as we were having a gin and tonic together the following evening, he said to me:

"Hey, David, do you fancy coming with me for a few days looking at the local rocks?" I said I'd love to, but I was afraid Gus might not allow it.

"You let me handle Gus!" Bill replied.

And the next morning at breakfast Bill turned to Gus and told him that he was going to spend some time prospecting the rocks of the Negev. He also said that he needed a vehicle to do it – there was a large Ford F50 which he pointed to and told him that was the one he would take. Gus started to object and Bill fixed him with a stare and said:

"Would you rather I was here, checking what was going on?" Gus was immediately quietened.

"And, oh, by the way, I'm taking David with me too. I take it you can spare him for a few days? Good, well then, that's settled. We'll be off in the morning."

That turned out to be the most propitious arrangement I made at Jemmeh, to go around the Negev with Bill. I remember several of the days very well, especially the one when we went down to Makhtesh Ramon, Ramon Crater, near the border with Sinai. Ramon Crater is a 500 metre deep gash which exposes a whole suite of early rocks which display fantastic colours and shapes. It's not really a crater but a deep ravine cut through these strata when the Wadi Arabah, the rift valley south of the Dead Sea, opened up about five million years ago. High and impressive mountains rise at the borders of the crater. There is a black hill to the north which was once an active volcano. A long-ago eruption covered it with basaltic lava. Smaller black hills in the southern part also constituted limestone covered by basalt. And in the centre of the 'crater' were some stone walls, the remains of a caravanserai built by the Nabataeans as part of their camel route from Petra to Gaza. I explained to Bill who the Nabateans were, Arabs who had controlled the extremely lucrative frankincense trade during the last few centuries BC from South Arabia to the Mediterranean and who had built the legendary city of Petra on the other side of the Arabah until their traffic was brought to an end by the Roman emperor Trajan around 106 AD. Bill showed himself to be very interested in the history and archaeology of the region.

But the day that will ever stick out in my memory is one when we didn't go quite so far. We drove east a bit and then walked down the Wadi Ghazzeh, some distance upstream of Jemmeh. There was another of Flinders Petrie's sites nearby, Tell Farah, another huge mound, this time perched on a sandstone bluff high above the wadi. I explained about Petrie's excavations here in the 1920s. We went up on to the top of the tell and I quickly worked out where Petrie had found the remains of an Egyptian Palace dating to the Late Bronze Age. We then descended into the wadi and I told Bill that I was actually working on some of the Middle Bronze Age tomb groups from Farah, from the so-called 500 cemetery, that Petrie had brought back to the UK and which now formed part of the collection at the Institute. I had all of Petrie's original notes and was proposing to use these as part of my PhD, along with the Jericho tombs of the same age. We were walking just where the Farah cemetery had been found and we stopped under a tamarisk tree for a rest. It was then that Bill turned to me and said:

"I've been really impressed with your archaeological knowledge. You shouldn't be working for a jerk like Gus, you know. He's a total waste of time.

You should be doing your own thing. Do you have a research project you'd like to start?"

I thought very quickly and said:

"Yes! Yes, I do, as a matter of fact I do. I'd like to conduct an environmental archaeological survey around here. You know, seeing how changes in climate have affected human cultural evolution and prehistory in the Wadi Ghazzeh and its hinterland, that sort of thing."

It was an idea I had been thinking fundamentally about in London, but that's all I'd been doing, thinking about it. Bill then said:

"Well, I tell you what. You direct it and I'll fund it!"

I was absolutely astounded, and I said so. And then Bill told me about this friend of his, Bob Citron, a volcanologist at the Smithsonian, who was setting up a totally new type of funding body called EEI, Educational Expeditions International, which would suit me perfectly, he said. The idea was that it placed adult students with renowned academics on field courses overseas, and in return for their participation and learning they would contribute to the Expedition funding.

And believe it or not, that's exactly what happened. Out of Bill's idea came the British Western Negev Expedition which I was to direct for the next several years and which was to explore totally new ways and methods of looking at the past. As an organisation EEI was eventually to morph into 'Earthwatch' and I was to be one of its first P Is, Principal Investigators, more of which later!

As we drove back to Jemmeh that evening I can tell you that I was in a state of considerable excitement.

\* \* \*

At this point I must digress to explain how I dreamed up the idea for the environmental project which I suggested to Moon-Rocks that day in Wadi Ghazzeh, an idea that had been fomenting in my mind for some years. In this present century of what I might style 'undisciplined climate change fear-mongering, both for and against, I think a note is needed to make clear the background to my interest in the subject in the early 1970s, a time before it was even a twinkle in the global political eye, never mind an uncontrolled football for the chattering classes to kick about. Let me say at the outset, for me there is no argument about changing global climates; it's been happening throughout geological time, for millions if not for billions of years, and

. changes will go on long after humanity has either drowned itself through the effects of greenhouse gasses or blown itself into oblivion with nuclear warfare. What is far more significant for me as an archaeologist, as it certainly was in the 1970s, is the question of to what extent human evolution, physical, cultural and economic, has been shaped by these colossal swings in climate and hence of the overall environment? When we have to consider how early humans made a living, how they survived generation by generation, it seemed to me essential to try to reconstruct what they saw around them when they awoke as the sun rose each day in the prehistoric past. What was the scenery like then; what plant species were available; what animals were their contemporaries in those primaeval mornings?

The fact that climates change had been established from as early as the beginning of the 19th century, if not earlier. The idea was especially developed in the alpine valleys of Germany, Austria and Switzerland, where it had been suggested that glacial 'erratics', geologically misplaced boulders, had been moved by now non-existent ice, giving rise to the concept of a past 'Ice Age'. Indeed, at the beginning of the 20th century two alpine geologists, Penk and Bruckner, advanced the concept that there had been four major alpine ice advances and contractions, and this was confirmed by geologists and geomorphologists in Scandinavian, Britain and North America. Thus by the early 1960s, when I was at school learning about physical geography, the idea of cyclical ice sheet advances and contractions was well established.

This was even more emphatically seared into my own imagination because the last major ice advance, known as the 'Würmian' in the alpine sequence, is known in Britain as the 'Devensian', after the River Dee (Deva Fluvius), which forms the border between England and North Wales, considered to be near the southernmost point to which that ice reached. The Dee flows about five kilometres north of the small border town of Oswestry, where I was born and brought up. It's a river in which I fished for trout when I was a boy. The immediacy of that fact was even more emphatic when I further discovered that my own home had been built on top of a terminal moraine of the same ice sheet. I was thus forcibly struck by the question of what my own back garden would have looked like during that arctic winter a mere 20,000 years ago – a very different place, I was sure, to the place I knew, a frozen polar desert with grinding glaciers and bitter, howling winds and the snouts of an ice sheet more than one kilometre thick covering the landscape. The countryside of North Wales, closely adjacent, is full of features left by the ice – 'U' shaped valleys, glacial pavements, lateral moraines, drumlins, eskers;

the whole paraphernalia of an ancient polar wilderness was on my doorstep. Thus began my constant question – what was the earth like when human evolutionary changes took place. And more importantly, was climatic change the engine of those changes?

Much collaborative work had been done on advancing and retreating ice sheets during the first half of the twentieth century. Similar features were found in the central United States and Canada, in parts of Norway and Sweden and in northern Russia. Glacial features abound all over what are now ice-free high latitudes of the northern hemisphere, and periglacial features such as glacial lakes and sub-glacial traces like those left by tundra have been traced as far south as southern France and Italy. It is impressive evidence of an ever-changing world. But for all these improvements in our knowledge, for me there was a fundamental drawback. The high latitudes of the northern hemisphere, the ones being studied, were definitely not where the significant elements of evolution, physical or cultural, had taken place. The onset of bipedalism (walking on two legs) , the beginnings of technology, (stone tool manufacture), the change from hunting and gathering to settled farming (the Neolithic Revolution) and the development of towns and cities and hierarchic government (urbanism), in short civilization itself, are changes that had taken place in the sub-tropics and tropics of the earth, in Africa and the Middle East, not in northern Britain or Scandinavia.

This led to the obvious and even more essential question - what had happened climatically here, in the sub-tropics and the tropics? There was no answer. With one or two conspicuously obscure guesses, no-one had really considered that problem. And anyway, it was incautiously thought, maybe there had been no climatic change around the mid-latitudes of the globe. In any case, all the methodology to study climate change had been developed to explain ice advances and contractions in high northern latitudes; so had the tropics and sub-tropics remained unaffected? It was a question that had largely been ignored. This was the question I wanted to pursue; climatically, what had actually happened in these areas? What had happened here during any globally cold phase of earth history? That was the background to my response to Moon-Rocks, my interest in any environmental changes that had taken place, for example, in Gaza and the Negev Desert.

CHAPTER EIGHT
# GLOBAL TOURS

*"The traveller is active; he goes strenuously in search of*
*people, of adventure, of experience. The tourist is passive; he*
*expects interesting things to happen to him. He goes sight-*
*seeing."*
Daniel J. Boorstin

For the two or three weeks Moon-Rocks was with us, he was kept happy with his geology, allowing Gus to resume his normal demeanour, though he didn't leave the dig for a moment while Bill was there. And it was just as well he didn't. The new mud-bricks turned out to be far more interesting and more challenging than even Gus, with his heightened sense of drama, could have imagined. The more they were articulated - that was the word he used to describe them being cleaned up - the more distinct they became. They were definitely canted over but they were in-situ, as he'd observed at the end of the previous season, but not because they had fallen like that. It was because they were the remains of the top side of a vault, a pitched-brick barrel vault which had acted as a roof over something underneath. It meant we were excavating through the ceiling of a building into a room below, and much of that ceiling was still intact. It was truly astonishing. As the structure gradually emerged, it became clearer and clearer. You could see the inside walls of the lower room, and the spring of the vault all around the edge. The centre part of the arching vault over the middle of the room had collapsed downwards. It must originally have been a two-storey building of which the whole of the lower storey had been preserved by fallen debris from the upper one. It had been in that fill that the little bowl had been found at the end of last season; presumably it had slid in from the upper storey. Gus had never seen anything quite like it. But I can say that it was thanks to his careful method of excavating mud-brick that he had managed to get the whole feature properly clarified.

And it was not just one room either. The same elements started to appear in some of the other squares, and in the end there were six of these little rooms, making a large rectangular honeycomb, each one with part of the stubs of their ceiling vaults still preserved. Presumably the lower storey rooms had been intended for storage as they had no windows, and the top surface of their vaults had provided the foundations for the floor for the upper storey which would itself have benefitted from more of the afternoon breeze. But what was this extraordinary building? We eagerly awaited Gus's next pronouncement. Of course as always Petrie had been here before us, and he too had found Assyrian Palace Ware in his excavations. He had uncovered a large building with a courtyard, around which there was a regular series of rooms opening off. There can be no doubt that this design was Assyrian in inspiration; there was nothing like it in contemporary Palestine, that is, in the eighth and seventh centuries BC, but there were a number of buildings like this in northern Mesopotamia which had been classified as Assyrian 'royal palaces'. Petrie's building might not have been quite that grand, but it could have been the residence of an Assyrian regional governor or some kind of high-up military administrative official and our vaulted rooms could well have been part of it.

During the early part of the first millennium BC the Assyrians had become an unstoppable military force in the Fertile Crescent. They hailed from the Upper Tigris Valley, in what is now north-eastern Iraq, where they had previously lived for centuries, trading with the lands round about them without any apparent tension or ill will, but soon after 900 BC they began to expand their sphere of influence by conducting a series of plundering raids on their neighbours, both southwards down the Tigris-Euphrates Valley into Babylonia and as far as the Persian Gulf, and west across Syria to the Mediterranean Sea, which they called the 'Great Sea of the Amurru Land'. Theirs was to become an extremely violent and vicious regime and they boastfully wrote copiously about their conquests; many of their cuneiform annals have been found. I knew a lot about them. I'd given lectures about their military exploits and excesses as part of my teaching in London. Their general foreign policy was to scare the living daylights out of their subject peoples by using the most brutal methods they could think of against them. All conquerors at the time practiced a policy of terror to a greater or lesser degree, but the Assyrians surpassed them all for sheer gratuitous malevolence. The Assyrian king who invaded Syria in the ninth century BC, Ashurnasirpal, was fairly typical. In his annals he seems to take great delight in describing the way in which he dealt with one recalcitrant city state and its inhabitants:

'I built a pillar over against their city gate. I flayed all the chiefs who had revolted and covered the pillar with their skins. Some I walled up within the pillar, some I impaled upon the pillar on stakes. I cut off the limbs of the officers who had rebelled against me. From some I cut off their noses, their ears and their fingers and of many I put out their eyes. Their young men and maidens I burned in the fire.'

But they didn't reach as far as Judah until the end of the following century, when they suffered their ignominious reversal due either to the intervention of the Angel of the Lord or to the depredations of field mice, depending on whom you read. So how did Jemmeh fit into that history, if at all? Gus was at first reluctant to be too specific. But the primary question he asked was that apart from the palace-ware pottery how was he to know that the vaulted buildings were really Assyrian at all?

The reason was found in his beloved mud bricks. First, the bricks that had been used to cantilever the vaults off the wall were square, a shape never used in Palestine but which was common in Assyria. Second, the vaults were pitched barrel vaults, again a design not seen at all in Palestine but which was known from Assyria. And third, the vaults were not semi-circular in profile, but coved, curved out from the wall and then laid somewhat flatter across the centre. To achieve this, the bricks in the middle of the vault had been made in the shape of *voussoirs*. They were a most unconventional wedge-shape in section which tightened the whole arch when laid, a design which was totally absent in the Levant but was known from the upper Tigris.

So where did the Assyrians at Jemmeh fit into the overall picture? Gus's later researches gave him the answer. After the ignominy of the defeat suffered by the Assyrians under Sennacherib in 701 BC, the Egyptians now got involved and began machinated politically in southern Palestine to try to stave off any further threat to their kingdom on the Nile. When the new Assyrian king Esarhaddon ascended the throne in 680 BC, he decided to conquer Egypt as a reprisal for their interference and the following year he began to fortify his southern frontier in the Negev in preparation, and on that frontier was Jemmeh. There is even an Assyrian name which Gus found for Jemmeh - Arza - known to the Egyptians as Yurza. Arza was sacked by Esarhaddon in 679 and then reconstructed as an Assyrian military frontier post. It may well be that it was at this moment that the palace and storage rooms at Jemmeh were built, in preparation for Esarhaddon's imminent invasion of the Delta which he then went ahead and launched. Arza would have been his forward headquarters and base. During his invasion in 671 he captured the capital of Lower Egypt, Memphis, from its 25th dynasty pharaoh, Taharqa, who incidentally was a Nubian, a black pharaoh. Two years later Taharqa seized the Delta back again.

Esarhaddon died, and his son, Ashurbanipal, was left to retaliate and again the Assyrians invaded Egypt, this time campaigning all the way south up the Nile to Thebes, modern day Luxor. But although they killed hundreds of Egyptians, taking masses of spoil and plunder in the process, Assyria's star was about to wane. In 655 the new Egyptian pharaoh, Psammeticus, defeated Ashurbanipal's armies decisively and then pursued them north into Palestine. The Assyrian domination of the Levant was finally over. In 612 in northern Iraq their last capital city, Nineveh, was destroyed by an alliance of the Babylonians, the Medes and the Scythians. The people of Judah were ecstatic. You only have to read their account in the Old Testament Book of Nahum, which incidentally has little if anything to do with any religious message but is a rather breathless rant about seeing Assyria destroyed once and for all. It's incredibly bloodthirsty and triumphalist.

'I will lift your skirts over your face and nations will look upon your nakedness. I will cast abominable filth over you and make you a gazing-stock … and all who hear about you shall clap their hands over you, for upon whom has not come your unceasing wickedness.'

Marvellous, unless you were an Assyrian of course! Incidentally, the elation that this turn of events encouraged among the people of Judah was to be short lived. One of the very armies who had done the smiting in Assyria, the Babylonians, then went on to turn their attention to Palestine and within twenty years Jerusalem had been totally obliterated and most of the population of Judah forcibly dragged off to southern Mesopotamia and exile, a piece of ancient history that still rankles with some fanatical nationalists to this very day.

Getting back to Esarhaddon and Ashurbanipal, they were the monarchs who probably represented the connection between the Assyrians and Jemmeh/Arza. As for Gus, he went on to excavate right down to the floor of the vaulted rooms, finding lots more Assyrian Palace Ware, though he came to the conclusion that although the pottery was the right design it hadn't been carted more than one thousand kilometres from the Tigris; it was probably made locally. But what a remarkable discovery the palace, or whatever it was, represented. And in one of those vaulted rooms there was even a complete doorway leading out of the complex, blocked by fallen mud brick of course, leading to … well, we shall never know. He didn't excavate through it. I like to think somewhat romantically that it would have led straight into the past, two thousand six hundred years ago.

\* \* \*

I made a life-long friend among the volunteers that second year, Alan Linden, who became known to me as Big Al. He came up to Jerusalem with me and was a frequent associate of the 'prayer-meetings' at the leopard-skin bar at the Ritz. He worked in Washington at the National Library of Congress in the Congressional Research Service and that's how he'd known about Gus and the Smithsonian expedition to Jemmeh. We were talking together one evening early in the season about life, the universe and archaeology when he said:

"You know, David, you should take some of us around these other archaeological sites you know so much about."

And out of that was born Tell Jemmeh Global Tours, a weekly weekend programme of unbridled fun in the sun by which I would organise a trip up to Jerusalem and then an outing the following day to see one or another of the archaeological sites in the country, and the volunteers would collectively pay for the taxis and by default for my hotel room at the Ritz in return for being taught what the sites were and how they fitted into the scheme of things. Every Thursday at breakfast-time in the eucalyptus grove, after Gus had given out his notices about the dig, I would outline the forthcoming weekend's planned attractions and by a show of hands would work out how many taxis we needed and how many rooms at the Ritz. That lunchtime I would phone through the details to Louis and he would set the whole arrangement in motion. By close of business on Friday morning Sami and the taxis would already be waiting at the gulag, engines running, and a few minutes later we were speeding on our way up to the Holy City. It worked the whole season long and it meant that I got to see and photograph all the main archaeological sites in Israel and the West Bank, none of which I'd ever seen before, although the troops didn't know that. Thus I was able to build up a marvellous slide library for my winter lectures at the university. It also meant that at the Ritz I was entitled to tour-leader's perks, such as being given one of their super-sized spacious suites when one was free. And in that the group were paying for all the transport and the accommodation for the whole weekend it meant I was able to hang on to even more of my freshly laundered green backs – a great arrangement all round I thought.

I dreamed up more and more elaborate tours each week and they became ever more popular, involving even more taxis and more suites. We made trips down to the sites along the coast such as the Roman remains at Caesarea, home amongst other things of Herod the Great, and trips up north through the hill country, through Ramallah, to Nablus to see Tell Balatah, site of ancient Shechem, and Samaria, capital of the Biblical Northern Kingdom. I knew just enough about each site from my studies in London that at each one I could interpret the various remains and put them into a historical context, even relating them where I could to the periods we were excavating at Jemmeh, though that was often not as easy – Persian and Assyrian remains were rare. By the end of each day's excursion we'd be back in Jerusalem ready for the evening's festivities. At the leopard-skin bar Al taught me a new trick to get the night off to a good start. He'd seen a bottle of Mariachi Tequila behind the bar, and the inner circle of we who were about to go out for dinner would order a round of drinks. The shots of tequila were all lined up along the bar, together with slices of lemon and a salt cellar. The idea was to moisten your left hand between finger and thumb, shake some salt onto it, then, all together, lick off the salt, smash back the Tequila and suck hard on the lemon slice. Two or three rounds of this and we were ready to hit the town and it was off to the Golden Chicken or similar hostelry.

As the season wore on my weekly tours became more and more adventurous, moving further afield, for example to Tell al-Mutesellim, the site of Ancient Megiddo, in a gap in the Carmel range. This was a really important defensive site in the Middle Bronze Age when, as I described it, the sides of the tell had been smoothed off and plastered to form a glacis surmounted by a wall. To get into the city you would have had to walk up a flight of stairs which started left of the gate, thus exposing your left side to the defenders on the wall, and then you had to make a right-angled turn through an 'I' shaped gateway. As I was describing this phenomenon in detail, with all the drama I could muster, while looking at nothing more than a heap of ruins, I remember some wisecrack piping up,

"Adds a new meaning to the term glassy eyed stare then!"

Walking to the top of the tell we looked at the excavations which had been completed by the Americans from the Oriental Institute at Chicago between the two world wars. They had intended to excavate the whole tell layer by layer, peeling each one back, but they ran out of cash. It's just as well because in trying to do this holistic archaeology they screwed up some of the stratigraphic relationships, mixing the layers with one another instead of separating them period by period. They managed to get some of their interpretations wildly out, like the attribution of the Solomonic three-piered gateway with the so-called Solomonic Stables – they were actually a couple of hundred years apart. But it all added to the drama of my description of the site.

On another weekend we made a trip right up to the Sea of Galilee to see the excavations of the synagogue at Capernaum, maybe it was even the one mentioned in the New Testament, and to the twin peaks of the Horns of Hattin overlooking the town of Tiberius. It was here on the 4th of July 1187 that the crusader knights led by Guy de Lusignac and Raymond of Tripoli were soundly defeated by Saladin. It's said almost twenty thousand crusaders were killed that day, ending their influence in Palestine for good and allowing Islamic forces once again to become the pre-eminent military power in the Holy Land. Saladin went on to re-conquered Jerusalem later that same year and the Muslims were to hang on to it for the next seven centuries. It was on that trip that we also went up to the Christian town of Nazareth, where Jesus was supposed to have been brought up in the carpenter's shop, as you know. Needless to say, no trace of the Nazarene carpenter's shop now remains.

But one of the best trips we made, for me at least, was to Mount Carmel and the northern Mediterranean Coast. On the south-western end of Mount Carmel there is a wadi, Wadi el-Mughara, the Valley of Caves. There are several caves here of supreme importance to the prehistory of the Middle East. The first and uppermost is Mugharet et-Tabun, the Cave of the Oven, which has a long sequence of the Stone Age dating back into the Lower Palaeolithic period, well beyond a hundred thousand years ago. It had originally been excavated by one of the great British female archaeologists of the inter-war period, Dorothy Garrod, who incidentally as a result of her field work here became the first-ever woman to gain a professorship at Cambridge. The site was currently being re-excavated by an American team under Professor Art Jelinek of the University of Arizona.

Another large cave in the same cliffs is Mugharet el-Wad which contained extremely important information in its uppermost strata about the Natufian Period, the Epi- Palaeolithic, which just like at Jericho's Natufian is the moment when agriculture first began. And lower down the slope is Mugharet es-Skhul, the Cave of the Kids, another cave excavated by Dorothy Garrod in 1928. The excavations also had evidence of the same Epi-Palaeolithic culture, characterised by the presence of abundant microliths, human burials and ground stone implements. But for me the real importance of Skhul was the discovery of a number of Neanderthal burials, people who had been present in the region from more than 200,000 years ago until about 30,000 years ago, during the last part of which they had lived alongside early examples of modern humans. All this terminology was totally new to the group and I had to go over it several times before they could fully grasp what was going on.

After an exhausting morning explaining the whole concept of human prehistory, I was ready for a good lunch and Sami suggested the port town of Akko, which still had a large Arab population and it was likely we could get a good meal there. We drove north around the Bay of Haifa and into the Old

Town. It was an amazing place. It had been a centre for the crusaders, when it was known as Saint Jean D'Acre. It was also associated with such well-known names as Richard the Lionheart, and in its day it was said to be wealthier than the whole of England put together. In the end it was the location of the last stand in the Holy Land of the Knights Hospitaller. It finally fell to the Mameluks in 1291. The old city of Saint Jean D'Acre was still very much in evidence and we found a picturesque restaurant right on the quayside surrounded by the old crusader walls. I looked at the fresh fish they had on display and talked to the owner. He advised we start with a host of meze followed by a number of fish dishes. The price he gave me for all of us - we were about fifteen - was very reasonable so I immediately agreed. He quickly set up a long table in the open on the quayside shaded with large umbrellas and we sat down and ordered drinks – he had everything - wine, beer, Fanta, Coca Cola, whatever anyone wanted.

I can remember that meal to this very day. It was truly sumptuous. There were endless meze – hummus, tahini, baba ganoush, green salad, pickled vegetables, black and green olives, the lot. And then came the fish - one huge grouper, various smaller fish, lobster salad, well, crayfish actually, but just as good. The wine flowed freely and everyone ate and drank well. There was baklava to finish, sweet dates and strong Arabic coffee flavoured with ground cardamom seeds. At the end of almost two hours we were properly replete, and I was musing on what a successful day it had been among the caves followed by such a memorable lunch. The bill came for the food and the drinks and it was so little that I just divided it by fifteen:

"That will be twelve dollars each" I announced, and that's when the trouble started.

"But I never had lobster, you had lobster, I didn't", this woman whined.

"There was plenty of lobster. You could have had as much as you wanted!"

"Well, I don't like lobster."

"There were lots of other things besides that you could have had."

"And another thing, you had wine, I only had Coca Cola."

"Coca Cola is more expensive than wine. They grow wine here. It's cheap."

"It's not like that in Pennsylvania. Coca Cola is much cheaper than wine there."

"Well, it's not like that here! Coca Cola is more expensive, and you had at least two cans, so pay up."

With extreme reluctance the woman who had been speaking paid up. I found out later that she was the wife of a wealthy goldsmith from Pittsburgh and she must have been rolling in it. But although she'd turned the end of the meal into something of a distasteful fiasco, the episode did give me a well-known phrase or saying. Forever after that, whenever anyone I am travelling with cavils about their share of the bill, I always calm myself down by thinking, 'But I never had lobster'.

* * *

After another archaeological extravaganza we arrived back at the Ritz and repaired to the leopard-skin bar for the traditional pre-prandial libations. We'd had another great day out and were looking forward to a few drinks and a good dinner. Al was in fine form again and we fell to talking about the political situation in Israel and the conspicuous lack of manners shown by most of its citizens. Almost universally I found them to be strident, disdainful and boorish, a combination of characteristics that I thought made them universally unlikeable. But we had some Jewish people among the volunteers who thought their would-be compatriots were wonderful. 'They're sabras you know, like prickly pears, uncomfortable on the outside but really sweet on the inside'. I wasn't sure about that analogy; I found them generally very unwelcoming and often downright disagreeable. I knew that Al was Jewish, and I asked him if he identified with the people and the country at all.

"Me? Hell no David! I wouldn't want to live with these crazies a minute more than I had to. I mean, to me they're really like foreigners. And this country? Well it seems to me to be so fucked up they can keep it as far as I'm concerned. Give me the old US of A any day. Cheers!"

We never mentioned it again, and went out and had ourselves a really good Arab dinner in Salahadin Street.

When we got back it was late, and we decided to have a nightcap at the leopard-skin bar. As we were quietly drinking, Louis came across from reception and said he was about to knock off for the night. It was midnight already and he was going home. But he then suggested we went with him. Al cried off with tiredness, but I was up for another adventure.

"I've got something in the Old City I want to show you. It's really interesting. I think you'll enjoy it."

With that I finished my drink and went out with him into the night, wondering what on earth it could be at this late hour. We walked along Salahadin Street and down Sultan Suleiman Road to the Damascus Gate. The Old City was totally deserted at this time of night, the light from the dim street lamps reflecting off the polished stones, burnished by so many centuries of human traffic. We continued along the empty, echoing alleyways. All the shops were shut, their roller closures pulled down and padlocked, and their upper storeys in deep shadow. We were walking towards the Platform, near the Bab al Silsila, the Gate of the Chain. Ancient doorways decorated with Moorish style stone arches were dimly discernible in the half light and their protruding wooden balconies of the houses were all obscured, shutters tightly closed. It was both eerie and magical by turns walking along these narrow abandoned thoroughfares normally so bustling with life. At a particular spot in an otherwise blank wall, Louis stopped and opening a door beckoned me to follow him inside. We walked down two or three steep stone steps into a semi-basement and there suddenly among huge Ottoman stone arches was a hive of industry illuminated by the light of a few weak, naked bulbs. It was a bakery, gearing up for the next day's demand for loaves. The bakers were busily working, loading the unbaked loaves onto large wooden spatulas and flicking them deftly onto the stones of the oven and then withdrawing the cooked loaves. Their faces were brightly lit from the oven's glare.

Louis spoke quietly to one of the bakers and passed him a few coins, and he in turn handed Louis a couple of newly-baked loaves of 'ka'ak'. This is a traditional bread ring, the dough for which has been leavened with fermented chickpeas and the outside covered with sesame seeds. When cooked they are like large puffy bread donuts. Jerusalem was apparently famous for its ka'ak. He gave me one; it was still warm from the oven. Louis then dug around in a bucket of sawdust at his side and pulled out two hen's eggs that had just been baked in the oven alongside the bread. They too were warm. He passed me a screw of newspaper in which there was a condiment to go with the egg which gave off a sort of lemony aroma – sumac. I peeled my egg and dipped it in the sumac and ate it with the newly-baked bread.

The combination of the ka'ak and the sumac-flavoured egg was unforgettable, a taste that I realised must have stretched back over many centuries. Louis and I sat there on a simple wooden bench in the semi-darkness of that room with its huge stone-built vaults, wrapped in the warmth from the open oven, watching the quiet, efficient movements of the bakers and I knew that this process had been going on here every day of every year since forever, back to the Middle Ages and maybe beyond. It was incredible in its simplicity and its cultural scope.

After a while, we got up and left, going back into the darkness of the Old City. Louis said his goodbyes at the corner of a nearby alley and I continued up to the Damascus Gate and the Ritz. As I walked I fell into a reverie, dominated by thoughts of a long cultural continuity now under threat from an alien world and an alien people. Al was right, I thought. Some of the Israelis I had met, mainly the newcomers with their unpleasant manners and their artless attitudes, were indeed in danger of screwing the whole thing up. How disheartening, I thought. How depressing!

CHAPTER NINE
# FLYING HIGH

*O little town of Bethlehem*
*How still we see thee lie;*
*Above thy deep and dreamless sleep*
*The silent stars go by.*
*Yet in thy dark streets shineth*
*The everlasting Light;*
*The hopes and fears of all the years*
*Are met in thee tonight.*
Words: Phillips Brooks, 1857. Music: 'Forest Green', Ralph
Vaughan Williams, 1906

For this second season at Jemmeh my good friend and confidante Vic had been replaced as the expedition photographer by Chip - Chip Vincent. Chip had worked the previous year in the wilds of Afghanistan with a Canadian archaeologist so he was used to rough conditions. He had brought with him his girlfriend, an English rose by the name of Felicity. In that neither he nor I had a trench to supervise we were naturally thrown together in each other's company, and the two of us, in fact all three of us, got along very well. One evening, Gus called us both in to his room. He said he had made arrangements for a special private flight over the tell so that he could obtain information about the site from the air in case there were some features he'd missed, and he wanted Chip to take the pictures. In the event that they wouldn't be able to find the site, as the site surveyor I was to go along as well to act as navigator to make sure we flew over the right spot. The flight was scheduled for the morning in couple of days' time, and Gus said that he and Ora would drive us to the airfield to connect with the plane.

Duly, that Thursday, after an early breakfast of the interminable tomatoes and cucumbers, we drove in Gus's Renault up to Lod Airport where the plane was already sitting on the apron waiting. We met the air charter owner who introduced us to the pilot, a real cowboy of a character, who said he could fly us wherever and however we wanted. We then sat for a while in the office; it turned out we were waiting for a pimply red-haired youth in army fatigues to arrive, and as he entered the room he announced that he was coming too. Apparently, so he told us, he was to act as the security operative, for want of a better title, and that he was there to prevent us from inadvertently taking pictures of any military or other sensitive installations over which we might fly. We then walked across the tarmac to the plane, a rather aging high-wing, four-seater single engine Cessna 206 painted in a dull camouflage green. The exceptional and certainly the most unnerving feature of this aircraft was that one of the rear doors had been completely removed, I suppose the better to allow for photographs to be taken from the back seats. The pilot and the security chap got into the front seats leaving Chip and me to clamber in the back. Gus and Ora watched through the office window. They'd told us they'd be waiting for us when we got back in an hour or two's time. It did cross my mind that Gus could have been the fourth member of the flying party, and I wondered why he hadn't exercised that option. Maybe he was scared of flying, I thought.

We were told to buckle up, which I did with great care, making sure the harness was properly secured to the fuselage and that the buckle wouldn't just open accidentally during the flight. As we sat there prior to take off, with the engine revving and the propeller whirring away, the pimply youth turned in his seat and told us that we were forbidden to take any photographs at all unless he said so. He implied that it would constitute a grave breach of security if we did, and that he would have to confiscate all our film from the whole flight should we not heed his strict instructions. Before we had a chance to argue, the pilot revved the engine, skewed the plane around and we were off. The noise was sufficiently deafening that any further discussion or conversation was rendered impossible, and a minute or two later we were bowling down the huge runway of the international airport gathering speed until the tiny plane flipped up into a clear blue sky.

We were soon flying south along the boundary of the hill country and the coastal plain. I had a map with me with the archaeological sites marked on it and shortly after take-off I recognised the tell at Gezer, an important Iron Age site, another of Solomon's fortified cities, which was currently under excavation. I attracted the attention of the pimply youth, waving my camera at him, but he shook his head and motioned back and forth with the flat of his hand in an entirely negative way. We flew on. Next, I noticed off to the left-hand side the tell at Lachish. Again I tapped the spotty youth on the shoulder and waved my camera at him; again he shook his head. I couldn't see anything that might even vaguely constitute a security risk and I began to form the impression that he was some sort of a control freak who just wanted to demonstrate his somewhat questionable authority over the proceedings. So, we continued to bump along picture-less and somewhat uncomfortably on the thermals rising from the hills.

By and by we reached the Wadi Ghazzeh and I motioned the pilot to turn north-westwards, which he duly did. Eventually Tell Jemmeh hove into view. I pointed to it and made him understand that this is what we had come for, gesticulating at him that he should fly in a wide circle around the mound. Being of a distinctly macho disposition, he put the plane into a tight turn to leave the site on our left hand side, the side Chip was on, but because he had banked so steeply I had an excellent view too. It was while we were negotiating this first abrupt turn that I noticed that the pimply youth was looking distinctly queasy, so after the first circuit I motioned again to the pilot to increase the altitude and decrease the turning circle which he did with great panache; powerful 'G' forces coursed through us as he gained height, the plane banking hard on its side. The pimply youth looked scared and distinctly off-colour. He made hand signals to the pilot who passed him a sick-bag into which he immediately threw up. I looked at him for a moment then indicated to the pilot to descend for a low pass in the opposite direction straight over the tell. The plane lurched downwards and the youth began to look a lot worse. Up! I signalled; Down! Around this way; around that way! The youth was in considerable and growing distress by now, his mouth open and his jaw slack, his head lolling from side to side with every movement of the plane. In the end he was beyond caring and just seemed to pass out altogether.

It was at this point that I motioned again to the pilot to fly east down the wadi, which we followed for some time before coming to the tell at Farah. I pointed where we should aim for and he efficiently interpreted of my instructions. I took a whole roll of pictures of the tell, the wadi and its surroundings before pointing back up towards Jemmeh. We again flew over Jemmeh and after a couple of turns during which Chip took all the pictures he wanted I showed him that he should continue flying further up the wadi to the coast. Gaza came into view, as well as the site of ancient Gaza, Tell Ajjul. We took loads more pictures and then motioned back to the hill country. We passed again over the tell at Lachish while I clicked away, and the same over a few lesser sites until we reached Tell Gezer. The pimply youth was out cold. After a quick flip over Gezer I indicated to the pilot that we were finished and wanted to get back to the airport. As we descended, I took the latest film out of my camera and put it in my inside pocket, leaving the camera empty. Eventually we made our final approach, affecting a good if somewhat cavalier landing, and taxied to the charter office. We stopped and the engine was cut; as we got out of the plane our hearing returned and we walked to the office where Gus and Ora were waiting. We had already left the building some minutes later and were walking towards the Renault when the pimply youth staggered after us. He had regained consciousness, though I must say he still looked dreadful. Haltingly he said:

"You didn't take any pictures did you?"

"No!" we both said. "You told us not to, so we didn't."

I showed him my empty camera and he stumbled off still dazed but seemingly placated. We by comparison had rolls and rolls of aerial shots in the can not only of Tell Jemmeh, but also of all the other sites we had flown over, and in particular I had a whole roll dedicated to Tell Farah which I thought would come in very handy for my planned expedition next year, not to mention for my PhD.

*   *   *

There were some interesting volunteers and staff on the dig that second year, or at least they had some interesting names. One of them was one of the site supervisors, Bill Potts. His full name turned out to be William T. Potts. When I asked him what the 'T' stood for, he said it didn't stand for anything. His father was a bit of a comedian, he said, and had put the middle initial in to make a rather weak joke out of his name – Bill Tea Pots. He wasn't amused at all. Another was a good looking but rather intense girl called Cynthia Anthony – she aspirated the pronunciation of both of the 'th''s. I inadvertently called her Anthea Cynthony one day; she wasn't amused either.

But the strangest surname of all was Annie's. Annie came from Danvers, Massachusetts and she was of Italian extraction. Her grandfather had emigrated from northern Italy at the start of the Depression and had arrived in the USA via Ellis Island. His surname had been Morosini, a famous Venetian name; the Morosini family had risen to the status of considerable nobility in Venice and some had become cardinals, statesmen and even doges. One of the most famous was Francesco Morosini who was made the Captain General of the Venetian Republic in the early seventeenth century. There is still a palace in Venice named after him, the Palazzo Morosini, on the Rio Dei Pestrin. But when Annie's grandfather arrived at Ellis Island, the immigration officials obviously hadn't heard of the name and couldn't even spell it, so they gave him the nearest English equivalent, and that's how Annie had got her surname. She was Anne Morose. But despite her rather glum appellation, Annie was great fun, always laughing and joking, always happy. I especially remember an incident at the gulag. Gus had erected a tented canopy at the back of our accommodation block, built with a concrete floor and metal uprights, which Ora called a 'souhaha', apparently the Hebrew word for a tent or booth. In the afternoons sundry volunteers could be seen sitting under the shade of the tent washing pot sherds from the excavation. The conversations among the participants sometimes became a bit raucous as they exchanged funny stories between them to pass the time, something that Ora took to be bordering on sacrilegious in the presence of Gus's precious pottery. On one such afternoon someone made a particularly ribald joke, causing peals of ensuing laughter from the rest of the workers, at which point Annie bounded up and in a loud and admonishing Ora impersonation shouted:

"Hey you people, what is this brouhaha in the souhaha?"

The assembly collapsed with merriment but Ora, who had been standing to one side slightly hidden from view at the back of the canopy was, alas, not amused.

\* \* \*

Now and again when I was at a loose end of an evening at the Ritz, Louis and I would go to Bethlehem for dinner. Provided there were no road blocks it was only about a twenty minute journey by cab. He had a friend there who owned a restaurant overlooking the site where it was believed the shepherds 'lay keeping their sheep, on a cold winter's night that was so deep'. In fact, rather obviously, his friend had called the restaurant 'The Shepherds' Fields' – at least that was slightly better than 'The First Noel', which I suppose he could have chosen. Anyway, the tidings of great joy which 'The Shepherds Fields' restaurant had to offer were some of the very best lamb chops I have ever tasted. Cooked over the open coals, they were small and trimmed of all fat so that just the eye of the meat remained on the bone and they were quite delicious. As I chewed on the chops and looked out of the open window across the dark limestone hills where no doubt the lambs had been raised, I just hoped that the certain poor shepherds who had been there two thousand years ago had enjoyed lamb chops anything like this good. But I have to say that as far as the little town of Bethlehem was concerned, it was one of the few genuine if somewhat convoluted parallels that I could ever think of with regard to the story of the birth of Jesus.

The Church of the Nativity in the centre of the town looks authentic enough from the outside, if a little over-fortified for a religious building. It had been built originally by the Empress Helena after another of her night visions. Inside, the Corinthian basilica which forms the main nave of the church is austere, evoking images of Byzantine churches in other parts of the Empire, and with the same history of destruction and reconstruction, the only indication that there is something different here being one or two large and very dusty Christmas tree decorations hanging near the chancel. But the real focus of the church is to be found in a small cellar underneath the altar which is said to be the very cave which had acted as the stable of the 'no- vacancies' inn, the one in which Jesus of Nazareth had been born. This is tricked out with the same tasteless jumble of religious bric-a-brac found in other churches in the Holy Land, though on a smaller scale – hanging lamps, innumerable icons and thick, embroidered drapes, heavy with the odour of incense. The nucleus of veneration here appears to be a marble slab with a circular depression in the centre surrounded by a silver studded star. Worshippers kneel with their bums in the air, heads under the surrounding curtains looking as though they are trying to find something under the bed. The grotto is operated by the same unholy trinity - the Greek Orthodox, the Armenians and the Roman Catholics - who administer the Church of the Holy Sepulchre in Jerusalem, with the same degree of hooliganism, scrapping and general squabbling. Quite how one evokes any kind of spiritual inspiration from the whole ensemble with all that going on is difficult to visualise.

Outside and presided over by a neon star is Manger Square, with the blank walls of the ancient church on the one side and a row of cypress trees on the other. Beyond that is the untrammelled commercialism of Christmas, three hundred and sixty-five days of the year - rows of curio shops which cater to the hundreds of thousands of tourists who flock to Bethlehem in search of an uplifting experience combined with the purchase of a few garish seasonal odds and ends. These quasi-religious emporia are piled high with rows of nativity figures of all shapes and sizes, mainly carved in olive wood – serried ranks of timber Josephs, Marys, shepherds, oriental kings on camels, cribs, miniature sheep, oxen and asses of all sizes – to be bought individually or as sets for your own personal Christmas pageant. There are rarer nativity sets in onyx, and even a few made of semi-precious plastic. And there are icons without number showing scenes of the birth of Christ, of the adoring angels and of the Virgin and Child. There are pictures of the Virgin of the Sacred Heart, standing eyes upward to the heavens in the anatomically curious position of holding her heart in her outstretched hands, and for the seriously undiscerning there are even ready-boxed light-up sacred hearts of Mary to be had, batteries, they make clear, not included. The tour guides push their charges through the shops hoping no doubt to supplement their own income by the sizable commissions on offer from the competing retailers. With all the multi-image iconography on sale in Bethlehem you could be forgiven for thinking that Christianity was a polytheistic religion based on the worship of idols, and to some of the visitors that's probably what it has become.

But I supposed there is one other rather startling historical similarity to those far off times when Jesus was laid in swaddling clothes in the manger. Whenever I was in Manger Square soldiers still patrolled the street corners as they must have done when Jesus was born, though this time they carried Uzi sub-machine guns rather than scabbarded swords and they wore combat jackets instead of silver breastplates. And nailed to the outside of the Church of the Nativity, the very place where the events of the New Testament were said to have taken place, stood a huge notice, written in the language of occupation, warning people of the penalties for civil unrest. It was issued by someone styling himself, The Military Commander of Judea and Samaria. It could have been in Latin instead of Modern Hebrew. It could have been issued by a Roman commander. It could have been there the night Jesus was born. It would have said the same thing. For me, and even more so for the citizens of Bethlehem, it would have had, as it still has, the same demoralizing effect.

*   *   *

On Sundays it was the habit of some of the staff among our diggers to assemble for lunch at a Greek restaurant in the Christian Quarter of the Old City. I think it was called Kosta's. It wasn't only the workers from Jemmeh who turned up there but diggers from other excavations in the vicinity, from Tell Gezer, Tell Hesi and so on. They were mainly Americans exchanging dig gossip and occasionally forming liaisons with one another before splitting up to return to their respective excavations the same afternoon ready for the forthcoming week's toil. It was a fairly simple restaurant which featured a small but attractive Ottoman walled courtyard at the back where the gang was wont to foregather. The specialty of the house, and actually pretty much the only main dish the restaurant served, was stuffed pigeon - squab stuffed with rice, pine nuts and tiny currants, all washed down with a robust Cotes de Cremisan, a red wine produced and bottled in the cellars of the Monastery of the Silesian Brothers just outside Bethlehem. The really intriguing feature of Kosta's for me was that as you sat in the courtyard tucking into the main course, all around on top of the high walls there were always live pigeons roosting and cooing and I always wondered, somewhat grimly, whether these might not be the next week's supply of the *specialité de la maison* waiting their turn for the pot.

I remember that we were sitting in Kosta's one Sunday lunchtime enjoying the usual meze and stuffed pigeon when an august-looking clerical gentleman came in on his own. We could see at once that he was clearly a man of considerable influence; the waiters scurried about clearing a space and setting up a table and chair especially for him. He stood to one side waiting for his place to be prepared, dressed as he was in floor-length black clerical robes tied around the middle with what looked like a satin cummerbund which served to accentuate his already rather ample girth. He was a fairly young man, good-looking in a Levantine way, his coal-black hair hanging down in ringlets and with a full curly black beard with which he idly played.

Eventually his place was ready and he sat down legs akimbo while several waiters brought him meze and wine, followed by the ubiquitous stuffed pigeon, all of which he ate heartily and with studied relish. We wondered who this imposing ecclesiast might be and what elevated position he held and in whose church. When he had finished his stuffed pigeon he pushed back his chair, replete. A finger bowl and towel were brought to him and he rinsed and dried his hands with considerable ostentation. A cup of Arabic coffee was placed before him and a boy brought out a hubble-bubble and set it down by his side. On the pan with the tobacco he had already placed glowing coals which he knelt down and blew, tending them with tongs until the wad of tobacco was properly smouldering before retiring. The well-fed Vicar of Christ leaned back and with hooded eyes drew leisurely on the water pipe, exhaling slowly in a studiously relaxed mood.

"Who is that guy?" asked one of our number to a passing waiter, pointing.

"Oh, that's the Armenian Patriarch of Jerusalem; his church is the richest in the city." came the hushed reply.

His Supreme Reverence was certainly the model for such a character, and he obviously enjoyed his position of great religious status as much as he had enjoyed his lunch.

Sometime later, when I was recounting this story to an Armenian friend of mine who had once lived in Jerusalem, she stopped me and said excitedly:

"I know who that was. I knew him. He was the man who tried to sell the Armenian Church chalices at Sotheby's in London, you know, with some of the priceless gold and silver plate. They were worth a fortune. It was so valuable that Sotheby's became suspicious and made some enquiries. They found that they didn't belong to him at all, but to the Church. They refused to auction them, and he was defrocked."

No more stuffed pigeon and hubble-bubble for him then.

* * *

The season was drawing to a close, my last season at Jemmeh. Gus had found his Persian granaries and his Assyrian palace with the vaulted brick store rooms, and he had acquired Ora too, whom he went on to marry, having divorced Colyn, and they remained together for the best part of 40 years, until Gus's death in 2012. He obviously never went back to South Arabia, which was thought by many in the academic community to be a considerable loss to the archaeological world. And though he was to work at Jemmeh for several more seasons he didn't really make any other startling discoveries and in any case he was constantly in the shadow of Flinders Petrie who had done it all forty years before. But with the ending of that season, Jemmeh, Gus and Ora passed out of my life.

Big Al effusively invited me to fly over to the States in the coming winter to visit him in his kingdom at the National Library in Washington, which I tentatively agreed to do. I'd never been to the US before but by now I'd spent three years working with Americans on American sponsored digs and I had really come to enjoy their easy confidence, their braggadocio and fast talking by comparison to the rather haughty reserve of the Brits.

I went with Sami that last Friday up to the Ritz to say my farewells to Louis, who was as always devastated at my departure.

"When are you coming back, my brother? When shall we see you again, *Habibi*?

I promised I would be back next year but in a rather different way. I said I'd call him and let him know. And with that Sami took me in the Peugeot down to the airport and I flew uneventfully back to London, my pockets stuffed with American dollars!

CHAPTER TEN
# PEDALING UPHILL

*Nobody's just arrogant. I've met people who are embattled*
*and dismissive. But when you get to know them, you find*
*they're vulnerable – that their hauteur and standoffishness is*
*because they are pedaling furiously underneath.*
Matthew McFadyen

Once I was back in London I ran into an almost universal wall of opposition
to my suggested field work at Farah. I explained what I was hoping to do but
the Middle Eastern specialists, if not the whole Institute, seemed to be against
it to a man. No-one there thought that it was a clever idea in any shape or
form. There was apparently an unwritten rule that to develop any overseas
archaeological research project originating from the United Kingdom you had
to have come up through the so-called British Schools system and I clearly was
not doing that. The development of the British Schools had been the idea of
Mortimer Wheeler and might be seen as his attempt to rule the archaeological
world. Brigadier Sir Robert Eric Mortimer Wheeler BA, MA, PhD, FBA, FSA,
Order of the Companions of Honour, Companion of the Order of the Indian
Empire, Holder of the Military Cross and of sundry other decorations and
accolades, TV star extraordinaire of 'Animal, Vegetable and Mineral', known
as 'Rik' to his mates and 'The Groper' to various female underlings and young
nubile sub-editors of publishing houses all over London to whom he'd made
advances in taxis, had, you may remember, actually created the Institute of
Archaeology almost single-handedly in the 1930s. Since then it had grown
and relocated from Bedford Lodge, Regents Park, to a brand new purpose-
built headquarters in Gordon Square WC1, hard by University College, but
Rik still had his hand firmly on the tiller. He was still in control. Amongst
his many other achievements and elevated positions Rik had been Director-
General of the Archaeological Survey of India, and, who knows, this may
have given him a taste for world domination.

There were already well-established British Schools and Institutes of
Archaeology in Rome and in Athens, and through Wheeler more schools
were created, in Ankara, Turkey; Baghdad, Iraq; Kabul, Afghanistan; and
Teheran, Iran; also in East Africa at Nairobi, and in Tripoli in Libya and, not
least, in Jerusalem. Palestine. Through Wheeler's hands passed all the good
and the great of world archaeology; 'that's how you climb the ladder', I'd once

heard him say. First you won a studentship to your chosen school and worked your backside off for them for a few years. If they, or maybe it was only he, liked you, you eventually rose to become the assistant director, and after another few years slogging away for a pittance in the God-forsaken outposts of the country of your choice you might be rewarded with the directorship. Being appointed to this heady position, you were entitled to direct your own excavations in your elected country, and if that had all gone well and you hadn't blotted your political copybook along the way, you were eventually brought in from the cold and awarded a professorship in London, at the Institute perhaps, or the School of Oriental and African Studies, or maybe a post at the British Museum, or even, if the wind was in the right direction, at an Oxford or Cambridge college.

Having reached such an elevated status you were then expected to preside over the next generation of acolytes and ensure that they too travelled along the same path, climbing the same ladder. And just to make sure the system worked, in other words to guarantee that this code of practice operated for ever, in perpetuity as it were, any and all available money for field work, any grants in aid or stipends for overseas archaeological research which originated in the UK would be rigidly controlled by the British Schools system. There was no other way. Plainly, I hadn't done any of this and therefore I would get no support.

However, for the establishment there was a more compelling reason for the opposition to my proposed project. It was about exactly where I had suggested I was going to work. The British School of Archaeology in Jerusalem had been established when Jerusalem had been under Arab control, and its academic remit covered the West Bank and the whole of Jordan. The Arabs were considered rather truculent but at least they were tractable, viz T. E. Lawrence for example. Peter Parr, my own tutor, had been the school's assistant director in the 1950s and had excavated at Petra under its auspices. That's how he'd gone on to get the job as Lecturer in Palestinian Archaeology in the first place – by climbing the ladder the Wheeler-esque way. When Kay Kenyon moved on from the Institute to St. Hugh's Oxford he took her place.

Now, although the Jerusalem school was just about on speaking terms with one or two Israeli archaeologists, there was no love lost between it and them, and when Israel invaded the West Bank in 1967 and took over east Jerusalem it left the school in a deep political quandary. If they stayed where they were, they would have to get on with the Israelis, who in any case didn't take kindly to the Brits or anything which smacked of British imperialism. The emergent state had fought against exactly that twenty years before. But if they moved the school to Amman, such a decamp would be a tacit admission that the Israelis had won and might even be construed as giving in to international theft and thuggery. That invasion had only happened five years before, and the school had not yet made up its mind what it should do. Feelings were still very raw in that respect. And now here was I, from the Institute and all it stood for, suggesting that I wanted to work in the Negev, which was patently in Israel. Never mind the environmental imperatives for working in the Wadi Ghazzeh, or that the climatic zonation of the whole of the east Mediterranean made it optimal to work in that precise region, something I'd quickly worked out which I'll explain in a moment, it was deemed to be in the wrong country, it was the wrong way of setting about it, and it was made absolutely clear that there would not be any financial support for any such venture as far as the Institute or any other British funding organisation was concerned.

But there was perhaps something even more fundamentally negative. The subject that I was proposing to study, an environmental survey of an area of southern Palestine, and the way I was proposing to go about it, involving as I intended both earth and life scientists in the field, went totally against the grain of the environmentalists at the Institute as well. We had a whole department dedicated to the study of archaeological environments – palaeo-botanists, palaeo-zoologists, palaeo-pathologists, snails experts, pollen experts and specialists in a whole range of other life scientists. But their function had always been to remain subsidiary to any actual archaeological excavations themselves. They were there to support digs when they took place, to analyse samples given to them by the excavators and to answer specific questions that he or she might ask to tease a little more information out of the trenches that had been dug, no less and no more. They were there to assist, not in any way to dominate. In other words, environmental archaeology was a service industry, not an end in itself. What I was in the process of proposing was an equal partnership of archaeologists with earth and life scientists from the very outset, a multi-disciplinary study where each would contribute in equal vision and measure to the question of what the environment of this particular region had looked like in the past and how changes in the climate, the rainfall, temperature and in short the whole of the natural world had contributed to the evolution, physical and cultural, of people who had lived there in ancient times. As I have already said, I was looking for the answer to a very simple question. When someone woke up in the Middle Bronze Age, or in the Neolithic, or at any other moment in the prehistoric past, what did they see? What was the vegetation, the wildlife, the sunshine, the weather like? In short, what resources were there for them to make a living? How did changes in the natural world affect their development, or otherwise? This was at the very heart of environmental determinism. And it was a question too far for the Institute's environmentalists, who said it couldn't be done.

And there was worse news still. Although the first director and professor of European prehistory at the newly created Institute, the famous Professor Vere Gordon Childe, (the ugly Australian as one commentator called him), had also been an environmental determinist, he had shaken the establishment to its foundations by demonstrating that European civilization had not originated in Britain, or France or Germany, but had actually come from the Near East. The reason, he said, was because the climate had gradually worsened at the end of the last Ice Age, and in the Middle East it had dried out, forcing humans there through their own ingenuity to adopt a new strategy of survival. They had invented agriculture to stay alive against a growing surge of aridity, which eventually led to them to live in fewer and fewer areas in bigger and bigger urban settlements, hence civilization. Their own struggle had saved them, Childe maintained, hence he called it the 'Neolithic Revolution'.

Wheeler and others saw Childe's Marxist interpretations as an anathema to the concept of European pre-eminence and he had been shouted down and forced to retire back to Australia, where sadly he committed suicide, directly as a result of this hostility so I was privately told by someone who knew him well. Anyway, the climatic changes he proposed, it was now believed, were nonsense anyway. There had been no such climatic deterioration in the Near East at any time in the past. That was the received wisdom in 1970. Climatic change was a feature of the high latitudes of the northern hemisphere, associated with the advancing and contracting ice sheets of the North Pole as they had affected the adjacent landmasses of North America and northern Europe. The effect of any such variation lessened abruptly as one travelled south, further from the Pole, so that by the time one reached Mediterranean latitudes it was non-existent. That was what people thought in the early 1970s, and the great high priest of environmental archaeology, Karl Butzer of the University of Chicago, had confirmed as much, so it must be true mustn't it! There was an end to it.

Everything but everything was against the expedition I was proposing. There was to be no money, no support, no political will, no academic reason for it and no evidence that it was even a viable idea. My plan was rejected in its entirety. It was all very discouraging, except, in my mind, for one tiny glimmer. Moon-Rocks Melson had said that support could be made available from the US through EEI. Was he wrong? Did he truly understand what I was trying to do? After all, he was a geologist and only really had a vague notion of archaeology, much of which I had given him anyway. Maybe it was all pie in the sky, or did US academics view the world more broad-mindedly? But when I dared to suggest at the Institute that such funding might be available, the shock and horror were even greater. I was proposing WHAT? - I was suggesting I could get commercial funding for my ideas? That I would go and sell the notion of archaeological investigation on the open market? To hawk the sacred trust of the study of man's past like a common peddler? It was made clear to me that that was an even more preposterous idea. It was beyond the pale! I was beyond the pale! The whole thing was ludicrous from start to finish – end of story.

But I had been given the spark of the idea from Moon-Rocks, and shortly I received an offer in writing from the offices of Educational Expeditions International in Belmont, Massachusetts no less to submit a proposal. I either had to give up all together then and there or I had to crystallize my ideas into a scientific proposition and submit it to them for their consideration. And it was at this time, at this precise moment, that I discovered the sheer serendipitous magic of the scheme I had casually outlined to Bill Melson months before in the Wadi Ghazzeh. The area I had chosen, the area around Tell Farah, was probably the most supreme location I could have selected anywhere in the Middle East for the study of changing earth climates; it was the epicentre of the most sensitive border between the three dominant eco-zones of the whole of the eastern Mediterranean.

Let me explain. The main zone of truly Mediterranean climate, at least as defined by its vegetation, is in today's world to be found around the shores of Mediterranean Spain, Italy, Greece and Turkey and the same zone continues in a narrow line down the edge of the Syrian and the Lebanese coast and ends just north of the Gaza Strip. Meanwhile, a second major zone, that of semi-arid climate, the Irano-Turanian Belt, which today covers vast swathes of the steppe lands of the Middle East from the plains of Teheran and beyond, comes west across the northern part of Mesopotamia and the Syrian interior then tongues down through northern Jordan, across the Rift and the northern part of Palestine and eventually peters out in the north-western Negev, right next to Farah. And a third zone, the arid heart of North Africa which stretches all the way across the immense tracts of the Sahara Desert from the Atlantic coast of Morocco to the Nile finally terminates just south of Gaza City. Farah is more or less where these three sub-continental zones met. That would mean, I quickly realised, that any shift in the climates of the past, however small, should first be detectable in this one spot on the planet before just about anywhere else. These zones would have ebbed and flowed, they would expand and contract, the one becoming dominant over the other two, in response to any changes in annual rainfall and temperature, which would then be evidenced in major shifts in the vegetation. That was it. There was no better place to base this study, irrespective of any political situation for which of course past climates would categorically be irrelevant. By pure fluke that afternoon with Moon-Rocks at Farah I had chosen the very best area to experiment with my idea; I couldn't have found one that was any better.

As I set this momentous discovery down in my proposal to EEI it all made total sense to me. The problem was how was I going to achieve this study? Who in God's name was going to join me? Where were my scientists going to come from? And even if I found the right people, how did I know that there would be any actual indication at all forthcoming to substantiate the idea of climatic change? This last issue was the one which really exercised me the most. What kind of evidence would be available anyway to show that there had been any climatic ebb and flow here in the past? The reason why this was my main concern wasn't difficult to find. As I was trying to get some answers by talking to the tamer environmentalists at the Institute, it became abundantly clear to me that the evidence they were used to looking for, and hence the methods they were using to find it, had all been developed with northern European and North American climates in mind, that is, in the high latitudes of the northern hemisphere. They were completely engrossed with glacial and sub-glacial climatic shifts, with permafrost and pine forests, with pingos and pollen, none of which was in the least bit applicable in the semi-deserts of Arabia.

There were no methods which had been invented specifically for examining climatic indications from the sub-tropical regions of the earth mainly because no-one had really looked there before. If you were looking at Appleton, Wisconsin or even, funnily enough, Oswestry, Shropshire, both of which were the terminal locations for the last glacial maximum, if you were trying to find evidence for climatic change in those places, you could analyse the pollen from peat bog cores or beetle wing cases from glacial lake deposits and thereby uncover what you were looking for. But there had been no glacial advances and contractions in the Negev or anywhere remotely near it. There were no glacial lakes just six degrees north of the Tropic of Cancer and certainly no peat bogs from which pollen cores could be examined and compared. It began to dawn on me at this point that I hadn't really got a clue where the evidence would come from, and hence I had no idea at all what methodology I might need, or if indeed it had even been invented. This led me to the inevitable conclusion that I had no inkling either about how to find the right kind of people for the job. I didn't know what I would be asking them to do.

But total ignorance being no excuse for inactivity, and armed with the irrepressible enthusiasm of youth, I set out on my quest. My first port of call was someone I barely knew. She was a person who was attending my extra mural archaeology classes at Goldsmith's College and all I knew was that she was some kind of botanist. Her name was Juliet Prior and she had a doctorate in botany from Imperial College London. I'd learnt that much about her when I had taken the class on a site visit to the British Museum that autumn and we'd been having a beer in the Museum Tavern afterwards, but for all I knew she could have been a horticultural specialist or a plant pathologist with no interest in the sub-tropics at all. She had recently found herself cast in the role of housewife in Blackheath and she wanted something to stretch her mental faculties, which is why she'd chosen archaeology. She'd turned up to my lectures out of sheer boredom, she'd said. I buttonholed her anyway at the end of my next Thursday lecture and suggested that we had a quick drink in the nearest pub, and she agreed. I explained that I had been working in the Negev for the last two years and had come up with the idea of looking for the evidence of climatic change in the sub-tropics. As I developed the idea, another convincing-sounding reason for doing this occurred to me.

"Look," I said, "The major events in human history, in human cultural evolution, didn't take place in the high latitudes of the northern hemisphere, in Britain or Scandinavia, did they? They took place in the sub-tropics. That's where agriculture began, didn't it? That's where the first cities were built. That's where the whole idea for civilization came from. But no-one's looked there properly for the climatic evidence. They've all been concentrating on the freezing north where no-one wanted to be in the first place!"

It sounded so plausible when I said it like that. And indeed it was true, even truer than I could have imagined at the time. As I was to discover some years later, even the initial advances which early humans had made, the actual very first steps they'd ever taken, happened to be in these same latitudes, although in the southern hemisphere. The whole of our physical evolution had taken place in the tropics and the sub-tropics of the earth, but that story was for another time (see 'Gazing upon Sheba's Breasts'). Right now, I was focused on the east Mediterranean. Juliet was a spirited individual and began to ask all sorts of questions I couldn't answer, about what the current vegetation of the Negev was like; about what the botanical indicator species of the Mediterranean assemblage were. I didn't even know what a botanical assemblage was, let alone how to discourse about it, but I couldn't let her know that. As the minutes passed she became quite excited by my ideas, saying that I should be looking for this kind of evidence and those kinds of signs; and did I know what sort of literature there was on the subject? I listened for a while and then gently introduced my main suggestion into the conversation. Would she, I asked, consider coming out to the Negev and taking a look?

"But I don't know anything about the area, or the archaeology, or the vegetation," she said. "I've never been there. I'd be hopeless; I wouldn't know where to start!"

"Don't let that put you off", I suggested weakly. I forbore to tell her that I didn't know where to start either.

"And have you got funding for this research?" she next asked, which I thought was a positive step, though I have to say that her tone was somewhat disbelieving.

"Well, yes, in a sort of a way," I countered.

I told her about Moon-Rocks and about EEI, blowing it up somewhat as though it was a major funding operation in the US. I didn't tell her that they had only just started out and had yet to field a single expedition … to anywhere. But it seemed to placate Juliet, and to reassure her that I was someone to be reckoned with. She had clearly not been to the Institute and felt all the immense pessimism to which I had been subjected over the previous few weeks.

"I could go and talk to the people at Imperial College for you, I suppose," she suggested. "There are some palaeo-botanists there, you know, and they might have some ideas about it. Anyway, they can give me some pointers, I'm sure. Leave it with me and I'll contact them and find out how the land lies. I'll get back to you next week."

So I left it at that. At least I'd made a start. The following week she came to see me after the lecture and said,

"I've spoken to the people in the Botany Department at Imperial. They're quite excited by the idea and were very encouraging. They've given me a whole list of references to look up and I've started to go through them. There's a lot written about those three areas you outlined. And you're absolutely correct in saying that they all meet around Gaza. But I'm not sure what evidence we should be looking for to evaluate where exactly these zones were in the past. It could be from pollen, though somehow I doubt it in the semiarid conditions, or it could be plant macro-fossils, you know, buried trunks of trees, leaves, that sort of thing. Or I was thinking, it might even be charcoal. That's chemically inert, you see, and can survive for hundreds, maybe even thousands of years."

The more she spoke the more animated she became, and her reference to 'we' looking for things was very encouraging. When she'd finished her exposition, I came to the testing point.

"Does that mean you will come out and take a look, then?" I asked.

"Oh yes, I think so. I wouldn't want to be left out. Of course, I could only afford to be there for a week or two, a month at the most. And there's a lot to do before I even think about going into the field. And you say you've got an airfare for me? And have you got permits to be in the area? And what sort of local contacts do you have?"

I didn't have any of those, except my contact with Louis of course, and I don't think that was the sort of contact she meant, but I couldn't let her know that. I covered my tracks by saying it would all be taken care of in due course, that I was still in the planning stages of the expedition and I'd let her know. I realised at that point I hadn't even got a name for the operation, let alone any idea of how we were going to proceed. I was now really flying by the seat of my pants, and I knew it. Over the next few weeks I tried to address these problems. I had written to the director of antiquities at the Rockefeller Museum, Moshe Dothan, the chap I'd met at Jemmeh who'd asked me about Masada, and miraculously he said he would give me a permit 'to investigate the environmental background to the Tell Farah area', making it clear that did not include any permission to excavate the tell itself. That didn't bother me; that wasn't something I wanted to do. But I'd got a permit and that was the main thing. I decided to call the expedition rather grandly 'The British Western Negev Expedition' and had a few sheets of headed note paper printed up to start the ball rolling. I talked to one or two students whom I was teaching at the Institute to sound them out as to whether they would like to join me in the Negev, and a couple said they would.

Slowly the B. W. N. E. began taking shape.

I even talked to a sort of geomorphologist at the Institute, someone called Peter Dorrell. I say 'sort of"' because he was actually an expedition photographer by trade but he knew the Middle East very well. He'd worked with Kay Kenyon and others and he was very familiar with Jerusalem. As an earth scientist he was self-taught but he had made a certain amount of effort to look at soils on other archaeological digs and he said he reckoned he would be able to give Farah a bash, as he put it. He was going to be in the area anyway, actually at the dreaded British School in Jerusalem, and he said he could spare us a few days. He'd never been in the Negev and said he was interested in Petrie's work. There was no love lost between him and Rik Wheeler either; he had known one or two of Wheeler's feminine conquests and he said that Rik had treated them abominably. Well, in a back-handed sort of way, that gave Peter an extra credential as far as I was concerned, rapidly becoming as I was the Institute maverick.

At this point I had the idea, the permit, the name, the makings of a team and even the headed paper. All I needed now was the money. I therefore thought that this was an opportune moment to make my first trip to the USA to commune with EEI to see if they were really genuine, and of course to spend some time with Big Al in Washington, so I looked around for the cheapest way of getting there, which was to fly via New York. Armed with my ill-gotten dollars from Jemmeh which Louis had let me exchange at the Ritz, suddenly I was going to America.

CHAPTER ELEVEN
# AMERICA THE BEAUTIFUL

*America! America!*
*God shed his grace on thee;*
*And crown thy good with brotherhood*
*From sea to shining sea!*
Katharine Lee Bates, 1893

Flugfélag Islands, Iceland Air, was the cheapest though perhaps the most convoluted way of flying from London to New York in early 1972. If you think about it, should you wish to change planes half-way across the Atlantic, it's the one way you can do it. But it was inexpensive, so that I was able to fly to the States as well as hang on to most of my dollars. When we reached Reykjavik, we had indeed to switch planes, and being in the middle of the winter the weather was quite arctic, with snow and ice thick on the ground. Imagine my surprise when I looked up at the plane standing on the runway for our second leg of the journey and saw that it was tricked out in the livery of Air Bahamas, incongruously embellished with a graphic rendering of a glowing sun over the middle of the fuselage and a waving palm tree up the tail fin. It must have been chartered by some wishful thinker or another, I thought. But it got us to JFK International Airport without incident sometime in the late afternoon of the same day.

When I arrived, after passing through immigration and customs control, I had been told that I should ask for a 'limo' to take me into the centre of New York City. It turned out this was a shared cab, which I located, and soon I was speeding down the freeway with that famous skyline of skyscrapers silhouetted on the other side of the East River against a setting winter sun. We plunged into the Mid-town Tunnel and re-surfaced in the middle of Manhattan at the limo terminal and when I asked how to get to my hotel, the driver just pointed to a line of cabs. I dragged my bag over and the cabbie motioned to the rear door. I pushed the bag in first and then followed. It was the least comfortable taxi I think I'd ever been in, a large yellow saloon with a thick Perspex partition cutting off the driver from the passenger section. He was sitting in comfort in the front while in the back there was barely enough room for me to squat, with my knees up. I bent forward awkwardly and gave the driver the name of my hotel through the ventilation holes and he careered off spring-less over the most execrable and pot-holed city roads I have travelled. My first impressions of New York were none too favourable. I found it ugly, overcrowded and grey and I have to say that further visits there later in my career did nothing to change that view.

The hotel I had booked at the same time as the flight was cheap but as it rejoiced in the name of 'The Royal Manhattan' I was expecting great things. I very soon discovered that there was no way it could ever have lived up to its regal moniker. It was located near the corner of 42$^{nd}$ Street and 8$^{th}$ Avenue, which turned out to be just about the most deprived and potentially violent part of Lower Manhattan. With flagging eagerness I checked in and went up to my room. On the back of the door, along with several impressive-looking locks, was a notice saying that I shouldn't open the door to anyone for any reason at any time except to go in and out myself. So, I locked myself in and went over to the phone to call Al. I rang the number he'd given me in Washington and miraculously he answered the call at once. When he discovered where I was staying, he gasped audibly and said:

"Jesus, David, what the fuck are you doing there? It's a hell-hole! Get outa there tomorrow morning as soon as you can and get your ass in a cab and go to La Guardia; ask for the Eastern Airlines shuttle to Washington. They go every hour on the hour. You don't need to book. Then you haul your ass into another cab at National and come up to the library. I'll see you tomorrow."

And with that I went to bed and to sleep. No-one attempted to batter down the door. The next day finding nowhere in the hotel I asked at the desk where I could get breakfast. Apparently the whole establishment was due to close down for good the following week and the restaurant had already folded, but the desk clerk pointed down 8$^{th}$ Avenue and said that about a block and a half away there was a diner in the Port Authority Building. I walked out into the street, looking furtively this way and that in case I was about to be attacked and robbed on my first day. In a fearful state I reached the said building and went into the huge lobby. It turned out to be the main bus station for New York City. I found the diner and entering, I sat at an empty table near the door. It was very busy at that time of the day with people coming and going the whole time. I took a look at the dog-eared one-sheet breakfast menu. A waitress came up to my table and spoke to me in what I assumed to be a New York accent.

"Hiya, wadayawana?" which I understood to mean what would I like to order. "I'll have the eggs", I said, pointing.

"Wadkinaeggsa?" she asked.

"Well, like it says here," I pointed. "'Eggs any style', I'll have those."

"Yutrynabefunny or sumin? Yuwana frieda, scrambled, poacheda or boileda?" "Oh, fried" I said.

"Yuwanemeasyover or sunnyside upa?"

"Whichever comes first," I replied, not wanting to become ensnared by a further linguistic imbroglio.

"English or French?" she asked again, seemingly about to write it down.

I had no idea why she needed to know my nationality for me to order breakfast. Maybe this was some peculiar American custom. Anyway, to show willing I said,

"I'm British actually!"

"Listenyou, yuwana English muffin or French toasta?"

"Oh, English then." I said, barely comprehending her rapid-fire interrogation.

She brought over the eggs and the muffin accompanied by a wrapped pat of butter.

It didn't look a bit like an English muffin to me, more like a fairy cake, but I didn't want to argue. She didn't ask me about the coffee. She just poured it into my cup. What was it G. K. Chesterton had said, 'Two countries divided by the same language'? It felt a bit like that. I must say that it came as something of a shock to find that these New Yorkers weren't anything like the bright young people I'd been working with at Knidos or at Jemmeh for the last three years. They seemed to me to be only semi-literate, or at least barely spoke English. I finished my 'eggs any style' and went back into the street to hail a passing cab. A moment later I was in another of those constricted leg-room taxis, but at least I felt secure, out of reach of the marauding masses that thronged the pavements – sorry, sidewalks.

We soon reached La Guardia and finding the Eastern Airlines shuttle desk I bought a ticket. The 'plane left twenty minutes later and I had a good view over Manhattan Island through the window. I thought at this altitude it looked a whole lot better than it had from ground level. One hour later we were descending to Washington National Airport. Our approach took us parallel to the Potomac River and as we turned for our final approach it felt like we were almost flying at the same level as the city, with the gleaming white dome of the Capitol in the distance. Even from the air Washington looked a lot more civilised than New York.

I climbed into another cab as Al had suggested and asked for the National Library of Congress. Shortly we were racing along the freeway over the Potomac, passed the Lincoln Memorial and the Washington Monument.

"Your first time in DC?" asked the cab driver, seeing me ogling the different sites.

When I affirmed that it was, he jerked his thumb at a large brick building on our right and said,

"Smithsonian Museum;. You ever heard of it?"

Had I heard of it? Hadn't I just. That was where Gus hung out, wasn't it, and presumably Moon-Rocks as well. A couple of blocks or so later we reached the library. I paid off the cab and walked up to the main entrance. At the reception desk I asked for Al. They looked his name up in a directory and dialled a number. Five minutes later Al appeared, so soberly suited I hardly recognised him.

"David, my old buddy! How are ya? Welcome to purgatory!"

The Congressional Research Service of the National Library where Al worked turned out to be a fascinating body of people. The idea behind the CRS was that it had been created to be able to investigate and answer any question posed to them by any member of congress, whether Republican or Democrat, using the library's limitless search facilities. Additionally the staff members were expected to be able to expatiate on any topic requested, from the tonnage of last year's banana crop in Cuba to what the current population of ethnic Uzbeks in northern Afghanistan was. To do this they had divided the world into regions and each region was represented by its own expert, someone who had either lived there, or spoke the languages and knew the people. I was introduced to some of them. They were all obviously highly intelligent. They were able to use the entire resources of the library as their database and then they would transmit the resulting information by hand to the relevant member of the House. Remember, this was in a world before the Internet, in fact almost before computers.

But speaking of computers, Al asked me if I knew anything about them. I told him that somewhat surprisingly I did. I explained to him that my developing PhD was about using computer programming to put various tomb groups in a rank order which might lead to a better understanding of their relative date sometime in the Bronze Age. To do this I had been allotted space on the University of London's computer in Tavistock Square - the whole of the university had only one machine in those days. It took up the space of an entire three-storey house. I was never allowed to see it; it was far too large and far too delicate, I'd been told. But here in Washington Al took me into the basement of the library and down a narrow corridor he unlocked a door and ushered me in.

"Welcome to the future!" he said, gesturing to what looked like a typewriter keyboard and a television set in the corner.

What he was showing me was an Automatic Electronic Systems programmable electronic text recorder. I suppose you could say it was the world's first micro-computer. It had a video screen with a keyboard, and information could be typed in and stored on magnetic disks. Texts could be retrieved from the disks onto the screen again simply by entering a password at the keyboard.

"This is like a personal computer," he told me. "It's probably the first one you've ever seen isn't it? It's not available yet, but pretty soon, you know, everyone will have something like this in their own homes. You will be able to write letters on it; do your accounts on it; keep track of all your personal affairs with it; everything! And in the end it will lead to the paperless office. You will file all your important messages on it and be able to retrieve them again without leaving your seat."

I couldn't see the value of it myself, personal or otherwise. What would you want to keep your accounts in the empty air of a box like that for? I didn't keep accounts anyway, but of course he was absolutely right. It turned out that Al was the CRS's pundit on the new subject of information technology, working out what the library, and indeed what the whole of Congress should do next in terms of storing and recovering data. He was looking at and testing the relevant new office machinery and trying to work out trends. Incidentally, along the same lines as the computer, a year or two later when I saw him at the library he showed me the first flat-bed scanner as well, again in a locked room in the basement. Again he let me into his vision of the future.

"This baby will soon make libraries redundant," he said dramatically. "Any third world country wanting to access the written word, from great fiction to yesterday's copy of the New York Times, won't need all the actual literature and stuff. They will one day be able to open their own personal computer and download the information digitally onto their monitor via a satellite link. All the pages of all the books on the planet will be digitised using flat-bed scanners like this and an OCR programme - 'optical character recognition' to you."

And of course he was right again, though it took a few decades to achieve this. But oddly he was wrong about the 'paperless office'. People still like to have hard copies of letters, contracts, receipts, agreements and such like. Years later I quizzed him about this and he said, somewhat regretfully,

"Yeah, you're right of course. We'll get the paperless office when we get the paperless rest room!"

But getting back to the computer, Al actually showed me how it worked. AES Laboratories, the company he was dealing with, was at that time at the cutting edge of this new technology. The company was based in Canada, and in this very year, 1972, they were just coming up with their first 'Word Processor', as they called it. The time saved by this extraordinary device was immediately obvious and remarkable, even to me. Pages of text no longer had to be completely retyped to correct simple errors, and projects could be worked on, stored, and then retrieved for use later. I was duly impressed.

In fact I was impressed with the whole of the CRS and its staff. They might have seemed on the surface like a fairly dull bunch of semi-academics just shuffling information on behalf of congressmen and senators, but in Washington information was power, and they had their fingers on the levers of that information, and hence they exercised an unseen authority. I came to learn this over the next year or two and found it so fascinating that I always made it my business when I was in the US to try to get to the National Library, especially at the end of a Friday afternoon when quite unofficially the moles in CRS were at their most impressive, when they were engaging in their collective end-of-the-week off-the-record recreational information-swapping. Because they were constantly being asked questions directly by politicians in the administration, they were in the habit of taking back-bearings from those queries and trying to work out why this or that member of Congress was asking such questions in the first place.

If, for example, five members of the House phoned up the CRS independently with a query about, say, the defensive capabilities of the Nicaraguan Air Force, you could surmise that there was a possibility that some imminent security issue was about to raise its ugly head with that country. If at the same time you had a colleague in the Nicaraguan Information Service, you could suggest to him the tentative connection you'd worked out and see if it played true. Washington was a governmental hothouse with information being the fertilizer that forced its plants. And CRS was at the very heart of this political horticulture; indeed, it had its sensors right on the growing tip.

Over the years I heard a lot of impressive exposures by the CRS of US governmental policies way before they happened, from Richard Nixon's impeachment over the Watergate scandal to the political annihilation of the peanut farmer, Jimmy Carter, because he'd tried to bring in his own country hicks from the deep south to run things 'inside the Belt-way', as it was called, something that no-one in Washington wanted. I was even there on the day after the famous occasion when in October 1974 Wilber Mills, chairman of the powerful Senate Ways and Means Committee and sometimes described as 'the most powerful man in Washington', was caught cavorting in a 'state of intoxication' as the police called it, near the Washington tidal basin with Fanne Foxe, the well-known Argentinian strip-tease artiste, which had fateful consequences for poor old Wilbur but which afforded a fountain of merriment amongst the CRS burrowers.

However, much of that was in the future. Right now I was going to stay with Al for a couple of nights, and at the end of a fascinating afternoon at the library we drove out of Washington to Alexandria, Virginia and to Al's apartment in a tower block called 'Watergate at Landmark'. That evening over a couple of large bourbons, a drink which, being really a gin man myself, I have to say I think is rather over-rated, I outlined my Farah ideas and told Al that I was going up to Boston to talk to the people at EEI. I explained to him the very negative attitudes with which my idea had been greeted in Britain, and he said that although he didn't fully understand what I was hoping to do, he did have a few contacts that might be able to help on the financial side. The following day I was introduced to Al's great mate, Don, with whom he'd worked in the past. Al explained that Don had been a high-flier in the previous administration, but that things had gone terribly wrong for him.

"I tell you, the shit really hit the fan for Don and he was out of a job, lickety split. That's why he's doing what he's doing now, President of the Puerto Rico Information Service. I mean, it's a front, of course. There's no such thing really. No, secretly he's still in the swim in Washington. You could say that Don's so far out he's in, if you see what I mean."

I must say that I didn't see what he meant. But Don was a great character, fast talking and very knowledgeable. Al told Don what I was doing in the US, trying to raise money for the proposed work at Farah, and by turns they both suggested to each other different people I should contact - Up-Town Charlie, Cross-Town Ronnie, and various other colourfully-soubriqueted philanthropists with whom they were both familiar. Although none of it ever came to anything, I have to admit that their sheer enthusiasm was infectious. But in the end I was going to have to bet everything on EEI, and with that in mind I got Al to book me on a flight from Washington to Boston the next day.

"It's two for one on Eastern," called Al from the phone. "Anywhere else you want to fly to?"

I told him I eventually needed to fly back from Boston to New York to catch my Iceland Air flight to London, and he booked that at the same time. He said I could pay for them both and pick up the tickets in the morning. I called my contact Barbara Sleeper at E E I and gave her the details of my flight the next day. She said she'd be at Logan to meet me. I assumed Logan was the airport for Boston. And with that, Al and I had another couple of bourbons, a good steak dinner, and went to bed. The next day I travelled in to work with Al and he dropped me off at National Airport on the way where I said a fond farewell to my good friend and caught my plane north to Boston.

\* \* \*

Boston, Massachusetts, as I soon appreciated, is the very heart of New England – Georgian-style mansions, clapboard houses, Regency churches and the Boston Tea Party. It's one of the few places on earth where the word 'colonial', far from being pejorative, is actually a term of discernment and good taste. Boston was home to the great heroes of the American War of Independence like John Hancock and Samuel Adams (there is even a local beer named after Sam Adams by the way). New England is certainly totally unlike New York; it's very much more upmarket and immaculately kept. And, of course, nestling in the Boston suburb of Cambridge is Harvard, that queen of American universities. I was impressed with Boston, and certainly with the little towns around about. Barbara from EEI picked me up from Logan Airport and we drove in her 1965 Chevrolet Impala Super Sport, to me the epitome of a 'big American car', along the Charles River to the offices of EEI at 68 Leonard Street, Belmont, Massachusetts.

I hadn't expected anything too extravagant, and I was right - they were located in three rooms above a dentist's surgery. By comparison to the grandeur of the New England style, EEI was a little understated, if I can put it that way. But, at least they were expecting me, Evie, Barbie, Sandy and Debbie, and we started talking right away about some of the projects they were hoping to fund and the scientific expeditions with which they were hoping to be involved. Bob Citron, Bill Melson's mate, who'd just created the whole thing, wasn't there, but I learnt a lot about him.

He had originally started an organisation called the Smithsonian Center for Short-lived Phenomena, on the basis that he was hoping to fund his own research visits to a number of recently erupted volcanos and other natural disasters by this system. He'd been a member of the Smithsonian staff at the time, and his idea for getting the public involved by looking at and recording these phenomena had been born out of a need to get to the location while whatever it was, be it volcano, earthquake, or some other catastrophe, was still active and measurable, or nearly so. Most funding for scientific research in the US, via the National Foundation for the Humanities, say, or through National

Geographic, took anything from a year to eighteen months to achieve, and only after there had been a long application process and exhaustive peer reviews, by which time his short lived phenomenon in question had probably totally faded away.

Alas the Smithsonian Center for Short Lived Phenomena itself turned out to be eponymously so itself. The management of the Smithsonian didn't take kindly to having its good name associated with anything so commercial as getting the public to pay for its own scientific research, and Bob Citron had to change by making his 'center' private and then rebranding it as Educational Expeditions International, in the process moving it from Washington DC to Belmont, Mass. I didn't care how it had got here myself, so long as EEI thought that they could raise the financial wind for my Farah expedition, which amazingly they said they probably could. Incidentally, EEI was to get bigger very quickly once it started. The demand for financial grants grew exponentially as government funding bodies on both sides of the Atlantic quickly dried up in the mid-1970s. Soon EEI itself was to be rebranded to become 'Earthwatch', which in no time developed into an organisation represented on three different continents, America, Australia and Europe. Bob Citron soon left all together and moved on to devote his time and talents to completely different commercial ventures, and Earthwatch was to appoint an investment banker by the name of Brian Rosborough, as its chief executive officer.

I was successfully to use EEI/Earthwatch as a source of funding for three separate expeditions over a period of more than twenty years, also funnily enough on three separate continents, in my case Asia, Africa and Europe, or at least, Turkey, so I knew it from the very beginning. Irritatingly, Rosborough went on to take the credit for creating Earthwatch, which of course he hadn't. Also, he came to treat Earthwatch like some vast multinational funding body for global environmental research, something like the Ford Foundation, which I have to say it never really was, and he was wont to spend money accordingly. But that's a story for another time.

Getting back to 1972 and to 68 Leonard Street, Belmont Mass., I suggested to Barbara that they might all like to see a visual presentation of the British Western Negev Expedition so they could appreciate exactly what I had in mind. I'd brought some slides with me from London that I had taken of the tell at Farah and of the surroundings, and I had made one or two extra slides of maps to illustrate the geography and the climatic zonation that I'd suddenly thought of when I had been talking to Juliet. A projector was hurriedly found, the chairs were rearranged and I launched into a supercharged orchestration of the history of my new idea, with helpful accompaniment by Vere Gordon Childe on violins and Flinders Petrie on woodwind. It sounded incredibly professional, I thought, especially when you consider that I hadn't actually done any work there at all yet and knew precious little about it. Nevertheless my talk scaled the heights of high-quality bullshit, something that I found I was getting quite good at.

What went down particularly well were the two dozen or so aerial shots of Tell Farah and the surrounding area that I'd taken with Chip the morning when we'd flown over the Negev with the supine security man during the last season at Jemmeh. The girls thought that the aerial reconnaissance was an especially professional touch, in that I'd seem to have taken such immense care to photograph the wadi from all angles, albeit at Gus's initiation and expense, which of course I didn't happen to mention. By the time I'd finished, they were totally sold on the idea, and they moved on to ask questions about the finer administrative details, such as the dates of the expedition, what sort of transport I would be using, where we would be staying, how the group would be fed, that kind of thing. I had to gloss over these because I really hadn't thought about them at all until now. But I quickly covered my tracks by saying that I was just in the process of finalizing all the minutiae and I would write to them as soon as I got back to London with all the information they needed.

The day ended for me on an all-time high. I'd won. I was going to be one of the first 'P. I.'s', principle investigators, for EEI As far as I was concerned, I'd got the funding for my new expedition, even though I wasn't actually in possession of a single cent yet. The girls at EEI suggested we all went to a fish restaurant to celebrate the deal so we drove to the Legal Seafood and Oyster Bar in Cambridge – whose motto I noted on the table mat was, 'If it isn't fresh it isn't legal!' It was an excellent choice. I had Oysters Rockefeller to start with, I remember, oysters served on the half shell and baked under the grill with a parsley butter sauce, followed by breaded New England lobster – a whole Maine lobster served with hollandaise sauce and a green salad - all washed down with a bottle of white Zinfandel from the Napa Valley in California. It was memorable indeed. Afterwards Barbara drove me to the Hilton Hotel at Logan Airport where I crashed out until the next day.

I caught my New York flight to La Guardia next morning and the transfer bus to Kennedy where at a restaurant on the concourse I treated myself to an extensive lunch with an appropriate alcoholic accompaniment. Suitably equipped with a post-prandial rosy glow, I poured myself on the Flugfélag Íslands flight to Reykjavik during which I slept the dreamless sleep of the just.

But I do remember one feature of the onward flight from Iceland to Heathrow. We were flying at 39,000 feet thereabouts over the cold North Atlantic. Dawn was breaking over the eastern sky as we approached the British Isles, and I had my headphones on listening to classical music. The outline of the wing of the plane was silhouetted darkly against the slowly lightening horizon, and blasting away in my ears was Dvořák's Symphony Number 9 in E minor, 'From the New World'. I was mesmerized, just as I'm sure Dvořák had been in 1893. Yes, I thought, it's a New World indeed.

As the panegyric continues,

*America! America!*
*May God thy gold refine;*
*Till all success be nobleness*
*And every gain divine!*

Amen to that!

CHAPTER TWELVE

# SIC TRANSIT GLORIA MUNDI

*'The future belongs to those who believe in the beauty of their dreams.'*
Eleanor Roosevelt

On my return from Boston I was agreeably surprised to find that the success I had enjoyed in my presentation to EEI suddenly bred more success in the UK and produced something of a reversal of opinions, at least among some of the people I spoke to. I realised I hadn't actually got any money for the Farah expedition yet, only a promise, but just the mention of the possibility of a grant from America, obviously not talking about the size of it or how it was to be achieved, even though the amount was pretty notional at this stage, made people immediately suggest other lines of funding, even including one at my own Institute, and this from people who had been so negative to the whole idea only a few weeks before.

"You should try the Gordon Childe Travel Fund," suggested one.

"You know, you might try the British Academy. They could well be interested," recommended another.

So I did. I obtained the necessary application forms and set out the potential of my intended research as I'd laid it out in Belmont. Interestingly, the Gordon Childe Fund, which was administered directly by the Institute, actually turned me down at first, something I had been quite prepared for given the connection between the Institute and the schools, but W. F. Grimes, then director of the Institute and known universally as 'Peter', deliberately reversed the committee's decision, much to their chagrin, and gave me a grant. It wasn't very much admittedly, but at £250 it was not to be sneezed at either; after all it represented two airfares. Maybe it was Grimes' way of getting back at the dominant and domineering influence of the all-powerful Rik; I don't think there was any love lost between the two. It was Grimes who also suggested that he would support my application to the British Academy, and with such a powerful reference they awarded me a grant too, £500, which was a lot to me at the time.

I was talking to Michael Borne, a student in my extra-mural class, who was a lawyer with a big West End legal firm, Stoneham, Langton and Passmore of Bolton Street, just off Piccadilly, and I mentioned to him how my applications were progressing. Mike suggested that if it would help he could set up a charitable foundation for me, *gratis*, through which I could channel any money that came in. I thought it was a bit of an extreme idea at the time, but I went along with it, and out of that came the 'British Western Negev Expedition Trust'. He was quite prepared to be on the board of this charity and to set up a client account at Stoneham's to make the whole thing not only legal but so much more impressive. The account was opened with £750, the only money I had at this stage.

I had another student in my class, Peggy Nuttall, who was then editor of the Nursing Times and apparently an influential force in the charity market when it came to the health of the nation. When I spoke to her in the Marlborough Arms in Bloomsbury over a beer or two after my class, she also became fascinated by the prospect of my potential work at Farah. She said she had some powerful friends with their hands on the levers of commerce and financial grants and she would sound them out. She did and so asked me to write an outline of the proposed project on half a sheet of paper, which I did. Out of this came an amazing grant of £1000 through Peggy's connection with Lisa Sainsbury, wife of Sir Robert Sainsbury, the grocery king. When I asked Peggy how on earth she'd done it, she said,

"Well, I told her that I had helped her with her charity (the Sainsbury's were wont to donate millions to various hospitals around Britain), and that it was time that she should help me with mine. That was all!"

Going to the supermarket took on a whole new meaning for me after that!

\*   \*   \*

It was obviously time to take matters more seriously. I had to start making proper plans if there was going to be any kind of an expedition. And I had to respond to EEI in Belmont, so during the next few weeks I quickly organised the various domestic aspects of the expedition. I had a contact at the Rockefeller Museum who suggested that we should stay in the town of Beer Sheba and commute out to the site every day. He knew of a cheap place we could stay too, a youth centre, which he said was empty during the summer months and probably would have rooms we could use. I wrote to the address he gave me and made a deal to hire rooms there, and they would provide all our meals too. I passed the details on to Belmont and amazingly they came back and said they may well be about to sign up a number of participants. They didn't elaborate on who they were at this stage, but said that they would join the expedition in mid-July, and for looking after them for three weeks we would receive $6,000. That was more than £3,000 at the going rate, and I might well be able to tease a little more out of the dollars through the money changers in Jerusalem.

My next consideration was transport – how did we get there, and how did we get around once we'd arrived? Then at just the right moment, a solution offered itself. That Easter there was an Institute training dig taking place at Bedfont, on the edge of Heathrow Airport. It was a rescue excavation of a Belgic Iron Age village in the middle of what was an aviation fuel depot, on top of which they were hoping to build several more storage tanks. I went along to teach surveying. The director, John Alexander, had been a lecturer at a nearby teacher training college in Hounslow and he arrived every day in his own mini-bus, one he had used to transport students around. During a coffee break one morning I asked him what it was like; how useful was it? He took me over and showed me inside; it was designed to take eleven people.

"I'm trying to sell it," he said. "You don't want to buy it, do you?"

And that's how I became the owner of a Ford Transit Minibus Mark I, lovingly built at the old Hawker Hurricane Aircraft factory at Langley in Berkshire. It was a fashionable dove grey in colour and he wanted £800 for it; it was only three years old, and it was ideal for my purpose. It had been designed by Ford to maximize the interior space, and it had a compact V4 engine under the bonnet. I named it 'Gloria', as in 'Sic Transit', though it was never really 'sick' the whole time I had it, but I did see a lot of the 'Mundi' in it. It took me to the Middle East and back a couple of times without complaining, and for two seasons provided all the transport I needed at Farah.

*　*　*

I organised air tickets for Juliet, and a couple of months later, with a route description provided by the AA, a couple of maps of Europe, and a pile of dollars from my fund I was off on what I reckoned to be one of the biggest adventures of my life so far – to drive right the way across Europe from London to Athens. I had modified 'Gloria' a bit for the journey by removing the rear-most seat and loading it forwards over the third row. This gave a larger payload in the back and with three people in the front that left the second row of seats to act as a driver's bed. There were four of us on that epic first journey – myself, and two of my students, Father Robin Duckworth who was a down-to-earth Catholic priest, and Martin Bidmead who was to become one of my site supervisors, and a girl who just wanted a lift to Athens.

I can't remember where she'd come from, but Martin was to act as general factotum on the journey and she was to be the sandwich maker. She also gave me a little money towards the petrol – I think in the end it paid for a couple of tank-fulls. Robin and I were to do all the driving turn by turn, two hours on, two hours off. At nine o'clock on a fine evening in late June we left London for Dover on the first leg of our momentous journey. I had booked the midnight ferry from Dover to Ostend and a ship at the other end from Athens to Haifa, otherwise the whole thing was unscripted. I had no idea how it would go that first time around.

Two hours later we were in Dover terminal boarding the ferry for Ostend, where our route across Europe was to begin. At 4am we were disembarking in Belgium and as dawn was breaking over the North Sea we were off, negotiating the roundabout outside the ferry terminal and away down the motorway. Our first hour or two took us past Bruges and Ghent, around the Brussels Ring and on to Leuven and Liege before crossing into Germany at Aachen and onto the Cologne Autobahn. I was worried about Germany. At that time the Deutsche Mark was very strong and to avoid unforeseen expense I planned that except for loo and fuel stops we should cross the whole of Germany in a day without resting. We had brought all our provisions with us; apart from petrol we didn't need to buy anything.

At Cologne we drove over the Rhine Bridge and out of the Rhine Valley across the Westerwald to Limburg and Frankfurt. Just outside Frankfurt we coasted to a halt at a petrol station to fill up, have a pit stop and change of drivers. Robin took over and I went to bed in the seat behind. We discovered that whatever we did it always took twenty minutes at any stop, to fill up, to empty out, to check the oil and water, to stretch our legs, anything – always twenty minutes. So after the statuary twenty we were off down the autobahn again, round Aschaffenburg, Würzburg and Kitzingen and across the Steigerwald to Nürnburg.

We had lunch en route as planned. Now, I happen to be a particular aficionado of tinned sardines and had bought a month's supply before we'd left London, so you could have any filling in your sandwich you wanted so long as it was sardine and tomato (optional). Another pit stop and another change of drivers saw us hammering south towards Ingolstadt and the autobahn to Bavaria. The day was wearing on. We hadn't really stopped since Ostende and the afternoon beckoned as we drove towards Munich. Around tea-time we were on the ring road leaving Munich on our right and heading for Rosenheim, then on down to Inn valley to Kufstein and the Austrian border which we crossed as the light began to fade. It was time for our first real break. Just over the border we came into the little village of Söll. There was what looked like a bar-restaurant by the side of the road and I pulled over and went in.

Inside it was absolutely archetypal, with a clutch of men in lederhosen and embroidered bracers drinking steins of larger around a fretwork-decorated wooden bar replete with cuckoo clocks. I asked if they knew of anywhere to stay and one of the men detached himself from the group and motioned me to follow him. What I didn't know, of course, was that Söll was a popular ski resort with quite a number of guesthouses and hotels all of which at that time of the year were virtually empty. We could have taken our pick.

We followed his car as he turned abruptly up a small track to an equally archetypal wooden chalet, the Gastehaus Edelweiss. A very hale and hearty hausfrau greeted us and was only too pleased to show us her rooms – they were all empty – so we checked in. After a few *weissbieren*, a good supper of *Wiener Schnitzel unt Gebratene Kartoffeln mit Zwiebeln* and a gentian schnapps to round off the evening we went gratefully to our beds. Next morning we awoke to sun streaming through the curtains and looking through the window I saw the superb mountains of the Austrian Tyrol, a landscape straight out of 'Heidi', complete with cows wearing large clanking bells around their necks in the pasturage all around the chalet. The ski slopes in June were of course all grass. After a quick breakfast we were back on the road again, winding our way through the Tyrol past St Johann, through the Kitzbüheler Alpen and the Felber-Tauern Tunnel under the main peaks of the Alps into the Ost Tyrol to Lienz, and then down the wonderfully scenic Unter-Drau-Thal to Spittal and Villach, where we made a sharp right turn up through the Karnisher Alps to the Italian border at Tarvisio. For twenty minutes we were in Italy before coming to an abrupt halt at the Yugoslavian border at Podkornen. In two days' driving this was the first crossing point we had really noticed. We were leaving Europe for the Balkans.

The border post was thick with *policija* who turned out to be a right pain in the *guzica*. We had to take everything out of the van, but I mean everything, including the sardine cans. And once it was all out and laid on the ground, they told us to put it all back in again without even looking at it. A minute examination of the passports followed, one by one - maybe they'd never seen a British passport before - until we were finally waved on.

"Longer than the statutory twenty minutes that bloody lot!" commented Robin as we set off through the Slovenian scenery towards Ljubljana and Zagreb in the last of the afternoon sunlight.

Just before Zagreb, in the growing dusk we pulled into a petrol station and road house where we booked a couple of rooms and checked into the shower for a long soak before reappearing in the bar for a few swift bottles of *pivo* and a dinner of *kranjska klobasa* with *idrijski žlikrofi* (sausage and dumplings) and a damson slivovitz to celebrate our progress. We were in the process of relaxing with the slivovitz when a German diner sitting next to the window suddenly leapt up shouting manically and rushed out of the door just in time to see his precious new Mercedes speeding down the road to Zagreb. That was the end of his good evening! I went outside and removed the rotor arm from the distributor cap of the Transit just in case.

Next morning 'Gloria' wouldn't start, until, that is I remembered about the rotor arm, and once it was replaced we were off again. Now, the map shows a motorway all the way through Yugoslavia known locally as the *autoput*. But wide it isn't. For the most part it's single carriageway, kilometre after endless kilometre of it, and there are a lot of kilometres between Zagreb all the way down the Sava Valley to Belgrade, passing interminable small village communes en route. After four hundred kilometres, with a couple of changes on the way, we drove around Belgrade and up the Morava Valley to Niš and on towards Skopje. One thing was particularly noticeable in Yugoslavia. Personal safety did not seem to be an issue with these people. They drove like there was no tomorrow, and indeed for some there wasn't going to be one. We passed accident after accident and home-made shrine after shrine, adorned with flowers and the buckled steering wheel or the crumpled bonnet of the car in which the driver had suddenly taken an unscheduled exit off the *autoput* into the next world.

It was getting towards dusk as we passed Skopje and headed into the Macedonian mountains towards the Greek border. I was driving when we came to a town marked as Titov Veles with still about eighty kilometres to go. It was now that I made a mistake and took an unscheduled right turn into the town. It was twilight by this time, but the town was in party mood, with hundreds of Macedonians thronging the main street, packing it from side to side. I drove in first gear, hand on the horn, until eventually we got out the other side, at which point Robin checked the map and said we'd have to go back; we'd missed the main road. I did a three point turn and locking the door I began the slow process of scything into the hoards again. On the way back through the press of people one over-zealous reveller climbed onto the running board and wearing an idiot grin started banging his fist on the window. Robin lowered the passenger widow just enough to shout through the gap and with extravagant enthusiasm said in his best priestly voice:

"Listen sunshine, if you don't get off there I'll knock your teeth so far down your throat you'll have to stick a toothbrush up your arse to clean them!" The vehemence of his threat was enough. The merrymaker alighted and we drove unscathed out of Titov Veles and back onto the main road.

An hour later we were through the Greek border, but it was already dark and we needed to stop soon for the night. At the border town of Polikastron I saw a notice saying 'Motel' and drove in. It was in total darkness, but when I beeped the horn, floodlights came on all around the building and an old man came out and greeted us in Greek. He indicated he had chalets free and we got out to inspect them. They were fine for the one night we needed them, and in drachma they were very cheap. I motioned to the tables in front of what appeared to be the bar and made eating signals. The old man nodded and indicated that something would happen in half an hour. We cleaned up and duly showed up at the bar. Rows of ice cold *Mpyra Fix Hellas* were brought while we waited for the dolmades, grilled haloumi slices and spanakopita followed by *kleftiko* with *fasolakia*, ending the evening with a comforting three-star Metaxa brandy on the rocks. Tomorrow we would reach Athens; we could relax, so we ordered another Metaxa to celebrate. The old man joined in the festivities by playing a few Rolling Stones numbers at full volume into the darkness on his speaker system.

Next day was easy. A late start after breakfast took us to the motorway at Thessalonica and down the coast to Larissa and Voulos, then around the Gulf of Malis past the site of the 480 BC battle of Thermopylae, the Gates of Fire – Leonidas and the three-hundred Spartans, 'here we stand' and all that. Soon we were approaching Attica and Athens. The great city with a liberal covering of smog hove into view and we followed signs to Piraeus. I found the offices of the shipping company and checked the tickets. We were told to be at the port at nine the next morning, so after parting company with our Girl Friday, Robin, Martin and I crashed out in a local hotel for the rest of the afternoon. Next morning, we drove to the port gates and were shown to the wharf where the 'Odysseus' was moored, the ship that was to take us across the Mediterranean. It was a ship was owned by Epirotiki Lines, one of the biggest ferry companies in Greece, and after a lot of shouting and indecision about the height of 'Gloria' they eventually let out the mooring lines to move the ship away from the quayside slightly so that the cargo door could accommodate the extra height of the Transit, and we managed to get 'Gloria' into the hold and we went to find our cabin in steerage. Our Mediterranean cruise was about to begin.

You would think that Greece, with all its islands and loads of sea, would produce probably the finest calibre of sailors in the world, what with the Battle of Salamis, Aristotle Onassis and all that, but this proved not to be the case, at least as far as Epirotiki Lines were concerned; their general seamanship left a lot to be desired. Actually, a few years later Epirotiki managed to lose three of their main cruise ships in the same year through sheer bad seamanship, including their flag ship. The most spectacular was the loss of the 'Oceanos' which sank in the Indian Ocean off the coast of South Africa, making international news when its captain, a certain Captain Avranas, was found by the South African police in a five-star hotel in Durban, having left the members of the ship's hired entertainment to supervise the passengers abandoning the vessel and taking to the life-boats. He was co-ordinating the rescue from his hotel room, he said. Anyway, as far as abandoning ship was concerned, we thankfully didn't have to do that on this cruise, but there were other moments of drama.

After leaving Athens, the first port of call for 'Odysseus' was Heraklion on the island of Crete where the crew had arranged a trip for the passengers to see the Minoan site of Knossos, so we went along. It was as we were leaving Heraklion that evening that we were involved in an alarming altercation. The ship was manoeuvring out of the harbour and there was already clear water between the side of the ship and the quay when for some reason the captain put the engines full astern. Just behind our berth there was a small fishing boat moored to the same quayside and the fishermen on the deck suddenly saw this great liner coming backwards at full pelt towards them. They shouted and waved frantically but to no avail until a collision was inevitable, at which point they scattered like cartoon lemmings, leaping over the side and diving into the water, while the stern of our boat crushed the trawler against the stone jetty with a sickening splintering of wood. Only then did the captain of our ship signal full steam ahead while his own crew gesticulated wildly at the men in the water seemingly blaming them for having moored their vessel there in the first place. Robin, Martin and I retired to the third-class bar. It was an odd affair, with banquet seats around the walls and small drinks tables, but no actual bar. The drinks were being served through a small hatch in the corner. I went over and had to bend down to give my order through the hatch – three beers please – at which point the barman on the other side of the hatch waggled his finger at me and said:

"For you, is'a close!" and shut the hatch.

We waited for a few minutes until he opened the hatch and started serving again. I went over and ordered the three beers again which this time he deigned to bang onto the counter. We soon finished these and it was Robin's turn to go up to the hatch, when to his astonishment the barman said again. "For you, is'a close!" and once again slammed the hatch shut.

I was relieved it wasn't only me. The whole evening went on like this, open, close, open, close. Maybe the barman was severely incontinent we thought and needed to relieve himself every few minutes. Or maybe he was moonlighting at another bar somewhere else on another ship. We could find no other explanation. Our way around the problem was that the next time it was my turn to order I asked for nine beers, and we were then able to relax, while the barman continued his opening and closing routine with all the other customers.

After a night at sea we arrived in the middle of the next morning at the Turkish port of Antalya to be greeted by a row of buses to take us on yet another excursion, this time to two of the best archaeological sites in the Classical region of Pamphylia. The first was Aspendos. It has a magnificent almost complete Roman theatre, with a reproduction wooden stage. Of course we had the usual clown in our group standing in the middle of the stage singing a bar or two of 'O solo mio' and asking his friends in the rear seats if they could hear him, to which the answer should have been 'Yes, but I'm not sure we really want to'. Back on the bus and along the main coast road again we arrived at Side, yet another Classical site, with yet another surprisingly intact theatre, this time built on flat ground with huge barrel vaults and interior staircases. More bars of 'O solo mio' from the would-be off-key tenor, more embarrassment from his companions. What did they think the Romans built the theatres for, for God's sake? Mime?

After a suitable time for a late lunch at a local kebab cafe, we continued to Alanya, another major port east along the coast where the 'Odysseus' had relocated, seemingly this time without sinking any of the local fishing fleet. As night fell we cast off to cross the sea to the Levant. That evening we were treated to more of the 'For you, is a-close' pantomime with the bar-man and the hatch, though we'd got his number by this time and always gave multiple orders on the rare occasions when the hatch was open. And after a suitable number of beers, we retired for our last night on board before our arrival in the Holy Land the next day.

Soon after dawn the next day the port of Haifa emerged through the early morning sea mist, the cityscape dominated by the Shrine of Bab, a golden-domed Bahá'í temple built at the beginning of the twentieth century. We hurried to the Transit in the hold ready for the disembarkation, which oddly wasn't long in coming and we emerged into the sunlight of Haifa's port buildings. Passing uneventfully through immigration and customs, I pulled into a petrol station near the harbour to fill up. This turned out to be a mistake, as I accidentally filled up with eighty-seven octane fuel. It was fine when we left Haifa by the coast road and along the base of the Carmel range, the roads being on the flat, but wanting to get into the West Bank as soon as possible we turned south into the hills at Jenin and then the trouble began – pinking. 'Gloria's engine started knocking like a badly-tuned tractor as soon as we were on any upward incline and we lost all power. I was reduced to shifting down into second gear, and even into first, on the simplest hills. Downhill was mercifully quiet but uphill she sounded like a Centurion tank without a silencer.

But it was a bright day and we were in high spirits, and eventually we passed through Nablus and on south through the limestone mountains to Ramallah and eventually reached the outskirts of the Holy City. Weaving our way around the narrow streets of East Jerusalem we finally turned into Ibn Khaldoun Street and drove up to the front door of the Ritz Hotel. Louis saw us from reception and came out to greet us. I'd come home.

CHAPTER THIRTEEN
# JOACHIM NEANDER GETS HIS MAN

*Behold! Mine brother Esau is an hairy man, but I am a*
*smooth man.*
Genesis 27:11

Whenever I was in the southern Israeli town of Beer Sheba, Bir es-Saba, meaning the Seven Wells, or the Well of the Oath, depending how biblical you want to be, it always occurred to me that the place was a bit like the wild-west – untamed and unruly. For several centuries during the Ottoman period it had been a small Arab village serving the disparate and obstreperous groups of semi-nomadic Bedouin who lived scattered about the central Negev Desert. But most of the people who had settled in Beer Sheba since 1948 were Jews who had come from the Arab world, especially from Morocco and Algeria. Surprisingly there were also thousands of Jewish immigrants who had originated in India, from around Bombay and also from south India, the so-called Malabar or Cochin Jews. None of them displayed the same confrontational self-importance and loud arrogance for which the European Jews, the ones who had migrated from Poland, Russia and the Baltic, were noted and who made up the bulk of the modern population. On the whole the Beer Sheba Jews were a much easier people with whom to get along. Ironically, despite claiming their unbroken lineage all the way back to Solomon, a full three thousand years of history, the Indian Jews were severely racially discriminated against by the majority of Israeli Jews from Europe who refused to recognise them as anything other than low class foreigners. Orthodox rabbis apparently even denied them the right to marry anyone who I suppose you might describe as a kosher son of Judah. What is it they say? If you have two Jews, you'll have three arguments?

In 1972 there were still some Arabs living in Beer Sheba who had moved in from the desert, and they even held a very colourful camel market once a week. By contrast the modern development which was taking over was untrammelled and drab, notable for its unfinished concrete buildings and cheap shopping arcades. Where we had elected to stay for our first season at Farah was no different. It was a colourless block on the edge of the town which served as a youth centre – which youth, and the centre of what, I never did learn; we were always the only people there. But it had enough twin-bedded rooms to accommodate our group, a plain school-room type of common room, and the food they produced was uninspiring but enough for our needs. Tell Farah was 30 kilometres to the west of Beer Sheba and it took us about half an hour every morning to get out to the site, leaving the youth centre at first light and driving westwards as the sun rose directly behind us.

Tell Farah itself is a large mound, especially distinguishable by its profile above the skyline; it sits up proud on a very noticeable sandstone bluff overlooking the Wadi Ghazzeh. Thomas Edward Lawrence had surveyed the area in 1913 as part of a covert intelligence-gathering exercise against the Turks, a part of his secondment to Bertie Clayton's Arab Bureau in Cairo during the First World War, and in 1928 Flinders Petrie had turned his attention to the tell after he'd finished excavating at Jemmeh. Petrie's aim was to study the connections between southern Palestine and the history of the Nile, and he found what he was looking for at Farah, which incidentally he called Beth Pelet on some rather dubious linguistic parallels. But he did find his links to Egypt, first in the fact that the tell had been fortified with a beaten earth glacis by the Hyksos, the Shepherd Kings, who had invaded Egypt and taken over the Delta at the beginning of the second millennium BC, and later by the discovery of what Petrie called an Egyptian Residency of the New Kingdom, dating from the reign of the 18th Dynasty pharaoh Thutmosis I around about 1480 BC. It had apparently been used until the reign of the Ramesside pharaohs of the 19th and 20th Dynasties, at which point the city seems to have been taken over by the Philistines, who had been part of the invasion of the 'Peoples from the Sea' at the beginning of the Iron Age around 1200 BC. The site was sufficiently large that Petrie worked for two winter seasons here, in 1928 and 1929, and during the second year he was joined by a separate team looking at prehistoric Farah, mainly a number of small sites on the opposite side of the wadi which dated to the late Neolithic period, just before the beginning of the Bronze Age. In typical Petrie style, both these and his own excavations on the main Tell were published, albeit rather tersely, by the end of 1930.

By the time we appeared on the scene, Petrie's excavation pit, over forty years old, was still clearly visible, if somewhat eroded. It could hardly be anything else. It covered a large area at the north end of the tell, but there were no obvious vestiges of his actual discoveries remaining. Nevertheless the scenery round about was impressive. Standing on the top of the tell and looking eastwards upstream the wadi curved around below in a huge S-shape under the side of the site. In the misted expanse towards the skyline was the country surface of the Negev, with a few acacia trees silhouetted like dark-coloured blots on the horizon. In the middle distance the bed of the wadi came curved like a huge dry river bed, in the centre of which were strips of gravel, flanked on the one side by long groves of young tamarisk trees and interspersed with beds of tall reeds clustered around a ribbon of fresh water which emanated from a perennial spring. And slightly to the left, to the north east on the opposite side of the wadi were a whole series of gullies that had been eroded into the landscape creating the appearance of 'bad-lands'. It was these gullies where we were going to make a start. They were to prove to be the making of our environmental survey and furnish us with the evidence that neither Lawrence, nor Petrie and his prehistorians, nor anyone else who had looked at the region had previously recorded. Archaeologically the gullies and their exposed contents were to provide the central magic of the Farah survey.

*   *   *

It was on about day three of our expedition at Farah that we made the startling discovery. We were getting the feel of the gullies first thing one morning, walking up and down them and realising that there was probably a climatic history tied up in the exposures of silt they represented, when we came across a scatter of chipped stones low down in the sequence, near the tamarisk grove on the side of the wadi. The flakes had seemingly washed out of the side of an eroded bank onto a slight apron. It was a small collection, hardly noticeable at first and half hidden in the mud. I picked up a couple of pieces, turning them over in my hand, and Peter Dorrell – you remember he was acting as the geomorphologist - did the same.

"You know something?" he mused. "I think that these might be Mousterian."

"What?" I countered.

"Yes, I think these are Mousterian. They're Middle Palaeolithic. You know what that means dear boy? Well, I'll tell you. It means that if they were in Europe they'd date from forty thousand, maybe fifty thousand years ago. These are old, and I mean old!"

We looked around more carefully. There were more flakes than we first thought which had trickled down into a small erosional cut. And as we brushed the mud away with our hands, Peter exclaimed,

"See, it's a Levallois flake. Look how it's made! That's part of the same industry."

cms

*Levallois flakes from near Tell Farah (© DPW)*

He held out a small triangular piece of stone

"It's even got a *chapeau de gendarme* butt, look!"

"A what?"

"A *chapeau de gendarme* butt; it's the mark of how the flake was prepared on the core. It's the indicator of the change in the way they made stone tools in the middle of the Stone Age. This industry is very early, at least if it was in France it would be. And there it's associated with Neanderthal Man."

"With who?"

"It's found with Neanderthal skeletons. It's well-known from southern France, from the Dordogne. The French are very fond of it; they have their heads right up their own arses about it. For them it only really occurs in France, and maybe in southern Germany and virtually nowhere else; you know what the French are like. The type site is an Abri, a cave-overhang called Le Moustier in the Vezere Valley near Bergerac. I mean, if this is what I think it is it could be really important."

We looked around more carefully and it was then that I spotted something that made the discovery even more dramatic. Among the debris and the flakes on the surface and mixed in with them were tiny white slivers. I drew Peter's attention to them and he pursed his lips and said,

"Jesus, you know what these are? They're fragments of bone. They're little pieces of bone that have eroded out with the flakes. It means there's a very good chance this whole deposit was originally *in-situ*, an open-air site with all the living debris still there. There may well be more of it. And you know something? The flakes are not patinated at all, the chipped surfaces are not clouded over. They're pristine. It means that they're even more likely to come from an intact deposit, one that may still be buried in the silt. Why don't we take a break and think what to do next?"

So we did. And in the end Peter was proved right; that's what this material was. We had come across a Middle Palaeolithic open air site, a Neanderthal hunting camp, right here on the side of the wadi and near the base of the whole sequence of sediments that made up the country surface of the Negev. What was even more interesting was that no-one had seen this kind of thing here before, even though Petrie had operated a whole season of prehistoric research in the area, and his colleagues must have walked over this place to get to their Late Neolithic sites on the surface above. As it became known what we'd found, it was to be one of the defining discoveries of the whole British Western Negev Expedition and it brought some welcome, and I must also say some unwelcome, attention. It was later to assume even greater importance when comparisons were made with other sites in the Levant and elsewhere, and in relation to new research and to new dates by others as well as by ourselves.

But right now, before all that, we decided to test three things. First, had this material truly come from an *in-situ* setting? Did it actually represent an intact deposit?

Second, where was it in relation to the depositional history of the Wadi Ghazzeh? Could we relate the overlying sequence of silts and sands to this Mousterian material, which would give us some kind of a date as to when things might have happened?

And third, were there any more exposure like this one? Were there any more sites from this period around the sides of the wadi?

It was this third question that I thought we should address first, and to that end I formed a small team to scour the gullies for several kilometres upstream and downstream from Farah. By this time several more of my extra-mural students had arrived to join us, and after I had showed them what we were looking for I sent them off for walks to conduct a site survey of the wadi. Every morning for a week they took off up or down the wadi, taking their packed breakfasts and some water with them.

They didn't return until it was time to go back to Beer Sheba for lunch. But the results they found were astonishing. They collected considerable numbers of flake samples in plastic bags from scores of locations from as far as almost ten kilometres away, all carefully labelled. So at the end of that week, when we could draw breath, we decided to review their discoveries one afternoon in the common room at the youth centre. Together we examined all the bags of flakes. The site survey group had understood by now what we were looking for, and indeed they'd been right on target. All the little bags contained Mousterian flakes. I was particularly impressed with their careful numbering and annotation system, Site MBB1, Site WAB3, Site TAB2, and so on. It looked very well thought out, very professional and scientifically based. I asked them how they had defined the nomenclature of the different sites - did the numbers refer to grid references perhaps, distance markers, or to height orientations maybe?

"Oh, those?" they said. "No, those refer to where we were when we found them – MBB1 was 'Monday Before Breakfast' site 1; WAB3 was 'Wednesday After Breakfast' site 3; TAB2 'Thursday After Breakfast' site 2 and so on. It's when we came across them really. Is that OK?"

Ah! My mistake! I'd forgotten these people were totally untrained in field techniques. The end result was that we had to walk the ground all over again to re-locate and to annotate them properly. But it was a worthwhile exercise too. Some of the sites were obviously completely washed out, but a significant number appeared to be derived from *in-situ* deposits. The Neanderthals, or whoever it was, had obviously been very active, or at least they had been there for a considerable length of time.

\* \* \*

The Mediterranean coast from Tell Aviv in the north southwards to the Wadi el Arish, just over the Egyptian border, experiences the highest rainfall gradient anywhere in the world. In a mere one hundred and twenty kilometres the annual average precipitation runs from almost twenty-five inches a year near Jaffa, more rain say than Athens in the central Mediterranean, to almost zero at El Arish just south of the Gaza Strip, which gets the same rainfall as the middle of Sahara Desert. And Farah is right in the middle of that gradient. That's the statistic that Juliet had to try to describe in her appreciation of the plant life in the Wadi Ghazzeh, and being Juliet she set about it with vigour. By the time she'd finished pressing and pickling her specimens that first season she'd collected well over one hundred different plant species which reflected the complex inter-relationship between the three sub-continental environmental zones I'd noted when I first began to describe Farah. The majority belonged to the middle eco-zone, the dry steppe which comes all the way from Iran across the northern Levant and down to Farah, but there were a few Mediterranean plant species too. What Juliet concentrated on doing was classifying the area around Farah in today's terms – what plants were growing here now. It would be later that she would turn her attention to how we were going to use any plant remains to interpret temperature and rainfall regimes of the past.

Peter meanwhile was concentrating his efforts on understanding the sequence of events which brought about the landscape as it looked today. The bedrock of the Negev at this point we knew was limestone from the Neogene geological phase, basically mid-Miocene, maybe dating to twenty million years ago. That lay beneath everything we could see. On top of this were a series of fossil dunes, like fossilised sandstones. One of these actually underlay the tell itself, and you could see the typical desert wind-deposited cross-bedding in the exposed slope of the dune just below the Tell. The dunes too were probably quite old. But of more interest was the next set of deposits. In the bed of the wadi were large spreads of loose gravel, made up of light-brown chert cobbles and pebbles, which is a kind of flint which eroded out from the limestone much further upstream. It was from among these cobbles that the Middle Palaeolithic people had obtained the raw material for their stone tools, the ones we'd found. But although the gravel was loose in the wadi floor, a closer examination along the sides of the wadi revealed that there was a hard, agglomerated bed of this gravel over the whole area forming a low terrace just above the present wadi floor from which the present loose gravels were being re-worked. Obviously at some time in the past the wadi, which had brought these gravels here, had dried out and the banks of deposited gravels had been cemented together in-situ with calcium carbonate. By the look of them this was some considerable time ago.

Overlying these was a very obvious and complex series of more or less horizontally bedded fine silt deposits which eventually attained a total thickness of almost thirty metres. It was in the lower parts of these layers that our Mousterian sites had been found. The more we looked at this material the more we realised that understanding this series was going to be the answer, at least in fairly recent geological time, to what had happened to the climate here in the sub-tropics, maybe over the past fifty to one hundred thousand years. And the more we examined it, the more detailed the sequence became. In the upper phases there were obvious fossil soils, chocolate brown soil horizons which we could follow horizontally for kilometres across country, which represented earlier surfaces of the Negev when the soil was not being deposited. Then deposition had begun again until the next pause, and the next soil formation. This would take a lot of working out.

But it was the Mousterian sites which attracted our attention most, and especially the one we'd found first. It was time to take a closer look at it, to find out if it really was in-situ and had truly lain here undisturbed for tens of thousands of years. It was time to make a test sounding. It was at this moment that the EEI volunteers were to arrive. There would be six of them and they would be our work force. We were in a state of high excitement waiting to begin; we wondered what experience of archaeology these volunteers might bring with them and how we might put that to use. And arrive the volunteers did, but they were not at all what we'd expected. They were not the eager participants who had given up their professional time to help us excavate the prehistory of the Levant. What actually turned up was a group of six teenagers of different sizes and ethnic backgrounds who had come straight from Chicago, three girls and three boys. All six were from the deprived areas of the central city itself and this was the first time they had ever been outside Chicago, let alone outside the US. The rest of the team were somewhat shocked. My first thought was to call Belmont to find out what had happened. When I phoned and asked how these kids had come to be sent to us, Barbara replied,

"Ah yes. They've arrived then. Well it's like this, you see. We had difficulty recruiting participants for your expedition, so we thought of another way we might fund you. We applied to the Inner Cities Program, you know, the LBJ thing, for funding, and this is how it happened. Sorry we didn't tell you earlier, but I'm sure you'll manage, David!"

The 'Inner Cities Program' was one that had been invented by President Lyndon Baines Johnson when he took over after J. F. K.'s assassination. He went on to introduce an ambitious domestic agenda into US politics which he dubbed "The Great Society." The most dramatic parts of his spending program concerned bringing aid to underprivileged Americans. He called on the whole nation to wage a war on poverty and he felt that America had not done enough to provide socio-economic opportunities for the underclass. He'd voted in a large budget to tackle these reforms, and though the idea was in its death throes by the time EEI got there, Bob Citron had managed to syphon off some of the last of these funds into his new organisation. The result was that we were now encumbered with these sixteenagers in the middle of the Negev Desert who had had no experience of living away from home, whatever home they'd come from, let alone of archaeology. Well, where they were now was certainly a very long way from Inner City Chicago, I have to say.

I felt there were two things we could do – either find something totally innocuous for the six to do, or to involve them as we had planned as though they were adults. We talked the problem through over a few beers in a nearby café in Beer Sheba run by a woman called Shoshanna who incidentally had a squint eye; the café became universally known to us as Cross-eyed Susan's. My decision was to treat these six as though they were grown up participants, to teach and train them and to let them become part of the whole expedition.

And that's what we did. I taught them the rudiments of what we were trying to do; I showed them the tell, I walked them through the wadi, I showed them the stone tools, the whole thing so far. And then I put them to work excavating the site, teaching them to use trowels, to sieve debris, to write notes on what they were finding. And I included them in our evening discussions about the work, and how our ideas were progressing. After a few teething problems and a certain amount of eye-brow raising among the older volunteers, and a general naivety on their own part, the six actually fitted in well and did all that was expected of them. I put one of my mature students with each couple of them as a sort of mentor. We opened up four separate metre-wide squares along the base of the ridge where we'd found the Mousterian flakes, and when we removed the small amount of overburden, we exposed what turned out indeed to be an in-situ deposit, with finished flakes, shaping flakes, cut bones and even charcoal, all buried as they had been left those many millennia before. We had a result. At the end of the three weeks one or two of us were even sorry to see the six EEI volunteers leave.

Curiously there was a sequel to all this. About fifteen years later, I was giving a talk in Chicago for the Archaeological Institute of America on our work in Africa at the prestigious Field Museum of Natural History – I'd moved on from the Middle East long since. There was a good audience, maybe a hundred or more strong, and I put on the usual show of our work to date. At the end of the lecture, and the after questions had finished, I was gathering up my slides from the visual aids operator, surrounded by well-wishers, when a young man pushed through the crowd and came up to me saying,

"Hi, Prof. I'm Danny, remember me? I was one of the inner city kids who were with you in the Negev all those years ago. I saw the advert for this lecture in the local paper and I said to myself, 'Hey, that's my Doc!' So here I am."

"Danny! How are you? What are you doing now?"

"Well, I could be doing better you know, and I sure hope to, but right now I'm driving a cab in Chicago. But I just wanted to say 'Hello' to you, and thanks. Doc, you changed my life in those three weeks. I'd been a hoodlum, you know, in a teenage gang and all that. But you treated us like adults. It made a big, big difference to me that three weeks we were with you, so thanks again!"

And with that he pushed his way back through the crowd and disappeared. I've thought about that meeting many times since then. You never know what effect you're having on anyone, do you? I'm so pleased that we did the right thing by Danny anyway.

The first Farah season drew to a close. At our last beer up at Cross-eyed Susan's we took stock of the whole thing again. We'd understood the basic sequence of events at Farah, in terms of the deposition of the sediments at least. Juliet had made a very good start on the botany and most importantly we'd discovered the Middle Palaeolithic sites around the Wadi Ghazzeh. That was the real breakthrough. What we now had to do was develop all the ideas further. We would need more details, interpretations and some actual dates.

I took all the equipment we'd bought, all the excavation gear, the picks, trowels, buckets and such like, to Jerusalem where Louis put them in a store-room at the back of the Ritz. We had one last blow-out at the Golden Chicken before driving back to Haifa to catch the Epirotiki Lines ferry to Athens. From there we retraced our journey uneventfully back across Europe, through Greece, up the *autoput* through Yugoslavia, along the autobahns through Austria and Germany before finally arriving at Ostende to catch the Dover Packet to Britain.

CHAPTER FOURTEEN
# SINGLE MALT

*Love makes the world go round.*
*But whiskey makes it go round twice as fast.*
Compton Mackenzie

Finding the funds to support the expedition was a never-ending campaign. No sooner had I arrived back in the UK than it began all over again, the interminable round of applications, the lobbying and cajoling, the endless statement and restatement of the aims of our research, and the constant reiteration of my conviction that it really was worthwhile. The effects of climatic change on the distant past wasn't the most attractive of archaeological subjects, It didn't have the immediate 'buried treasure' appeal, the 'lost civilization', the 'earliest' this or the 'oldest' that. But I found that with a liberal element of undimmed enthusiasm and a certain amount of high-quality creativity I could frequently win the day and attract people's attention in the face of a whole barrage of other people's projects, good causes, fascinating discoveries and new ideas that were on offer. And nowhere did it work better, funnily enough, than among my extra-mural archaeology groups. In particular I had a couple of Americans in my class at the Institute, Paul and Mary, who were very taken with the idea of what we were doing and they invited me to dinner to discuss the whole thing. They lived in a very spacious apartment on the Marylebone Road, directly opposite Harley Street, so thither I went to explain things further.

Oddly enough, the one feature of the expedition so far which rang bells with the average man in the street was the Middle Palaeolithic sites we'd uncovered. Well, not exactly the Middle Palaeolithic sites, you understand; no one who wasn't already a totally committed prehistorian would be able to relate to such an abstruse piece of information, but they would know something about Neanderthal Man, the character who was normally to be found with tools from this period. The image that Neanderthal Man evoked always held something of a fascination for people in general, despite, it must be said, many holding on to continuing misconceptions and misunderstandings. The first Neanderthal skulls had been discovered as early as 1829 at Engis Cave in what today is Belgium and again some twenty years later at Forbes' Quarry in Gibraltar but they went unrecognised at the time and were certainly not called Neanderthals. That didn't happen until 1856 when the bones of three individuals of what today is taken as the type specimen of the form were unearthed at the Feldhofer Cave outside Düsseldorf in north Germany. The cave was located in what had become known locally as Neander's Valley, named afterthe seventeenth century Christian mystic, Joachim Neander, who had lived as a hermit there, hence Neanderthal, Neander's Valley. At the time they were found, many people assumed that the bones were not very old. Some thought for instance, with perhaps understandable ignorance, that they might be the skeletal remains of badly wounded and mutilated soldiers who had died sheltering from a battle during some long-forgotten Prussian war. Others pejoratively saw them simply as the remains of itinerant Dutchmen, on the basis that all Dutch people were thought, especially by the French, to be significantly backward.

But on more informed reflection these discoveries were felt to constitute the very first evidence which could support the notion that modern man might have evolved from an earlier, more primitive form. This was indeed a highly explosive idea in the middle of the nineteenth century, especially among the biblically entrenched and theologically fundamentalist clergy of the day. Indeed, although the Feldhofer specimens had been found three years before Charles Darwin was to publish his famous book 'On the Origin of Species', curiously he didn't mention the Neanderthals at all. You'd have thought he would, wouldn't you? Maybe the perception they implied, of evolving humans, was at the time just too graphically inflammatory even for him. Nevertheless, as the theory of evolution gained ground in the latter part of the nineteenth century, Neanderthals began to fascinate the scientific world as being one of our possible ancestors, and by osmosis, they captivated the general public too.

But in 1911 a French palaeontologist by the name of Pierre Marcellin Boule published an extremely crude-looking reconstruction of a decrepit specimen of a Neanderthal from a site called Chapelle aux Saints in the French Dordogne region, representing it as abnormally primitive, with a brutish ape-like face and a body covered with long hair, a portrait which at once gave Neanderthal Man his simian reputation. It's really because of this one reconstruction that as a word in English, 'Neanderthal', is now taken, quite unwarrantedly, to be synonymous with utter stupidity and boorishness. Despite this, by the time we were working at Farah in the 1970s there had been something of a rehabilitation of the status of Neanderthal Man. It was pointed out that usually they were equipped with a large brain, up to half as big again as the modern human brain, and as a result the name once more began to gain a certain caché, and the idea that at Farah we were looking at the culture of Neanderthals, or at least at elements of their life-style, seemed to awaken people's imagination. It was something to which they could relate.

That's the story I gave to Paul and Mary. I told them what we had discovered and how significant it was, and they in turn suggested something I wouldn't otherwise have thought of, not remotely – a support group which could help the finances of the British Western Negev Expedition in return for being given privileged up-to-the-minute news of any new discoveries, and the possibility of visiting the expedition on site when we were in the field. This was a new idea to me. In fact it was very much an American concept, that members of the general public would become involved with academic research. It was an extension of the notion of public support for museums, or operas, or theatres, something which was alien to a British audience who thought these cultural organisations ought to be paid for by governments or by some other public body, but in the US apparently it was common, especially among the wealthy. You would boast of which particular causes you supported, and the more cerebral, the more impressive.

"It's braggability, that's what it is, you see," said Mary. "Everyone wants to demonstrate to their neighbours that they are supporting this, that or the other good cause. Your what-d'you call-it, British Negev Expedition or whatever, would be perfect for it. We could form a 'friends' group, you know, 'Friends of the British Negev' thing."

"But where would such 'Friends' come from?" I asked naively. "Who would know about it and who would want to belong?"

"Oh, you just leave that to us. We know lots of people who would be only too pleased to put their hands in their pocket-book and join in. Why, we know of an organisation that's just been formed in California, what, about two or three years ago, to support the work of the Leakeys in Kenya, and that's much older stuff they're looking for than you. We could do exactly the same."

And so was born the 'Friends of the British Western Negev Expedition Trust', or the 'Friends of Farah' for short. It was to operate for most of the rest of the time we were working at Farah and it proved to be a very good source of supplementary funds as well as giving opportunities for general junketing. One of the first 'functions' for the new 'Friends' that Paul and Mary held was a caviar party, of all things. At the time Paul was working as a senior manager for the ITT Corporation which had a large stake in Iran – it was a time when the Shah was still around – and he was going backwards and forwards to Tehran constantly and talking to some very senior people there who were anxious to hold his attention.

Every time he came back, he would be told by the British Airways stewardesses that a frozen package had been delivered to the aircraft for him and they had put it in the first-class fridge. On arrival back in London, they'd hand him the package and inside would be half a kilo, or sometimes more, of the best Beluga caviar from the Caspian Sea. After a few weeks Paul and Mary had accumulated a ton of the stuff and their friends and acquaintances were invited to pig out on the result. They ordered a case of champagne, put the caviar in large dishes, made a pile of melba toast, and off we went each armed with a champagne glass and a desert-spoon and helped ourselves, heaped spoonfuls at a time. It was wonderful. At an appropriate moment during the proceedings I was asked to give a presentation about Farah, which I did with all the four part harmony and orchestration I could think of - slides, maps and diagrams – and I gave a very upbeat assessment of how incredibly important the work had been so far and how world-breaking the next season would be. It might have been the champagne talking, but it certainly sounded impressive - to me anyway.

And blow me down! It worked. The money came rolling in, the product of the smooth talking and arm twisting that Paul and Mary were really good at among their friends. I don't know what the party would have cost if you'd had to buy all the caviar and the drinks, certainly hundreds, but it didn't seem to affect them. The coffers of the British Western Negev Expedition Trust were swelling as I watched. I went to see Mike Borne at his lawyers' offices off Piccadilly to ask him how the balance was looking, what with the residue saved from last season and now these new funds. He was very blasé about the whole thing, until I asked him to check his client account to see exactly how much was in it.

"Just a minute, my secretary has just fetched the papers. Yes, here they are... Blimey David! Do you know how much there is in this account? There's almost eleven thousand pounds, that's how much. What have you been doing? Making the stuff? That's amazing."

"Well," I asked, "what do you think we should we do about it?"

"Open another branch at once!" came his laconic reply. "No, seriously, that's amazing. You are doing very well. Start planning next the season at once."

\* \* \*

I had become involved that winter with a dig at a place called Coldingham Law on the east coast of Scotland, just over the border from Berwick-on-Tweed. The excavator was a fellow lecturer with the extra-mural department, a Scot by the name of Duncan Noble, and he told me he was in desperate need of a surveyor. The Scottish Ministry of Works were on his back about it, he said. Could I please come up and plan his excavation for him – he was apparently excavating a Mediæval priory there. So I agreed to do it on condition I could fly up to Edinburgh and back, and that I stayed at a local hotel. It turned out that there wasn't actually a hotel anywhere nearby, but there was a tiny pub in the village called the New Inn, and they had a couple of rooms to let, so with some reluctance I agreed to go.

Now, I knew that in the coming Easter I would have to be back to Jerusalem to arrange the next season's permit as well as a place to stay for the 1973 field work – I didn't fancy another sojourn at the youth centre. I'd spoken to Louis on the phone and worked out what I should do. I could accomplish everything there in about four or five days provided I flew out and back from London. I'd already organised my ticket to do this.

It was while I was staying at the New Inn prior to my international flight that I thought of something rather out of the ordinary. Sometimes, when I had been staying at the Ritz, it had been a practice of Sami ed-Dhib my taxi maestro on the occasional Saturday or Sunday to invite me to lunch at his home in Bethlehem with his family, and the central feature of these lunches had been a bottle of scotch whisky which was placed in the middle of the table with a bucket of ice and surrounded by a whole variety of meze. Invariably the party always drank the same brand of scotch, Johnny Walker Red Label, a cheap blend which was commonly available in the Middle East. The idea I dreamed up in Scotland was to take Sami a bottle of single malt whiskey, something I have to say I had never seen in Bethlehem before. I thought it would be a great treat for them all.

Armed with this idea, while I was staying at the New Inn I went into the bar where I had my evening meal and after it was finished I asked the owner, George, which he thought was the best malt whisky in Scotland. This turned out to be a rather foolish question. He made certain recommendations and the other rude mechanicals in the bar like Hamish the Baker and Ewan the Plumber added their tuppence-worth as well. George suggested that I should try the various brands – he had rows of bottles lined up at the back of the bar.

"Well, David, you should maybe try a wee sensation of this one."

And with that he poured out a shot glass of Old Fettercairn ten-year-old single malt. It tasted like burnt car tyres to me. "Or maybe this one perhaps?"

And he poured out another shot, this time of 14-year-old Glen Goyne. After that it was the Lagavulin sixteen year old, then the Glen Moray, then the

Glen Kinchie and on and on up and down through the various highland glens and lowland Trossachs of Caledonia until I could hardly stand. Somewhat overwhelmed I bade them goodnight and said I would try again the next evening.

Next night the same thing happened, an alcoholic tutorial in the geography of the highlands and islands, from this loch to that brae, from Aberlour to Auchentoshan, until I could barely distinguish what I was drinking let alone make any informed decision. Hamish would swear by this one, and Ewan by that one, but to tell the truth I had no palate at all to appreciate any of them. In the end I turned to George and I said,

"George, I want to take a bottle to Bethlehem. In your honest opinion, which would you choose? Now, be honest!"

"Well now," he said, after careful consideration, "I think I would take the Talisker. It's the only single malt Scotch whisky rugged enough to call the Isle of Skye its home, and more importantly, it's the whisky that the doctor, Doctor Mackenzie, drinks so it must be good mustn't it? That's the one I recommend."

So that's the one I bought from George. He wrapped it up well and the next day I flew back to Heathrow carefully cradling the golden elixir. The next weekend I was due to fly to the Middle East and I packaged the bottle of Talisker in my hand luggage – you could do that in those days. I felt very pleased that I would be able to repay some of the wonderful Arab hospitality I had enjoyed, and I also mused thoughtfully that I was carrying this magic potion from one end of the Roman Empire to the other, from Caledonia to Arabia Petraea. How interesting! On arrival at Lod Airport, Sami was there to meet me and we drove up to the Ritz. He said that the next day, which was a Sunday, I was invited for lunch at his home and I duly went along with his special present, gift wrapped.

All my old friends were there sitting around the table in Bethlehem, and I ostentatiously handed Sami the bottle, saying that this was a very particular offering that I'd bought for the party. As he unwrapped it I explained that this was a single malt, not a blend, which had come all the way from its place of birth in Scotland, that that's where I'd bought it, so that everyone could experience the taste of the real 'water of life' after all the many years they'd spent drinking a very ordinary blend. This was the very best, I said.

In due course the dishes of meze were brought out from the kitchen and put on the table, and then as everyone got ready, out came the glasses and the ice, and as always a bottle of the Johnny Walker Red Label was placed in the middle. I was just about to protest when Sami brought from the kitchen an individual glass of Talisker, just for me. When I remonstrated with him about what he was doing he said blandly,

"Well David, you are our honoured guest aren't you, especially having come so far, so you should be the one to have the very best whisky. We'll carry on with the Johnny Walker if that's alright with you."

And with that he opened the bottle of Johnny Walker and poured them each a glass. I was never sure if that was really what he meant, the business about the honoured guest, or whether they were so used to the blended whisky they didn't fancy having their Sunday lunchtime drink up spoiled by some foreign flavour.

\* \* \*

First thing the next morning I went to the Rockefeller Museum and picked up my new permit which was already waiting for me and then I headed back to the Ritz to meet Sami. Today we were going to drive to Beer Sheba to try to make a deal with a small hotel there that I'd already spoken to at the end of the season before. We drove south through the beautiful hill country of the West Bank past Bethlehem and past the Dheisheh Refugee Camp. Sami told me that it had been created to house the people from several dozen villages west of Bethlehem and Jerusalem who had fled the fighting in 1948. It was supposed to have been a temporary measure, he said, but it was still here. There had originally been about three thousand refugees there but now there were more like ten thousand. It was yet another indictment of the present political system wished on the area by the Israelis.

"You know, David, in years past the people living here used to climb to the top of the mountains over there and look down through the barbed wire at their old villages on the other side. Before they were forced to flee, the older people had lived there all their lives. The Israelis came and bulldozed their houses flat so that there was nowhere they could return to. It must have been heart-breaking for them."

We continued on, passing other quaint stone-built Palestinian villages surrounded by olive groves, fig orchards and fields of carefully tended grape vines picturesquely set among the limestone hillsides. The landscape exuded a sense of great calm and ageless peace, which alas turned out to be a completely erroneous façade. Just down the road was Hebron, a town which has proved to be as much a flashpoint for profound hatred and inter-racial violence today as it was in the past. It's all to do with the so-called Cave of the Patriarchs. According to the Old Testament Abraham bought the cave from the Hittites, though quite what these Anatolian mountain men were doing there at that time God only knows; they hadn't appeared anywhere else yet. But because it was none other than Abraham that was said to have acquired the cave, he being perceived to be the grand-daddy of the whole Jewish nation, whatever the historical truth of the matter some Jews asserted that this place gave them the primary right to claim ownership over the whole land of Judah. It seems it was the first time that their nomadic forefathers had settled anywhere in their long peregrination from Mesopotamia, and that could have taken place as long as some four thousand years ago. It meant that however insignificant the cave might have been at the time, if you believe the Old Testament, it constituted actual Jewish real estate at Hebron hundreds of years before Moses and Aaron were even thought of, let alone before any victory of Joshua's trumpeters outside the Walls of Jericho.

Not only that, but Abraham, so they say, went on to be buried in the said cave, making it the one place on earth above all others which must be quintessentially Jewish. What could Abraham's final resting place possibly be other than absolutely and categorically holy, they argue. The only problem with this idea is that Abraham, or Ibrahim as he becomes, is also equally revered by the Muslims who have gone on to elevate this shrine at Hebron to the fourth most holy place in Islam. But alas, it's not the moderate, free-thinking Jews and Muslims who are considering their position with regard to the Cave of the Patriarchs at Hebron, or rather, the Shrine of the Patriarchs as it has inevitably become, but the screaming lunatics from the extreme right wing of both religions.

Various head-banging rabbis from extremist orthodox communities in Brooklyn and elsewhere have urged their fanatical followers to lay absolute and sole claim to the shrine, and with it the whole area, much to the unspeakable fury of their Islamic counterparts who happen to be in charge of it at the moment. The result, as you can well imagine, is an explosive mayhem! All was not well even before Israel occupied the West Bank in 1967. But since then, various deranged clerics have encouraged their overwrought followers actually to go and live in Hebron, hence the fortified settlers' village of Kiryat Arba, the so-called City of Four, just on the outskirts, about which there have been more terrorist incidents than you can shake a machine pistol at. If you had wanted to ensure universal bad faith from all quarters, building such a settlement was the exactly the way to do it!

Anyway, that morning we were able to bypass Hebron - Al Halil, the Beloved One - eschewing all the religious fanatics and their unholy works as we drove on south past Dahriyeh and through the army check point at the 1948 armistice line and on to the wild-west town of Beer Sheba, the *soit-disant* gateway to the Negev. The people there that I'd spoken to before owned a small establishment on the outskirts of the town called the Hotel Zohar and I met the same people again that morning. They were happy to see me and we quickly made all the arrangements for the season. It was going to cost me exactly the same per person as it had done at the youth centre the previous year, but the rooms and the restaurant were a whole lot better, and lo! I quickly discovered that they actually had a bar as well. We completed the business in no time at all and then Sami and I went for lunch. We ended up with a *shawarma*, a pita bread sandwich of chicken, salad and pickles, bought from a local Arab street vendor.

At the beginning of the afternoon we retraced the road back to the West Bank, and it was as we were approaching the village of Dahriyeh again that Sami said,

"I've got a friend here, you know. We should go and see him. You'll like him; his name is Abu George."

So we drove off the main road and up a dirt track to a rather fine-looking Arab house on the hill-side. Abu George was just saying goodbye to a group of people who'd been visiting, and then he came over to us.

"*Sami Habibi. Marhaba! Kaifahalok*?" – "Sami my dear, hello. How are you?"

We were ushered into a sitting room decorated in flock wallpaper with chairs and settees all around the walls, in front of which were small wooden tables decorated with lace doilies. I was about to experience the ultimate in Arab hospitality, though I didn't realise it for an hour or more. As I watched Abu George's women-folk clearing dishes away, I thought 'well, they've obviously just had lunch so maybe they'll bring us some tea'.

"Please, sit down. What will you drink? Sami? David? What can I get you? Beer? Whisky? What would you like? I have everything."

So I settled for a beer and Sami for a fruit juice. Abu George went into the kitchen and came back with a bottle of Amstel, a glass of orange juice and a few plates of nuts. He sat and talked for a while, asking me what I was doing in Palestine, how I knew Sami.. I could hear noises from the kitchen which I assumed were the ladies washing up after lunch. Time passed. I finished my beer, and Abu George immediately went and fetched another cold Amstel, and some more nuts. The afternoon wore on with more talk and banter. At one point Abu George excused himself and went through to the kitchen again. I whispered to Sami that we ought to be going now. Sami looked quite put out and said that we couldn't possibly leave at this juncture. At that stage I didn't know quite what he meant, but just kept quiet and ate some more nuts. Another beer was brought, and another hour passed. I was a little confused as to what was happening until the kitchen door suddenly opened and the ladies of the house came in bearing trays full of dishes of meze, salads and a chicken dish called 'kabseh bi djej', an Arabian recipe comprising a whole chicken on a bed of rice. This is what the ladies had been doing for the past two hours, preparing all this food. The bowls were arranged on the little tables in front of us and Abu George encouraged us to begin to eat while it was still warm.

"Come, my friends. Eat! Eat!"

I looked at Sami and he shrugged and took a helping of hummus and another of baba ganoush. I did the same, but just helped myself to a small amount of each. Abu George was in expansive mood.

"Come, you must eat. Who knows where the next meal will come from? Come on, eat!"

With that he pushed the bowl of chicken and rice in my direction, ladling a generous portion of rice onto my plate and breaking off half a chicken for me. I looked at it in despair. We'd already had lunch in Beer Sheba, and what with the beers and the plates of nuts I'd eaten I was now full. I picked a little at the chicken, and then Abu George looked me straight in the eye and shouted the most devastating encouragement of all.

"Come my friends, you must eat. The more you eat the more you bless my family!"

I was at a total loss. Although I was full, I knew I couldn't see him lose face, so I had to soldier on until at least some of the chicken and rice had been consumed. At last he seemed satisfied, and I felt utterly gorged. In the end Sami and I staggered out of the house and got back in the Peugeot. Waving our thanks and goodbyes to Abu George we bumped down the dirt track back to the main road and up to Bethlehem and Jerusalem.

"You see," said Sami, "We couldn't have left when you said. In our culture it would have been a huge insult to Abu George and to his household. It's typical Arab generosity, especially among the Bedouin. If you are a stranger and you turn up at their tent unexpectedly, even if they hate you they have to offer you their protection and their hospitality, even if it means they themselves will go without for weeks afterwards."

I understood what he meant, I think.

## CHAPTER FIFTEEN
# SPOOKS

*The other day upon the stair*
*I saw a man who wasn't there*
*He wasn't there again today*
*I think he's with the CIA*
Anonymous

As we were gearing up for the next full season at Farah we discussed a new 'must have' botanical investigative technique which was being used by some archaeologists at the time called, prosaically enough, 'the seed machine'. The idea had been developed by a group of people at Cambridge University for the purpose of examining Neolithic sites for any evidence of early agriculture. The way it worked was that every bucket of debris excavated from such a site would be washed through the machine. The apparatus consisted of a tall drum of water through which a spray of fine bubbles was passed and as the excavated earth was decanted slowly through the drum hopefully any seeds in the deposit would be caught by the bubbles and would slop over the rim into a gutter around the top of the drum from where they would be caught in a fine-meshed sieve. The resulting seeds could then be examined to see if they showed any sign of domestication. We thought we might use this machine even for our pre-Neolithic sediments. We surmised that in such a dry environment as ours seeds might have survived for thousands, if not tens of thousands of years. With this in mind I drove to Cambridge and bought one of their used drums with its bubbler. They told me where they'd had their compressors made - an engineering company in Carshalton - and I went there too and ordered one – it comprised an air pump driven by a small Briggs and Stratton lawn mower engine; all very scientific.

Juliet meanwhile had been busy talking to her friends at Imperial College. They had chatted a lot about pollen, one of the main ways in which palaeo-environments were then being determined, and they'd all come to the conclusion that in arid conditions such as ours, being somewhat aerobic, pollen probably wouldn't survive for very long so we would be unlikely to find any. That should have been the end of the palaeo-botanical story. But Juliet had then asked them about using charcoal for identifying plant remains instead, and they said they didn't know if it would work; no-one had tried it. There was a technique which they'd recently developed whereby they were in the process of examining modern charcoal using a scanning electron microscope; they could even identify particular species from the shape of the internal cellular structure and by the pitting on the individual cell walls, but they didn't know if ancient charcoal would be of any use. The charcoal they'd used for their experiments had been prepared at low temperature in the controlled conditions of their laboratory, but they felt that ancient charcoal, which they assumed must be the result of a bonfire, would probably have become overheated and the cell walls would therefore be so badly deformed that nothing diagnostic would be recognisable any longer.

Juliet said it was still worth a try, and with that in mind she said she was determined to collect specimens in the field from all the woody species she could find and by comparison to see if she could recognise any ancient charcoal when we unearthed it. We knew for example that the Middle Palaeolithic sites contained charcoal. I can reveal that this was the beginning of a brand new method which Juliet invented and went on to refine that was to be a substitute for pollen as a way of understanding past environments in the sub-tropics.

While Juliet was involved with that, I was recruiting more people to excavate, and I had a new student, Jonathan Tubb, who said he would be interested in joining the team. He had trained as a pharmacist but had given that up in favour of Middle Eastern archaeology. I'd obviously had discussions as well with a number of prehistorians and stone tools specialists at the Institute and elsewhere and I had established that the material we'd found at Farah was indeed Mousterian, but that as far as anyone knew, these were potentially the first in-situ open camp sites of the period to be excavated in the Middle East. There had been several cave sites excavated, for example at Mount Carmel, especially es-Skhul, and also near the Sea of Galilee at Wadi el Amud as well as in the Lebanon at Ksar Akil, a cave just north of Beirut, all of which contained Neanderthal remains, but seemingly nothing had been found in the open. This represented good news and bad news. The good news was that we'd found the first Mousterian open-air hunting camps ever to be discovered in the Levant. The bad news was that they might not be comparable to any of these other sites in terms of its stone tools; they may have been different in some way, on the basis that such an open site may have involved different activities from the enclosed cave sites. Anyway, I thought that we'd cross that bridge when we had a large enough sample.

*   *   *

The middle of the year came around and we were off again, with Robin, Jonathan, Peggy Nuttall and myself driving in 'Gloria'; the rest of the team were going to fly out. I'd bought the necessary airline tickets cheaply through a company I'd got to know, Project 67, just around the corner from the British Museum. The agency was run by two people of my own age, David Mezzetti and Ashley Jones, with whom I got on really well. They had special deals with El Al, the 'Ethnic Airline' as they called it. But I quickly got the impression that there was no love lost between David and Ashley and the majority of their clients, who all seemed to be Jewish teenagers going to Israel to work on various kibbutzim.

"Ooo! they're bloody dreadful, these people', confided Ashley. "They'll complain about the slightest thing, you know, and ask for money back, or they want extra discounts and things. They write us such illiterate letters you wouldn't believe it. But we've found a way to get the better of them. Oh yes! We charge them a special price which is ten per cent more than anyone else, then we take that off if they make a fuss to make it seem like they've got a cut rate. We call it the 'Levy' levy! They go away thinking they've got something for nothing. Marvellous don't you think?"

As far as I know I bought my tickets at the right rate. But before the fliers took off, 'Gloria', the seed machine and the more intrepid of us left for the next trans- European fandango - across the Channel, over the Rhine, under the Alps and down the Yugo-Put, adorned as it was with wayside shrines commemorating the fast and foolish of the Eastern Bloc. Finally we arrived in Greece again. The seed machine did cause some perplexity both going into and coming out of Yugoslavia . In our non-existent Serbo-Croat it was virtually impossible to explain what it was, and even our mute charades, however ingenious and animated, failed to convey its proper subtlety - but in the end we made it to Athens without mishap. The sea voyage on Epirotiki Lines was thankfully uneventful and we reached Haifa on time and motored up to Jerusalem. As always Louis was pleased to see us, and amongst other things made sure I had enough local currency for our first week in the field. The following day we drove down to Beer Sheba and the Hotel Zohar.

I had decided during the winter that we should enlarge one of the Mousterian sites to open a broad area on which to work and to this end I enquired at the hotel about hiring a digger, a JCB or similar, to remove the three metres or so of sterile overburden. The same afternoon a character called Yavi came over and offered his services. We arranged a price and he said he'd be there at nine the next morning. We duly drove out next day and waited on the side of the wadi. I was expecting a small back hoe which we would be able to control with some precision. What appeared over the horizon and then came down the track from the tell was a huge articulated wheeled Caterpillar excavator with a two and a half metre wide front bucket. It was truly massive. We had no option at this stage but to show Yavi what we wanted and hope he didn't destroy the delicate archaeological horizon. He roared up the gully and positioned himself precisely where we had suggested he should start. In a matter of minutes he had taken off most of the overburden in a five metre wide swathe. We slowed him down as he came just above the deposit and with what I have to say was incredible precision he took off centimetre by centimetre of the remainder until the very first stone tool appeared at which point he backed off without damaging the site at all. It was a genuinely masterful demonstration with such a large and powerful machine. The whole thing had only taken him about twenty minutes, at which point he reversed down the gully and drove off. He might have been something of a cowboy but he certainly knew intimately how to handle his machine.

The area he'd exposed was about eight metres by five and it would keep us occupied for several seasons. The only downside for the excavation was that in the strong sunshine the matrix of the site was wont to become rock hard once it had dried out, making it difficult to be gentle with it, but I bought some small, lightweight hand picks which helped immensely. It was a very fragile deposit but it seemed to cover the whole forty square metres, replete with stone tools, masses of chipped stone debris, various fragments of charcoal and lots of pieces of broken bone. It was exactly what we had predicted the previous season and it promised to be very informative, more of which later.

\* \* \*

I'd been told by EEI to expect a photographer from the US to put in an appearance with the first group of volunteers that season. He was going to make a film about the participants on the dig, so I was informed, which the people at Belmont maintained they would be able to use for further publicity. It seemed like a good idea at the time and I said I'd go along with it. Duly one evening I got a phone call at the hotel from the said photographer.

"Hi, David. This is Benny. Benny Aaronson. I'm the film guy. I'm staying at the Desert Inn (a rather upmarket lodge on the outskirts of the town). You going out to your dig tomorrow? Can you pick me up? Great! See you then."

I told him we started early and the next morning he was ready in the lobby of the Desert Inn at dawn with a massive tripod and camera and a host of other gear.

"We going to Gaza today?" he asked as we drove off.

"No." I said. "We're going to the Wadi Ghazzeh, where we're working with the EEI volunteers."

He was quiet for a bit, and then he asked again, "You ever go to Gaza? You know, the Strip at all?" I again told him where we were going.

"But it's close, isn't it? I mean, like real close?"

I explained to him that the border with the Gaza Strip was about ten kilometres across the desert as the crow flies and that seemed to keep him occupied for a while. I was bemused by his interest in the Strip. He seemed more exercised about that than the about the EEI participants.

When we arrived at the dig, Benny spent about an hour 'setting up', as he called it, fiddling with his tripod and adjusting his camera. Then with the whole thing attached he climbed up out of the wadi onto the top of the tell, 'getting the feel of the place', as he said. He spent most of the morning playing around up there, and we left him to it.

When the time came to return to Beer Sheba, he dismantled his equipment and climbed into the minibus.

"Damn shame that," he complained. "I got a problem with the camera. It's not working properly. It's the focus you know. Just won't do what I want."

We arrived back at the Desert Inn and he got out, unloaded his gear, and gave me a wave.

"I'll call you, you know, when I've sorted this camera out. Maybe take a day or two, mind you. But don't worry, I'll give you a call. OK?"

And with that he stomped off through the hotel door.

"Funny guy that," said one of the older volunteers. "You know something? I don't reckon he was a photographer at all. He had the wrong kind of lenses, did you see that? And he wasn't at all interested in what we were doing, was he? I'd say he was CIA. Well, it's obvious isn't it? Written all over him, didn't you think? Yeah, that's it. CIA, that's what he was. A spook! I've seen them before. He might as well have had CIA tattooed on his forehead. Wonder what he was really interested in, though? Gaza maybe? I don't think we'll see him again, anyway."

I don't know whether he was a spook or not, but that's the last we ever saw or heard of Benny Aaronsen.

*   *   *

The most important development in the 1973 season was the focus on the geomorphological aspects of Farah, the changes in land-form that must have happened over the many millennia. It was abundantly clear that there was a sequence of sediments covering the whole region; we could see it. It was perhaps as much as 30 thirty metres thick, and at some time in the past it must have been emplaced by a different environmental regime because we could see that this wasn't happening today. The whole succession was currently eroding away aggressively and was forming the 'bad-land' gulley landscape on the north side of the wadi. What we needed to find out first was if this sequence was totally in-situ, in other words, whether or not it had accumulated without any significant interruption.

We were interested in the process, the start date for the whole deposition, how it had come into being, and what were the mechanisms and the forces that had brought about its build-up. Perhaps the most important questions were over what period of time it had happened and when it had ended. And finally we wanted to know whether we could determine the environmental conditions under which it had taken place. We could clearly see ancient soil horizons, thin chocolate-coloured layers at various levels in the middle of sequence which visually we could follow horizontally for many kilometres across the exposed landscape and which must represent at least some periods of hiatus in the depositional process, so we guessed that it probably had a complicated history. What we needed to do was to analyse the whole column from top, the most recent parts of it, to bottom, the most ancient.

*View of the Negev near Farah with palaeosols (© DPW)*

With this in mind Peter and I searched for some days up and down the gullies and finally found a suitable location where we could expose a vertical section, given a dog leg or two, down through the whole series. We started to cut a half-metre wide step trench down from the present Negev surface metre by metre, sampling the undisturbed sediments revealed in the section for soil analysis. It was going to be a long process. We'd talked to one or two local soils people who had given the area nothing more than a cursory glance and they had said 'Oh it happens all the time; it's just loess,' just wind-blown dust. But we suspected it held a much deeper secret than that, and anyway, even if it was only just dust blown here by the wind, how and when had that happened? Loess is normally found adjacent to the outfall of a glacier or an ice sheet, where the volumes of rock perpetually being ground to dust by the ice are released as moraine when the snouts melt. It's then wafted away by the strong glacial winds blowing off the ice and deposited as fine sediment some distance away. Well, what was the source of the material which had allowed thirty metres of sediment to form? Where had it come from, because it certainly wasn't from any moraine? No ice had ever remotely affected this area. And there wasn't any answer to the problem in today's environment either.

With regard to the time period during which all this had happened, we hoped that we would be able to find enough archaeological evidence to give some kind of idea when this thick deposit had been laid down. We knew that the cemented gravels alongside the current wadi underlay the whole sequence and at some point we would need to examine those in detail. We also felt that the Mousterian sites were likely to be very close to the bottom of the whole column of sediments, though we didn't yet have a clear idea of the date of these sites. Also, what would be helpful archaeologically would be some idea about the date the whole process ended. When had the whole regime of deposition, however it had happened, stopped? With that in mind we scoured the country surface all along the edges of the gullies and indeed did come up with some useful clues. We found a circular stone-lined pit dug from the present surface which Jonathan sectioned and found that it was a cistern with a plastered sump, part of a farmstead perhaps, all over the bottom of which were large pieces of amphorae which had fallen into the cistern and broken. Fairly simple ceramic analysis of these cylindrical and bulbous vessels gave a date of sometime during the early Byzantine period, perhaps around 600 AD, just before the Arab conquest of the Middle East in 634. The present surface of the Negev was certainly well established by then.

But there were also the sites that Petrie's prehistoric team had examined, which they had named Late Neolithic and which were now called Chalcolithic, the Copper/Stone Age, the very end of the Neolithic just before the Bronze Age. On present estimates they would date to the 4th millennium BC, between six and seven thousand years ago. His team had discovered them somewhere on the top of the Negev and we now relocated them to see what the exact relationship they had with the Negev surface.

There were a number of them and they were quite easily found, but the dwelling areas which they contained had been semi-subterranean. Had those been cut from the surface, or just below it? We indeed established that these too had been cut from the present surface, so the whole deposit of sediments had been emplaced before seven thousand years ago. It was beginning to look as though the 'loess' or whatever it was had been deposited during the Pleistocene, the penultimate geological period from the present which had ended some ten thousand years ago, and it was that which was in the end to prove highly significant.

Certainly the present erosional process of the 'badlands' was several hundred, if not several thousand years old. We discovered a couple of silt dams which had been built low down across the mouth of two of the eroded gullies. They had been intended to catch the wet silt that was washing out every winter during the rainy season and which would have provided a small patch of damp fertile soil in which to grow a crop of wheat. They were probably Bedouin in origin we reckoned. Both had been breached long since, but in the exposed section of one of them we found a sherd of Mediæval green tin-glazed earthenware which probably dated to the Abbasid period, as early as the tenth century AD. Obviously the whole gulley system had been well established by then; erosion was well under way.

In another attempt to understand this whole process of bracketing the dates of the depositional sequence, while the team were beginning to cut the step trench on the north side of the wadi, I thought it might be helpful to check what was actually at the base of the tell itself, on the south side of the wadi, where the earliest occupation levels must also have been built on the country surface. This would give us more data on the original soil horizon of the Negev from at least five thousand years ago. Was it the same on both sides? To this end I'd dug a narrow step trench about fifty centimetres wide, stepping down in metre pits about four metres in total. I'd already started digging it some days before and was just coming to the critical junction of the Bronze Age debris and the all-important ancient soil, the real interest of the test pit. I had returned to the tell on my own one afternoon to finish this off and was crouching in the trench cleaning the section when I suddenly heard gunfire, several shots in a row, from what sounded like a machine gun. I leapt up and shouted some suitable expletive at the empty wadi when another series of shots burst around me, this time close enough that I could hear the bullets ricocheting off the surrounding earth, as one might hear them pinging off the rocks in Western films. I dropped down to my knees again in the trench, not wanting to provide a target for any would-be fanatic or trigger-happy assassin.

The shooting stopped, or at least, I couldn't hear any more bullets. But just in case, I stayed crouched there in the trench wondering what the hell was going on. I didn't know what to do next. Then a few minutes later I heard a vehicle driving around on top of the tell and I peered out to see what it was. It turned out to be an open army vehicle with a machine gun mounted on the bonnet being driven by what looked like a uniformed soldier wearing a great coat, gauntlets and goggles. He looked for all the world like a member of the panzertruppe driving a Kübelwagen, some Hauptmann Himmel or other left over from Rommel's Afrika Corps. I got out of the trench and was about to challenge him when seeing me in shorts and bare chest he shouted, "Vot are you doing hier?" Mein Got, he even had a German way of speaking.

"I could ask you the same question," I replied, pulling out my permit and handing it to him.

"Vy didn't I know about this? Nobody informs me of anything. I could have shot you, you know this thing? Vy am I always kept, how do you English say, 'in ze black'?"

I was quite pumped up by this time, and visibly annoyed.

"Listen, Sunshine, I don't know who you are or what you are doing here, but if you want to go around loosing off machine guns at all and sundry, I suggest you go and do it somewhere else. And in any case, you have no business driving onto this mound here. It's an archaeological site of great importance and you are causing it irreparable damage OK? So why don't you just shove off!"

I don't know if he understood the whole diatribe, but the vehemence with which I'd delivered it must have been enough, because he got into the jeep and without another word roared off in a cloud of dust. I never saw him again.

\* \* \*

But that was not the only encounter I had with armed soldiers. One Saturday morning during that year just out of interest we took a trip north of Jerusalem to go and look at the site of Phasaelis, an estate founded in the Roman period by King Herod on the edge of the Jordan Valley and named after his elder brother Phasael. After he'd built it, for some reason he gave it to his sister Salome, she of the seven veils fame. When we'd had a walk around the site we decided to drive directly south to Jericho down a dirt road along the fence line of the border with the Kingdom of Jordan just west of the river which meant that we could reach Jericho and then go back to Jerusalem up the main road. We'd only been driving for a few minutes when an army check-point came into view and a soldier in army fatigues carrying a heavy machine gun leapt in front of 'Gloria' and brought us to a halt. It seems we were driving on a military road, not a clever thing to do in this part of the world as I now realised. He stood and looked long and hard at the front of our vehicle, and then nonchalantly sidled round to the driver's side and, instead of reading off a list of military dos and don'ts, he looked straight at me and gave me a huge smile.

"Hello! You lot British then are you?" he asked, in an incongruously broad Lancashire accent. "I couldn't help noticing the number plate, y'see. It's English isn't it?" he said, leaning on the side of the door. When I answered that we were indeed from Britain he continued, "Well, would you believe it? I come from Manchester myself, you know, well near it anyway. Well I never! Fancy me seeing you lot all the way out here!"

Looking at him standing there with this huge gun in his hands looking distinctly naïve and self-conscious I just couldn't resist the obvious response. "Oh," I said, "so you're just down for the shooting then are you?"

And with that he stood aside, creased his face up in a puzzled kind of a way and waved us on.

\* \* \*

The expedition progressed well. Juliet did a lot more collecting of her flora, the Mousterian site started to be excavated and proved to be even richer in animal bones than we had imagined, as well as stone implements, and Peter took soil samples from the long section through the sediment. So our second season came to an end and we began to pack up ready to drive back to the UK. Louis came up with a particularly good idea during the time we were there. I came to rely on him more and more, for advice, for money to tide me over when I hadn't had time to cash traveller's cheques and for general support. His great idea was that he had a friend in Jerusalem who was willing to hire out a new Volkswagen Combi to us for following the season. I spoke to his contact and we arranged a price which was very beneficial to us. It would avoid the cost and the inconvenience of the journey across Europe and back, the cost of the ferry, and the insurance. It also meant that we could all fly back and forth. With Project 67's magic airfares it would be no more expensive and very much easier. So I agreed.

And with that we loaded up 'Gloria' for what I thought was going to be the very last time and set off for Haifa and the Mediterranean ferry.

## CHAPTER SIXTEEN
# A MOMENT OF HAPPINESS

*Both light and shadow are the dance of Love. Love has no*
*cause; it is the astrolabe of God's secrets. Lover and Loving*
*are inseparable and timeless.*
Mevlana Rumi - 1207-1273

The journey back to Britain that August was going to be a bit different from the year before. This time I thought we would go back a different route, through Cyprus and Turkey. But this was to cause its own problems. When we arrived at the port in Haifa the Greek officer in charge of loading the ship we were to take was particularly small-minded, I thought, and he said we had to take all the equipment out of the back of the minibus and place it on a special pallet. The reason, he said, was that at Limassol in Cyprus the whole lot would have to off-loaded onto a lighter and then floated into the harbour. I didn't quite grasp what he meant, but with rather poor grace we all did it anyway. It was only the following morning that I understood the full purport of what it was he was driving at. As we arrived off Limassol a tug pulling a large barge appeared by the side of the boat and to my mounting horror I saw 'Gloria' being lifted high into the air by the ship's crane out of the hold and then dropped with a bang onto the pitching barge in the open sea, followed by the pallet with all our equipment and samples. Obviously, the crane had a weight restriction.

We hurriedly followed down a gangway. The barge was heaving up and down in the heavy swell and I feared for our own safety and that of all our belongings, but despite displaying what I considered was a particularly cavalier attitude to the whole affair, the tug's captain towed us into Limassol Harbour without incident and we disembarked by the more normal way of driving onto the quayside and then we had to re-pack the vehicle all over again.

We had decided to drive straight to Famagusta on the east coast. There was a ferry there which linked Cyprus with Turkey which when we arrived we discovered was due the following morning. We found rooms in the Greek part of the city at a brand new tourist hotel which had only just opened for business. That evening we decided to go into the old Venetian walled city to see what it was all about, and to find out if there were any restaurants there where we might find dinner. Duly cleaned up we were walking through the ancient city gate when a voice suddenly shouted in English,

"Ere you, where the 'ell do you think you lot are going?"

It was a Turkish Cypriot policeman in uniform. Unbeknown to us we had crossed an imaginary line into Turkish Cyprus. The officer came over and at once discovered that we were British.

"Oh, that's alright then", he continued, in a totally incongruous Cockney accent. "My name's Ali. You can call me Al. Where you from then? London? I spent ten years in London, in Stoke Newington. Marvellous it was. Lovely people, you know. Really friendly and all that! What you doing here then? You want somewhere to eat, do you? Well, you want to try Mustafa's, that's what you want to do. He's bloody good he is. You'll get a good dinner there, you will. 'Ere, why don't I take you there? It's only just around the corner, over 'ere on the right."

And with that he strode off and led us up the ancient street into a maze of Mediæval houses. He stopped outside one of them and opened the door. There wasn't a sign anywhere but he called out;

"Ere, Mustafa? You in there, mate? Got some customers for you, I have,"

At which a stooping elderly gentleman appeared in the semi-darkness of the hallway and very quietly motioned us in and through what I take it was his living room into a small courtyard at the back of the house as Ali said his goodbyes. In the walled garden there were one or two tables set up as though for eating but it was otherwise empty. Mustafa beckoned us to sit down. I wondered quite what we were doing there, but I asked for a menu anyway to make sure we were in the right place.

"Oh, I'm afraid I don't have a menu", Mustafa replied diffidently. "But you are welcome to have what I have got, if that's alright."

I enquired if he at least had a wine list we could look at and he said again,

"I'm sorry I don't have such a thing. But why don't I bring you the wine from my village, if you would like it, that is? My family make it from our own grapes, you know."

With that he disappeared into the house and soon reappeared with some plates of Turkish meze – peanuts, olives, goat's cheese, white beans in olive oil, fresh bread and a large jug of red wine with four glasses.

I raised my eyebrows a bit and then took a swig of the wine. It was absolutely delicious. It seemed to embody all the sunshine and the fullness of the unadulterated Mediterranean countryside in summer, a truly enchanting flavour the like of which I had never tasted before. The others filled their glasses and joined in.

"Şerefe, Mustafa!" I said to him. "To your honour!"

Mustafa looked on and smiled, pleased that I'd greeted him in his own language. He lumbered back into the house and we began to tuck into the meze. They were equally wonderful, home-made and perfectly flavoured in every respect, so reminiscent for me of Cengis' *cayhane* at Knidos. As we relaxed in the flickering candle-light we looked about us at our surroundings. All around the ancient walls trailed bushes of flowering white jasmine and the garden was filled with their heavy fragrance, which created its own calm and exotic atmosphere in that warm evening air under a clear and starry sky. By and by Mustafa brought more plates to the table, filled with freshly cooked lamb shish kebabs and lightly spiced köfte finished with aromatic herbs, as well as a dish of cooked buttered rice and a bowl of mixed green salad, together with another earthenware jug of his exceptional country wine. We ate heartily and drank even more so. It was most enchanting and we began to shuffle off the cares of the expedition and the travelling and simply immerse ourselves in the loveliness of the moment. More kebabs appeared until we were satiated, at which point Mustafa brought out a plate of home-made, honeyed baklava for us to share.

"You know Turkey?" he asked me. "Do you know the Mevlevi? The Whirling Dervishes of Konya? I have one or two Mevlevi flutes. Would you like to hear me play one for you?"

We were intrigued. He went into the house and emerged with what appeared to be a couple of long tubes with finger holes in them. He sat by our table and was about to apply one of them to his mouth when he quietly said,

"I made these flutes myself. I would like to play for you some of the Mevlevi music, from what they call the 'sema', the mystic whirling dance the Dervishes perform where they try to achieve oneness with God. They do this following the example of their founder, Mevlana Jelaleddin Rumi. It is through this dance and this music that they believe he was able to achieve a divine ecstasy, you see. It's very old. It dates from the thirteenth century."

And with that he lifted the flute to his lips and began to play and as he did so the deep, sad, husky music of his home-made flute filled the garden. We were at once completely entranced, a feeling no doubt heightened by the fumes of the country wine and the scent of the jasmine, and replete as we were with that simple but superb dinner. After a while the music came to an end and with a brief pause Mustafa picked up a larger flute and began to play again. The resonance of the music was even more profound and even more soulful than before. I felt that in its way this was perhaps the most haunting sound I had ever heard as it echoed through the stillness and around the walls of the shadowed courtyard. It could have been like the very breath of life itself. As he played, it seemed to me that the evening was gradually turning into one of the most mystically beautiful nights I had ever experienced.

The music ended again and as it did so Jonathan leaned over and spoke quietly to Mustafa, after which he drew a small case out of his bag in which he kept his own silver flute. He put it together and also began to play, part of a Bach partita I think it was. The impression of the previous transcendent Oriental strains combined with the complexity of this baroque contrapuntal composition was overwhelming. As the cadences of each intertwined in our memory, we were transported onto another plane. For a short while time seemed to suspend its inexorable motion, a time during which the two flautists exchanged their musical reminiscences. After what seemed an age, alas we had to get back to the hotel. The next day was going to be a long day. We said our poignant farewells to Mustafa and to the scented garden. What a discovery it had all been. It was a truly uplifting experience.

The next day our journey continued without incident. We caught the ferry to the Turkish port of Mersin near the Syrian border and then drove up through central Anatolia visiting the sites in the Taurus Mountains, Pammukkale, with its warm springs, and the adjacent Roman city of Heiropolis. We travelled down the Meander Valley to Aphrodisias and Nysa, to Miletus, Priene and to Ephesus, before we finally turned north along the coast towards Troy, the Dardanelles and Europe.

I remember another remarkable dinner on that journey. It was at a small hotel near Ayvalık on the north-west coast on our last night in Turkey. The hotel had a restaurant in the basement called 'Cadır', The Tent, which had just been opened by what I suppose you'd call today a celebrity chef from Istanbul. There were very few foreign tourists in Turkey in those days. Ephesus, for example, had been virtually empty when we visited it. Most holiday resorts catered only for the most discerning visitors and they were Turks who came mainly from Istanbul and Ankara. The Cadır Restaurant was aimed at them. We selected a table and chose some of the courses first from the chiller cabinet – fresh prawns, calamari, grouper – and then as we waited for them to be cooked we went out and sat out on a grass verge opposite the restaurant and drank an aperitif watching the sun sinking slowly over the sea.

One of the assistant chefs had brought out a long cylinder full of ice next to us and was quietly churning cream in a bowl to make home-made ice cream - *dondurma*. It was a slow process but obviously a labour of love. When the ice cream was almost ready, he added fresh fruit to the mixture. As the sun set we went into the restaurant and enjoyed a magnificent sea food dinner followed by the fresh home-made ice cream which was quite the most exceptional I've ever tasted, a fond memory which kept us going for the next week or so as we drove out of Turkey and right the way across Europe to the Belgian coast. I can't remember all the details of that part of the journey, but I do remember that at the end of it we had a celebratory beer at a bar in the ferry terminal at Ostende, and the barman saying to me, as he pushed the glasses across the counter,

"That'll be fifteen!"

To which I said something like, "Fifteen what, exactly?" In my wallet I had US Dollars, Israeli Pounds, Turkish Lira, Greek Drachmae, Yugoslavian Dinars, Italian Lira, Austrian Shillings, German Marks and one or two also rans. I'd become international! I think he accepted some US Dollars, following which we finished the beers and caught the Channel ferry to Britain. Another season had been brought to its successful conclusion.

* * *

1973 proved to be pivotal for me. Around about Easter time, I had taken a group of extra mural students to Paris. The reason for spending a weekend in that glorious city was that there were several archaeological collections on display in the museums in and around Paris which were relevant to the first three years of the university's Diploma in Archaeology, part of which I taught. There were the prehistoric collections at the Musee de l'Homme at the Palais de Chaillot for the first year students, the superb collections from Mesopotamia and Persia at the Louvre for the second years, the year for which I was a lecturer, and the Prehistoric Europe collections at the Musée d'Archéologie Nationale at St Germain en Laye which were important for the third years. Amazingly I had sixty students who'd booked up for that weekend. I'd chartered a whole aircraft, a Douglas DC4, from Dan Air Skyways, and I'd also organised the hotels through them too. Of course I had already met all the second and third year students. I'd taught most of them. But I hadn't yet encountered any of the first years and I noticed that some of them had signed up as well. To get a better idea of who they were I asked one of the first-year tutors, Desmond Collins, if he knew any of them. He scanned the list and immediately picked one out.

"Oh wow," he said, "Now that's interesting. I see you've got Susan Vickery coming with you. She's something really special, she is. Not your common or garden student, I have to say. She's much too good for you, Price Williams, if I may say so. She's a real stunner!"

And he'd been absolutely right. I met her first at Dan Air's reception office at 33 Elizabeth Street, Victoria when she came to join the coach that would take us to the airport. She was indeed a real stunner as Desmond had said - tall, poised, well dressed, blue-eyed and with a voice like dark honey. Above all, she was outstandingly beautiful. I remember her so well when her group visited the Louvre on the second day. I put in a lot of extra effort describing the Sumerian and Babylonian displays to her party in the hope of catching her attention, but when we finally reached the room where the Assyrian Palace reliefs were at the end of the visit and I asked how they'd all enjoyed it, I noticed she remained distinctly aloof.

That autumn, when I'd come back from Farah I was anxious to see if this lovely creature would turn up in my class, or could she have chosen another lecturer and another class instead, which of course she might well have done. I arrived in September at my Tuesday evening class at Hampstead Garden Suburb and to my great delight there she was sitting at one of the desks with the rest of the students. I gave that first lecture, 'Introduction to the Middle East', exclusively for her, at least, that's what I hoped she'd think, and at the end of the class she came up to me and said that some of them normally went for a drink after the lecture to the Bull and Bush on Hampstead Heath and would I like to join them? Wouldn't I just, I thought, but I had made other arrangements that first night, though I did say that I would come out with them the following week. The next week came around and, wonder of wonders, at the end of the lecture she invited me to join them again, which I did. And that was the beginning of it. It was not long before it wasn't just a drink we were meeting for, but dinner as well, just she and I. She invited me to her house in Putney, and pretty soon after that we weren't just going out together, we were staying in together too, which turned out to be something even more exciting.

I talked a lot to her about our work in the Middle East and about the concept that I was exploring, namely trying to find new methods to understand paleo-environmental changes in the sub-tropics, and about the Mousterian sites we'd discovered, and the work Juliet was doing - the whole multi-disciplinary approach. She was fascinated by everything. I introduced her to the 'Friends of Farah', to Paul and Mary and the others, and she took a great interest in the 'Friends'. Afterwards she said that as she'd recently come into some money she would like to make a donation as well, which she did, handsomely as I remember. I was overwhelmed. A number of the 'Friends' were going to come out to Farah the next season to get a 'hands-on' feel for what we were achieving, so nothing loathe, I asked Sue if she'd like to come as well. I suggested that perhaps she would like to experience the thrill of our newest discoveries actually in the field, and to my utter astonishment she said that she would. She was going to join us in the Negev.

But that wasn't the end of my discussions with Desmond Collins whom you remember had been Sue's first year tutor. He and his wife had invited me to a dinner party at their home in Belsize Park and before I went I recalled that he was of course an expert in Palaeolithic Europe. He'd taken his degree at the University of Cambridge under that great exponent of prehistory Grahame Clark who held the Disney Professorship there, the same position that Dorothy Garrod, the woman who'd excavated the Carmel Caves had held, so I thought he must also know about the Near Eastern Mousterian.

I accepted Desmond's invitation and said I would be bringing a friend with me. Imagine his astonishment when I turned up on the doorstep with Sue. I could see he was impressed that we'd become so close. Anyway, not to be side-tracked, I launched into a discussion about Farah and the Middle Palaeolithic of the Near East, using what little I had gleaned already, and I asked him if he would be interested in joining us for a season to look at our sites. I told him we needed an expert, someone who could identify the various stone tool industries of the Mousterian, and he said he could certainly do that and would be willing to come out for a week or two and have a look. He would be another string to our bow, another member of the team.

And thinking about the Mousterian sites, we had uncovered a considerable amount of bone within the excavation so far, and there promised to be lots more. The site had clearly been a Mousterian hunting camp, but we had no-one to examine the remains of the animals that had been butchered there. An analysis that the fauna represented must surely have a bearing on their contemporary environment. I asked Juliet what we should do and she said she knew someone, Dr. Caroline Grigson, who had studied with her at Imperial College and she was indeed a palaeo-zoologist but she was currently acting as a curator of the collections at the Hunterian Museum, the museum of the Royal College of Surgeons in Lincoln's Inn Fields. She might well be persuaded to help, she said.

Duly, I contacted Caroline and went along to the museum to meet her. What a place! It's housed in a very imposing building on the south side of Lincoln's Inn Fields. The museum preserves one of the oldest collections of anatomical, pathological and zoological specimens in Britain, based on the items assembled by various medical people over the last several hundred years. When I went inside to meet Caroline I was greeted by rooms-full of anatomical and pathological preparations of all sorts in large glass jars set on racks around the walls - bits of actual dissected spinal columns, deformed limbs in formalin, orthopaedic specimens of all sorts on open display. It was very unnerving. Before we got down to the business of the meeting, Caroline showed me skeletons with acromegaly, gigantism, as well as the bones of midgets and various grossly malformed people in between. I didn't think I really wanted to know about all these so I eventually came to the subject of our discussion and to my delight she leapt at the chance of getting back to the topic in which she was really interested, namely her archaeo-zoology, as she called it. She told me she had friends at the Natural History Museum in South Kensington through whom she had access to their reference collections which she would be able to use to compare and identify our material. Another member of the team had joined up.

But that wasn't the end of developments that winter. After I had published a preliminary report of our work at Farah the previous year, I was now approached by an eminent geographer from University College, Dr. Claudio Vita-Finzi, who was already well- known for his work in the Mediterranean in combination with another great Cambridge archaeologist Eric Higgs, a true believer in the analysis of palaeo-environments. Together they had developed an approach to prehistoric sites that was becoming all the rage. They called it 'Site Catchment Analysis', the way in which local geographical circumstances dictated how humans would live and respond in relation to the scenery around them and how understanding these factors could lead to a better grasp of how humans had evolved culturally. Claudio said he had a third-year student who needed a subject in physical geography for her dissertation to complete her degree and did we have anything appropriate for her to study? I told him I would like to meet the said student, so one afternoon I went along to his office and sitting there was a most attractive young girl waiting to see me. Her name was Rita Gardner who incidentally was later to go on to become the first female Director of the Royal Geographical Society, but that's another story altogether. Long before any of that, we discussed the field work with which we were involved at Farah and I said that we desperately needed a geomorphologist, which she was, to complete the analysis of our section through the Farah sediments. Peter Dorrell had told me that alas he would be unable to join us for the next season and in any case we needed someone more dedicated now that we'd partly understood the stratigraphic column, someone who could draw the whole thing together and make a final interpretation. Rita fitted the bill very nicely, and Claudio said that he would help with the whole project as much as he could too, which given his track record, would be extremely useful.

The team had expanded even more. It was becoming a very impressive line-up, and the 1974 season beckoned.

CHAPTER SEVENTEEN
# ARGUMENT AND COUNTER ARGUMENT

*'Twas blow for blow, disputing inch by inch,*
*For one would not retreat, nor t'other flinch.*
Byron: Don Juan. Canto VIII. Stanza 77.

Our third season at Farah got underway with the emphasis more and more focused on the soil profile in the badlands. It was now very clear that the cemented gravels underlay the whole sequence, and after an exhaustive investigation of the few exposed sections of the un-eroded material that we could find on the sides of the wadi we managed to locate a couple of fairly obvious Lower Palaeolithic un-rolled hand-axes stuck into the matrix, which meant of course that these gravels originally might well be old. Just how old they were was a matter of some debate, but they could be as much as a quarter of a million years old, if not older. It was something with which we couldn't really progress at present. The Mousterian sites were stratigraphically not far above these, and they were certainly near the bottom of the whole badland sequence, though they may of course be very much younger than the gravels. I'd sent off radiocarbon samples of the charcoal from the Mousterian excavations of the previous season to the Carbon 14 laboratory in Groningen in Holland and they'd come back to say the samples fell outside the range of C14, beyond fifty thousand years old or more, as we'd perhaps already begun to suspect. We adopted a working date for the sites of about sixty thousand+ BP (before present). This would agree with other recently acquired C14 dates and other estimates found elsewhere in the Levant.

The newest evidence from Mousterian sites found in other sites in the Levant also seemed to indicate that there may have been two different kinds of humans around at the time, the Neanderthals themselves and a type palaeontologists were now calling Archaic Moderns, who were apparently slightly less heavily built. It was not known if they exactly co-existed with each other or had come in and out of the area at different times. We had no human remains at Farah and were unlikely to find any, our sites having been in the open air, so we had no idea which of the two types of humans the makers of the stone tools at Farah were, but we were at the beginning of a theory which was to gain more and more ground in the decades to come, namely that in some way the Middle East had been the land-bridge across which not only very ancient representatives of the human family had first crossed more than a million years ago, but that modern humans had also crossed from Africa into Europe again, much more recently, gradually becoming the dominant population as the pure Neanderthal genes became reduced through inter-breeding with the newer forms.

It was time to ask Desmond what he thought. He'd looked at the stone implements and the debris that we were uncovering, but apart from telling us it was Mousterian, which we already knew, he didn't at first add a great deal more.

"You see," he said quietly, "The Mousterian of France, which is very well known, is divided into several industries according to the kinds of retouch applied to the edges of the implements - the scrapers and such like - and here you just don't get any retouch, so it's virtually impossible to compare the one with the other. It's impossible to fit them into any sequence. There's a big literature on this, you know," he rather gnomically continued. "I have to say I haven't studied it carefully so I can't say any more at this stage. I would guess that the reason they didn't re-sharpen their tools was that they didn't need to. There was enough raw material to be found in the chert cobbles on the wadi floor to make new ones when they went blunt."

But he then went on, "There are two things I can say, though. As you know you've been finding a lot of Levallois points in the site, these are very characteristic convergent triangular pieces, as well as flakes similar to them but where the axis of final percussion is offset by forty five degrees, what I call pseudo-Levallois points. By comparing your assemblage with other sites, especially in the Mount Carmel area, I've found that this distribution seems to appear late in the Mousterian, which would give us a date for the Farah sites of, say, between seventy thousand and forty five thousand years ago. And by the way, those other sites are usually associated with Neanderthals, if that helps. The other thing I can say is that the sites at Fara are sites definitely in primary deposition. They're not secondary sites, you know; the flakes are not washed in from somewhere else. Therefore, they do date the sediment in which they're found. I've been able to piece fragments of the implements together with the chipped stone debris and the remnant cores and make them all fit. The tools were made right here, on the side of the wadi or whatever it was at that stage."

Considering he'd had problems understanding our sites, I was amazed he was prepared to go so far. These were two considerable steps in the right direction, although we had already suspected the material was in primary deposition, but his comparisons corroborated the date we'd estimated from the C14 dates.

Meanwhile Caroline was busy looking at the fragments of bone from the Mousterian site. She confirmed what Desmond had said about the in-situ nature of the main site, that the bones hadn't been rolled around or washed in in any way. They were found exactly where they had been left. Some of them were too cut up or too small to be certain of an identification, but she was able to suggest that we had horses at the site, or equids of some description anyway, and she had a number of end bones she recognised as ungulate, from hoofed animals, and in one case specifically from a hartebeest. And whilst she was at Farah we uncovered a very obvious horn core which she immediately identified as coming from an aurochs, the extinct wild ancestor of the modern ox, which was much bigger than our domesticated cattle.

"I think it's the springs in the wadi which attracted these large game species," she went on. "That and probably open grassland mixed with wooded areas as well. Does that fit with anything?"

Well, it did actually. Juliet had been working on the modern flora in which the edges of the springs in the wadi were fringed with thick tamarisk groves. But while she was evaluating that, we found something for her which was much more exciting. Deep in one of the gullies, very close to the base of the whole column of accumulated sediment and just above the gravel beds, we discovered a stream bed that had been filled in shortly after its creation by thick mud, and in the mud, now hard and clayey, there were a considerable number of what were quite clearly leaf impressions. Juliet was ecstatic. It was the very best palaeo-botanical evidence she could have hoped for. She photographed them and took the pictures to show some of the botanists she'd been corresponding with at the National Herbarium in Kew and they were in no doubt what they were.

"You know what, David," she began eagerly when she'd got back, "There are two species represented here and they've positively identified both of them. One is a species of *Salix* and the other is *Populus euphratica*, that's willow and poplar to the likes of you. You know what that means, don't you? It means that if you've got the stratigraphic relationships right, then during the time the Mousterian people were around there was deciduous woodland down here in the bottom of the wadi. There must have been permanent water here too. That fits with Caroline's interpretation doesn't it?"

While all that was going on Rita applied herself energetically to the geomorphological aspects of Farah. She checked and re-checked the stratigraphy of the sediments on top of the gravels and came to the conclusion that above the muddy infilled stream bed the overlying sediments were the product of one continuous sequential deposition, all twenty five or so metres of them, with a small number of still stands from time to time which accounted for the ancient soil horizons. But there had been no down-cutting. There was no evidence anywhere throughout the whole sequence of any further stream formation or interim gullying. It was a complete uninterrupted sequence and one which probably represented a long period of climatic stability but a climate which was very different from the present modern semi-arid climate, the one which was accounting for the aggressive erosion we saw all around us today.

Nor was it the same as the climate when the Mousterian people were around. The chemistry of the sediments indicated that wherever they had come from originally they had been laid down in an arid environment, certainly in conditions much drier than today. There were horizons of calcrete, calcium carbonate formations, which clearly pointed to a climate lacking in rainfall, though the sediments themselves had been laid down in an aqueous regime. Rita visualised it as a series of rarely occurring flash floods taking place in a desert environment, the floods themselves accounting for the horizontal bedding we could see and also for the lack of gullying, meaning that water was only available for extremely sporadic depositional events, like the creation of alluvial fans, but insufficient to causes erosional features to form.

It was during this 1974 season that the next set of radio-carbon dating results came in. We'd found a small hearth in the stratigraphic column the previous year, about half the way up. It was the only evidence of human activity that we found throughout the period despite exhaustive searches. The dates for the hearth turned out to be all around about twenty eight thousand years ago. So with all the data we had now accumulated we felt we could go on to suggest what was happening. When the Mousterians were around, sixty thousand years ago, the climate had been much the same as the present, if not a little wetter and perhaps warmer. World-wide that coincided date-wise and climatically with a warm phase in the middle of the last ice age which was well documented in the evidence from western Europe. It had been recorded many times.

This was followed by the emplacement of all the sediments. With a basal date of more than fifty thousand years ago, a mid-date of somewhere at or after twenty eight thousand years ago and a surface date of around ten thousand years ago, we were looking here at a period for the sedimentation which coincided in Europe with the end of the Upper Pleistocene, the latter part of the last ice age, and more especially it included the moment of the last glacial maximum around about twenty two to eighteen thousand years ago, which was the coldest moment that the Earth had experienced in recent geological time, when ice had formed sheets in northern Europe over one kilometre thick. The outfall from this ice sheet, the moraines around Oswestry and the boulder clays of the adjacent Shropshire Plain, indicated its actual snouts. And coincidentally, as you may remember, it was these features that had started me on the search for ancient climates in the first place when I was in my teens!

Perhaps I was harking back to my initial interest in geology. I felt, rather grandly, that I could now make my own contribution to the sum total of our knowledge of recent earth history by describing what had happened in the sub-tropics of the earth during that same period, the Devensian. Here at Farah everything pointed to the fact that after a warm, moist phase the climate had become much drier, hyper-arid in fact, and extrapolating from that we could suggest from our evidence that when the earth became cold, resulting in a major ice advance in the high latitudes, the sub-tropics became abnormally dry, at least in the Levant. Fascinatingly, this was in opposition to what that great environmental guru Karl Butzer had been saying at the time, namely that there had been no appreciable climatic change at all in the sub-tropics during the last ice age. Ice ages, he reckoned, were only a feature of high latitudes, and in particular the high latitudes of the northern hemisphere.

Even more importantly, our interpretation was diametrically opposed to what Gordon Childe had thought, namely that during glacial periods the Middle East had been very cool, moist and verdant and that at the end of the glacial it had become hot and arid, forcing humans to find another way to live and compelling them to invent agriculture. Conversely, however, if we were right, then the Levant had been cold and very dry for long periods during the last ice age and had only become moist and hospitable again when the ice age had finished about ten thousand years ago. That would mean that the first agriculturalists, the people who first domesticated wheat and barley, as well as sheep and goats, did so in a climatically ameliorating world. This was a completely new way of looking at the beginnings of civilization. It wasn't Man struggling against ever-declining climatic conditions, the Neolithic Revolution, as Childe with his Marxist thinking had called it, but rather that modern humans in the Middle East were taking advantage of the ever increasing resources that the invasion of post-glacial grasslands would have represented. In other words, they hadn't been pushed into the beginnings of civilization, they had jumped of their own accord. Yes, we were still in the realms of environmental determinism, but for the opposite reason to the one which Childe had envisaged, and with the evidence to prove it. Now here was an idea that was truly revolutionary, for modern archaeology at least. But the full drama of that is a story for another time.

\* \* \*

This was our second season staying at the Hotel Zohar in Beer Sheba and we were getting on famously there. We'd got to know the owners and the few staff they employed pretty well by that time and I have to say they looked after us all very ably, such that our day to day living was a whole lot better than on many excavations I have known. What was particularly impressive was dinner time in the restaurant. Actually, the restaurant itself wasn't particularly salubrious; it was rather nondescript in fact. It was the content of the meals and their presentation that was so notable. The restaurant staff had all come from Tunisia which, being a Francophone country, meant that they'd been trained in France at premier establishments on the Riviera or in Paris before they had decided to emigrate to Israel. Their approach to the hotel business was therefore very professional and considering we were paying discount rates for everything the food was fantastic. The chef, Yves, lovingly prepared our dinner each evening. Even if it was only a humble chicken stew it would appear at the table as a *Fricassée de Poulet au Vin Blanc*, wonderfully garnished. Simple stewing lamb he would present as *Tagine d' Agneau Marocaine* with apricots and raisins, or as *Navarin Printanier* with fresh vegetables, or *Ragout Provencale*, with tomatoes, peppers and garlic. The more we applauded his food, the more effort he put into it. And our waiter, Charles, was equally outstanding. He served everything with a great flourish, however simple, as though it was *haute cuisine*. Yves would often prepare some extra *hors d'oeuvres* for our amusement, simple but impressively presented, and Charles would bring them to the table with studied panache. Charles would act as the wine waiter as well and though the choice of wines was extremely *vin ordinaire* he would serve them as though they were great vintages from Bordeaux or Burgundy. It nightly lifted our spirits substantially.

One night I asked Charles why he and Yves took such trouble with us every evening. The Zohar was a cheap hotel, but the attention these two gave to our welfare was conspicuously exceptional.

"Ah," he replied, "We 'ave so few guests who appreciate what we do. I tell you something. We 'ave these large parties coming to our 'otel, school kids, you understand, Americans mainly, from New York. The government sends them to us for weekends as part of their learning about Israel and we 'ave no choice; we 'ave to accept them. They are all Jewish, of course, just like us. But they are awful. They treat us like shit. 'I want this! I want that!' No 'please' or 'thank you', you know, Just 'Gimmee a Coca Cola' or whatever. They are really 'orrible to us. Yves and me, we 'ave been trained at some of the best 'otels in France, and 'ere we are made to feel like pigs, except for your group, of course. You, you are so grateful for everything. You really like what we do n'est pas?"

But that wasn't the only revelation to which we were given access into the lives of Yves and Charles. We were coming back from Farah to the hotel in the middle of the afternoon one day and we saw Yves standing behind the reception desk in the lobby talking to a couple of Israeli soldiers. He had his chef's apron on and was no doubt about to go into the kitchen to start the evening meal when he suddenly snatched one of the soldier's guns and with lightening speed broke it down into its constituent parts on the counter in front of us, and then equally quickly he reassembled it and handed it back.

"You see," he complained, "That's what I 'ave to do. You know we Israelis, we all 'ave to spend some weeks of every year in the army, and that's my job there - weapons drill. I mean, I was trained in one of the best kitchens in Paris to become a chef, and this is what I am made to do. It gets me so angry sometimes. I don't want to kill anyone, I mean. I'm a chef. I cook good food to make people come alive. I create interesting dishes, isn't that so?"

We whole-heartedly agreed. And that night Yves excelled himself yet again on our behalf. I was pleased we were offering both him and Charles an opportunity to show their real worth, and we certainly enjoyed the result!

\* \* \*

1974 saw a conspicuous rise in the numbers of United Nations forces in the region, specifically patrolling the border with southern Lebanon. The Israelis were concerned about the upsurge in Al Fatah, the militant arm of the Palestine Liberation Organisation, so the UN had offered to keep the two sides apart. Some of the UN officers choose to stay at the Ritz during their time off and as I was there every weekend I got to know a few of them well, drawn alike as we were to the attractions of the leopard-skin bar. A couple of them whom I used to see every week were Canadians, Phil and Russ. They were on the Lebanese border five days a week from Monday to Friday and came down to Jerusalem on Friday afternoons for their weekend recreation.

One of the benefits which Phil and Russ added to each weekend as far as I was concerned was that they had PX rights with the UN stores, wherever they were, and they could obtain copious bottles of scotch, and especially gin, at very cheap prices. The result was that every Friday night was party night in one room or another at the Ritz. It was tremendous fun, smashing back the duty-free liquor and talking about Lebanese-Israeli politics.

But I remember one particular Friday when they were not quite as full of the bonhomie they usually exuded, in fact Phil was downright morose, and it wasn't long before I found out why. They'd been patrolling the border as usual and it had all started uneventfully. They drove around in specially painted white four-wheel drive vehicles with a huge black UN painted on the sides and the roof so there could be no mistaking who they were.

"We can pick up some problems with that too," said Russ. "Now and again the guerrillas hi-jack one of our jeeps and high tail it up and down the border scaring the living daylights out of everybody but it usually ends up by the Israelis blasting the crap out of them with heavy artillery, or the PLO get tired of doing it and just leave the vehicle stranded in no-man's land."

"Yeah, but this week was different, wasn't it Russ?" said Phil. "I mean, shit, we were driving along the border as usual and came near this Lebanese village. Russ reminded me that someone had asked us if we could pick up a bottle of Haddad arak, the best arak in Lebanon, if we found ourselves the other side of the border and we said there should be no problem with that. We do it all the time. So, we drive into this Arab village and stop at the village store. I go in and I'm just in the process of paying for this fucking arak when this young kid comes in with a Kalashnikov and points it straight at me. I mean, Christ, he couldn't have been more than fourteen but he tells me to get out of the store and into the street. Russ is waiting in the jeep, and he points this gun at him too and he gets out as well. The guy's waving the AK at us and telling us both to walk up the street and onto this piece of waste ground by a broken-down wall. We've both got our hands in the air and I for one was scared shitless, I don't mind admitting it. I can see this kid has the safety catch off and his finger is on the trigger and I'm thinking, if this guy gets spooked by something he's gonna drill us both and we're dead meat. Holy Mother of God! I thought my last moment had come.

We were stuck in this stand-off for what felt like an age until some older guy comes tooling round the corner having seen our UN vehicle and shouts at the lad in Arabic but the lad is reluctant to give up until he gets clipped round the ear and told something like that they don't mess with UN forces.

The old guy takes his rifle away from him and bows and scrapes to us and tells us to go. Man, I couldn't get out of there fast enough. We jumped in the vehicle and drove off at high speed until we're back on the border line, when Russ here says to me, in all seriousness, 'Well, did you get the arak then?' to which I told him that he could shove his arak where the sun don't shine, 'and I'm not going back there if that's what you're thinking' I told him. That was a fucking close-run thing, I can tell you. Cheers!"

They had a UN mate of theirs, Ron, who was British and who used to join us at the bar from time to time. He was slightly older but more prone to overdo the booze, especially on a Saturday night. He was married, and he kept showing us pictures of him and his wife Cheryl back home in Rotherham and saying how happy they were. But Ron had one overwhelming problem. He couldn't stay away from women, whoever they were. We'd often leave him drinking on his own and go out for a meal and by the time we got back he'd be chatting up some old bag or other at the bar, deeply involved. We'd wish him goodnight and leave him to his own devices. The next day was always the same. Ron looked like death warmed up and screwing up his face he'd ask what happened, and then tell us that he'd had a go at this bag, and he'd ask us what she was like. He couldn't remember, apparently. When we told him she was well the wrong side of fifty, which was invariably the case, he'd wail, 'Oh no! Not again. Oh shit. What's Cheryl gonna say? I didn't mean to do it, honest I didn't. I just couldn't help it. I won't do it again, I promise. You've got to believe me.' I don't know what he thought we could do about it, but the following week would be a repeat performance of the same thing. Ron was completely incorrigible.

*   *   *

Our season came to an end again. It had all gone remarkably well. We'd finally made the environmental breakthrough I'd been hoping for. We now knew that there had been major climatic change in the sub-tropics and that it did have an effect on human cultural evolution. When the earth gets cold, we'd discovered, the sub-tropics become very dry. And if you advanced that argument further you could say that the so called ice ages, when ice had clearly advanced from the poles, were only a symptom of a much bigger global phenomenon, rather than being events in themselves, albeit an aggressive part of it. If we had our time over again to name these shifts after the global evidence rather than what we tended to find outside our back door in North

America or Shropshire, then looking from where we were now standing we might instead be talking of desert ages rather than ice ages. After all it was in these mid-latitudes, in the tropics and sub-tropics, that the main events of human evolution had taken place, both physical and cultural, not in the freezing north. I'd say that was a pretty dramatic result.

And to crown it all, Sue had been out with us as well. She could only spare a couple of weeks, but she saw the size and scope of the operation and how we had progressed. I hoped she was impressed. And I'd shown her all around Jerusalem and of course I'd introduced her to the Ritz and to Louis, who was captivated with her I must say.

"You've got a good one there, my Brother," was his comment privately to me. "You want to try to hang on to her if you can."

And I thought, "You know something? I think you're absolutely right"

CHAPTER EIGHTEEN
# ALL CHANGE

*All changes, even the most longed for, have their melancholy,*
*For what we leave behind us is a part of ourselves.*
*But we must die to one life before we can enter another.*
Anatole France

That autumn it had been arranged that I should travel to the US again, this time to give a series of lectures for the AIA, the Archaeological Institute of America. They'd invited me to give talks to a number of their 'chapters', their local societies, mainly based at various universities dotted about the states. The subject of my lectures was going to be Farah of course, and I called it 'Recent excavations in the Negev', a bit of a broad heading but at least it wouldn't put people off in the way it might do if I chose a more scientific title. But the AIA also asked me to contribute an article for their popular journal 'Archaeology', which I went on to write for them, calling it 'Science and Archaeology' in which I described our innovative methodology at Farah and the way we were working as a multi-disciplinary team. This lecture tour enabled me to visit EEI in Belmont again and also to spend more time with Big Al and his team mates at the National Library in Washington DC where I would no doubt be regaled with the latest scandals on Capitol Hill.

On this trip the high point was to be my final lecture at Princeton, one of the eight 'Ivy League' universities in America, itself famous for providing a home to everyone from Albert Einstein to the actor Jimmy Stewart, no less. I flew in and checked into the Nassau Inn, Princeton's premier colonial-style hostelry, and in due course a member of the Classics faculty, who acted as secretary for the local AIA there, picked me up to take me to dinner at his home before the lecture.

"You'll be pleased to know," he said as he was driving, "a great friend of yours is going to join us for dinner tonight, Homer Thompson; he's so looking forward to seeing you again."

Homer who, I thought? I have never heard of this person before let alone ever met him, as far as I knew. I didn't say anything at that stage and we reached the professor's home slightly ahead of the due time. His wife was there and as we chatted she too extolled the fact that my 'great friend Homer' would be there at any moment and how much he'd said he was looking forward to being with me again. I remained totally in the dark. In due course the door-bell rang and with cries of "That'll be Homer!" the wife went to answer it. I could hear voices in the hall-way as the said Homer was taking off his overcoat and a moment later he came into the room, at which point it at once became perfectly clear to him, as it already was to me, that until that very moment we had never previously clapped eyes on each other. But rather than admit to the fact, neither Homer nor I let anything slip to dispel the illusion created by our hosts of our strong mutual chumminess, and we kept up this charade all the way through dinner. At the end of it our host was so taken with our apparently momentous reunion that he said to Homer that he was sure we had so much more to reminisce about that Homer should take me to lunch the next day to the Princeton Faculty Club, which we arranged to do. After that I was whisked away to the lecture room where my talk about Farah was well received.

The following day I pitched up at the Faculty Club and we sat down to lunch. Still neither Homer nor I admitted to each other that this whole fellowship was a nonsense, and after lunch we walked together across the hallowed lawns under some impressive cedar trees to Homer's office at the Princeton Institute for Advanced Studies. He was obviously someone of importance, I'd gathered that much. Coffee was brought in after which it was soon time for me to leave. I felt I really ought to know by then with whom I had been teamed up, at least notionally. I temporised a bit longer and then hit on a brain wave. He knew exactly what I did; he'd been to my lecture the night before after all. But what the hell did he do?

"So tell me, Homer," I launched out, somewhat deliberately, "How is your own research progressing then?"

"Oh well, David," he replied, "I've decided not to get involved in the publication of the thirteenth volume of our excavations. I feel I've done enough, don't you?"

I raised my eyes to the bookshelves behind him and there, right the way across the middle shelf were the first twelve volumes entitled 'Excavations of the Athenian Agora', by Homer A. Thompson. Homer was 'Mr. Athenian Agora', and had for many years been the director of one of the most prestigious and significant excavations in the Classical world. Did I feel foolish? Absolutely, but I covered my tracks by saying how remarkable the dig had been and then mercifully for me it was time for me to leave, so I said my goodbyes and hurried off much chastened by my own ignorance.

*   *   *

During that winter Juliet persuaded me that she needed an Easter visit to Farah to finish her reference collection of the botanical material. The charcoal work was going well, but just for completeness of the whole survey she wanted to check the spring flowers. We arranged to do that and flew out together. We weren't going to excavate anything so I didn't think we needed a permit, but I informed the director of antiquities anyway. However, one evening while we were there I received a phone call at our hotel in Beer Sheba from the office of the director of antiquities about the summer season's permit, which I thought a bit premature. His secretary was asking me to call in at his office in Jerusalem, and so the following Monday morning I stayed up in Jerusalem and went to see him.

"We have a problem," he began. "A hard-core group of prehistorians from the Hebrew University are upset that you are excavating what they consider is their own Mousterian site at Farah. They've sent a deputation to me to protest. They think they should be excavating it instead. It's an Israeli site in Israel is their argument. You know, 'Israel for the Jews', that kind of thing. I've tried to reason with them but they've got pretty het up about it. And they're also complaining about the fact that you call your expedition 'British', you know, the 'British Western Negev Expedition'. They think it smacks of the British Mandate all over again, a sort of neo-colonial re-annexation of the Western Negev. What can we do, do you think?"

"Do they consider that our Neanderthals at Farah are specifically Jewish?" I countered, hardly crediting the logic. With a quiet irony I continued, "I'm afraid I'm not really expert enough to tell if sixty thousand years ago they indulged in the practice of circumcision or not! But it does seem to me there's a lot of deliberately targeted political nonsense flying around here. What do you suggest?"

Over the few years I'd been there I had come to realise that Israeli archaeology was generally characterised by an overbearing political desire bordering on the fanatical to prove that the Old Testament was one hundred per cent true, the underlying intention being to demonstrate that the Jews had physically been in Palestine for absolutely eons to the exclusion of anyone else. It was an approach which was often thoroughly detrimental to any other archaeologically represented phases of human endeavour they might encounter, which of course they tended to ignore as being completely irrelevant. But proprietorial claims to the Middle Palaeolithic seemed to be taking things to extremes, I thought.

"I know it's totally preposterous," continued the director, "but I have to try to pacify them. They've got themselves very wound up about the whole thing. Now, in that you are not specifically interested in the Mousterian site for its own sake, you know, but as part of the wider environmental survey, what I suggest is that next season you take an Israeli prehistorian with you on the dig. That way, they can't complain it's a purely British expedition and they'll have to shut up. I've got just the man in mind, a quiet but determined young archaeology graduate who actually studied at the Hebrew University, so they can't say anything against him can they? Leave it to me. I'll introduce you to him."

I went back to the Ritz and an hour or two later the director called me again and set up a meeting for later that afternoon. After lunch I turned up again and was introduced to a young archaeologist named Itzaak Gilead. We talked about the site, and the wider aspects of the survey we had already conducted, but by that stage I already decided two things. The first was that I would hand the whole excavation over to him, and second, the summer season would be my last in Israel. I'd had enough. Although Itzaak seemed to be perfectly reasonable, I knew that I didn't want to have to treat with his countrymen any more. Since the occupation of East Jerusalem and the West Bank in 1967, it was obvious that many had become even more confrontational and possessive and that they had absolutely no intention of making any kind of a deal with the Palestinians. They'd seized their land, razed their houses, appropriated their fields and imprisoned tens of thousands of their young people when they'd tried to oppose them. For me, the way events were unfolding had become distinctly unpleasant. I walked back to the Ritz with a heavy heart wondering how I would explain this to Louis. He'd become so much of a friend to me he was like my own family.

As it turned out, events came to my rescue. Louis came up to me in the Ritz the very next day and asked me if I would walk with him to his house in the Old City. There was something he needed to discuss, he said. He looked very sombre. I'd been to his house many times before of course and I always enjoyed being there, not least for its historic location. It was on the top floor of an old stone-built Ottoman tenement block which comprised several apartments with inward-looking balconies surrounding a paved courtyard. It was reached down a passage off one of the main streets not far from the Dome of the Rock. I always got the feeling that the families who lived there were very neighbourly. We walked down together and reached his home. His wife Nura was there but the children were out playing in the yard.

"I've got something very serious I want to talk to you about, David," he began. "Nura and me, with the children of course, we are thinking of leaving Jerusalem and emigrating to the States. I don't think we can take what's happening to the little ones any more. Mazi comes home late from school several times a week every week now and says he's been stopped at gun point in the street and pushed around by the Israeli soldiers. I mean, David, this is our city, these are our streets, and they are the intruders here. What do they think they are doing? Well, the last straw was yesterday when it happened to Mary as she was coming home from kindergarten. You know, she goes to a kindergarten run by the Lutherans on the Mount of Olives. The soldiers asked her who she was, where she lived, what she was doing. She came home crying, David. I won't have it. I don't mind if it happens to me, but to the children? They're only little and they don't understand what's going on. Why do we have to put up with these sons of bitches – sorry Nura. I'm upset about it. My brother Fuad lives just outside Miami with is family. He says he can sponsor us if we can get the papers together. We need you to help us to fill them in. Can you do that for us?"

I was of course shocked and deeply saddened by this turn of events. Louis and Jerusalem had become inseparable for me. I knew then and there that there could not be one without the other. I thought for a bit and then turned to Nura who was sitting saying nothing.

"Nura," I began, "I understand the pressure you're under with the kids. I can see that clearly. But are you sure that you want them to be brought up in America? If they go to school there they're of an age when they will forget all about Palestine, all about Jerusalem, and they'll become little Americans. They will speak with American accents. Maybe they will even forget their Arabic. Can you take that? Your family has been here for generations. Can you see yourself making a new life in Florida?"

Nura looked at me with a steady gaze and said quietly, "I can't take any more of this hatred that the Israelis show to us. I'd rather leave and make a new life for us all in Miami. I know it will be difficult, but Fuad has a hotel outside Miami and Louis can work there and the kids can go to school in peace and quiet. I'll be fine with it. I really will. I would rather that than go on with these problems every day."

I could see that they had been turning the idea over in their minds for weeks and they had already made their decision.

"It will take at least six months to complete all the formalities, David," Louis continued. "In any case even you have been saying for some time that you probably only have one season left anyway, so I won't be leaving you alone here, *Habibi*. While you need me, I'll be here. It's my city for you, you know that. In any case, you are also finding these Israelis more and more difficult to take aren't you?"

I had to agree. I'd talked to Louis about it many times before, but as things were turning out I'd made a decision too. The whole atmosphere was becoming more and more soured by what I had witnessed as a collective separatist and vaunting ambition among the occupiers. The majority of these people didn't want to fit into the Levantine world at all; they made no attempt to. There were those among them who only wanted to dominate it. Supported by the armed might of America, Israel had become the most over-militarised country in the world. I was aware that there were a significant number of Israelis who were conscientiously opposed to this idea, but yes, Louis was right; personally I had already made the decision the previous day that the coming summer season would be my last. We had more or less completed what we had set out to achieve and in any case I'd come to a natural fork in the road.

After a minute or two I spoke again. "Well, Louis," I said, "Maybe we're all going to change soon. You're right, of course. This coming season is going to be my last. But there's something else you should know. I am going to ask Sue to marry me. What do you think of that? Do you think she'll have me?"

"That's marvellous, *Habibi*! You are made for each other, really. And you know my answer. I think she will be a fantastic wife for you. She's the one who will look after you, you know that. All the other girlfriends I have seen you with were rubbish. But Sue, she's the very best, the top! She'll make you into a real man, David, believe me. Where are you going to get married? Wait a minute, why don't you do it right here, in Jerusalem? I can arrange it for you, at our church. I can arrange everything. You would be married in the Holy City. Think of that. I could be your best man. Nura could be Sue's bridesmaid. It would be really wonderful, honestly, David, I'm telling you! I won't leave for the US until you're married, I promise. How's that? We'll both leave together."

"It's a deal, Louis. If Sue agrees, I'll do what you say. The only thing is," I smiled, "it would be an arranged marriage then, wouldn't it? Very fitting I'm sure."

\* \* \*

Juliet and I finished our brief spring season and flew back to Britain. On the way back the more I contemplated what Louis had suggested the more I thought it was a great idea, though I had no notion of what it would entail, even if Sue were to be in favour of it. But I knew that if we were going to do it, I would have to ask Sue fairly soon, so at an appropriate moment I rather prosaically proposed to Sue that she might like to get engaged. For one heart-stopping moment she said that she wouldn't, get engaged that is, and then she continued that she'd rather get married once and for all. I rather hesitantly told her about the plans that Louis and I had discussed and she didn't turn a hair at the possibility of getting married in the Old City of Jerusalem; in fact she thought it was an excellent plan.

"My parents couldn't be there anyway. They couldn't afford to fly from southern Africa. You don't want to tell your Mum and Dad either. So it's ideal. We just go off and get married on our own. It's our very own day, and we'll keep it like that."

I phoned Louis in Jerusalem to tell him the good news, and he was delighted. He said he'd take the matter in hand at once. Meanwhile, Sue and I had some thinking to do. Amongst other things we needed a wedding ring for Sue and so we went to Hatton Garden, centre of the London jewellery world, and bought one for £50. That was about as much as I could afford at the time. I didn't know what the legal position was about getting married in the Middle East, so with some reluctance I phoned the Israeli Embassy in Kensington. I described that I wanted to get married in Jerusalem, and was told to hang on while I was put through to an advisor.

"Hello, how can I help you? You want to get married in Israel?"

"I want to get married in Jerusalem. What should I do?"

"It's very simple. You contact your rabbi and he will arrange it."

I told him I didn't have a rabbi and he replied that it wasn't a problem. One could easily be fixed up, he said, to which I replied,

"But I am a Christian. I certainly don't want a rabbi. I want to get married in the Israeli-occupied part of the Old City in East Jerusalem."

At that point I heard the phone at the other end being slammed down. So much for them, I thought. I would have to trust to Louis's judgement on the legal matter. Sue fared a little better and was told that she could register herself as a spinster at Wandsworth Town Hall.

There wasn't much more that could be done in Britain. I'd just have to wait until I got back to Jerusalem. Meanwhile, there was the 1975 summer season to plan, with arrangements to be made for the scientific team. Everyone was again going to fly out and I had my vehicle hired and waiting. Soon after the beginning of July everything was ready. Knowing this was going to be my last season, my heart wasn't really in the expedition as it had been before, and in any case we'd already made the major breakthrough on the environmental front the year before. Also I was quite prepared to hand over the running of the Mousterian site to Itzaak, whom I was sure would be only too willing to take up the reins.

\*  \*  \*

Once I'd got back to the Holy City my mind turned to the forthcoming nuptials. Louis had been as good as his word and had organised everything. The church we were going to use was Louis's own, the Greek Catholic Melkite church. But he said to me,

"Unfortunately I couldn't get our Patriarch, Hilarion Capucci, to marry you. He was arrested by the Israelis at the end of last year and is in prison in Ramleh for smuggling guns between the Al Fatah guerrillas in Lebanon and the freedom fighters in the West Bank and Gaza. They say that quantities of weapons and explosives were found hidden in the doors of his Mercedes car. But I've got our acting priest, Peter Boutros, to do it. He's a lovely man. You'll like him."

The troubled Middle East was never far from the surface, I thought, whatever you were doing. But I met Peter Boutros and he was indeed a fine man, a true man of God. He reminded me of my own father. I talked to him at length about my background, my desire at one time to enter the church myself, and my change to archaeology. He assured me everything would be well on the day, which we now fixed for the morning of 25th August, scarcely four weeks away. He suggested that with my schooling in Greek I should read the Gospel at my wedding. He thought my Greek would be better than his, but I declined his kind offer. I told him that on the day I would be too nervous.

In case I'd missed anything, I went to see the British Consul in East Jerusalem to ask whether he could add anything to the procedure for getting married in the West Bank. The Consulate was a two-roomed upstairs office not far from the Ritz, with the staff comprising just one British employee, the consul, a rather lacklustre young man who obviously felt he'd got stranded there. The only other person there was an Arab factotum who acted as his driver and male secretary. I explained that I wanted to get married in the Old City, and the Consul asked,

"And where was your wife-to-be born?" to which I answered, "Alexandria".

"You mean in Egypt?" he continued rather incredulously, with raised eyebrows. "Well, I must tell you that as a rule these mixed marriages are a thoroughly bad idea. They seldom last, you know. It's the cultural differences that cause the problems, you see, those and the bride's family, of course, who invariably interfere. I would strongly advise you to think very carefully before taking such a bold step. It might seem like a good idea now, but give it a year or two, you know, and you're likely to wind up regretting it. Oh yes, I've seen it all before, I can tell you. We have to try to sort out the mess when it all goes wrong. Believe me it's not easy for us."

He seemed more concerned about his own administrative problems than answering any questions I was asking him. I explained to him my fiancé was British, at which he looked distinctly sceptical, until I told him in no uncertain terms that her father had been a wing commander in RAF Intelligence in Egypt during the war and that amongst other things that's why she was born there. I also told him that I'd been working in this part of the world probably rather longer than he had and through my contacts I had the church, the priest and the ceremony all arranged. If he didn't know any more about it, that was fine by me, but I told him very firmly that I was going to go ahead and get married anyway, with or without his advice.

"Goodness me," he replied, rather cowed by my outburst, "You do seem to have got it all sorted out, don't you. We haven't seen a case like this before. Perhaps when you've actually got married you could come and tell us how you did it. We'd like to know, I'm sure. The only thing I can suggest is that you post the bans in our office here just in case anyone has any objections."

I couldn't imagine who on earth might come into the flea-blown British Consulate in East Jerusalem to find out which British citizen was getting married to whom, or who the consul thought might be casually passing through their insignificant first floor office in its back street and say, "Oh, look at that! I see David is getting married", but I said I'd adopt his suggestion anyway that he should post the bans. He asked me what my address was in Jerusalem so he could put it on the document. I thought for a second and then said proudly that it was the Hotel Ritz, in Ibn Khaldoun Street. It really and truly had become for me a home from home.

CHAPTER NINETEEN
# NUPTIAL COTTON WOOL

*My advice to you is to get married;*
*If you find a good wife, you'll be happy.*
*If you get a bad one, you'll become a philosopher.*
Attributed to Socrates

My dancing day was rapidly approaching and of course I'd been preparing for it for weeks. I'd had a suit specially made for me by an old Arab tailor near the Ritz. I'd bought the cloth in London, from Dormeuil of Regent Street, and taken it out with me. It was fine navy blue wool worsted with a threadlike wine-coloured stripe to which the tailor added a rather conspicuous light baby-blue silk lining. I'd also been to see a well-known Armenian jeweller in the Old City, Momjian, and he had hand-crafted a special wedding ring for me, so between the two I was well kitted out. I'd kept Sue informed by telephone on progress at the church. Louis's own church, the Greek Catholics, or Melkites as they are known, is perhaps the oldest continuous Christian community in the world, and certainly the dominant one in the Middle East. They originated in Antioch, in Syria, at the very dawn of Christianity and they still followed a Byzantine form of service stretching back across almost two millennia.

The main Melkite church, the Patriarchate Church in Jerusalem, the Church of the Annunciation, had been closed for almost two years. Although it had only been built in the early 19th century, the frescoes of the interior had apparently faded and were being restored by two Romanian church artists who understood the proper artistic styles and techniques to use. The congregation had been squatting at another church in the Old City in the meanwhile, which is where I'd first met Peter Boutros. But Louis told me he had obtained special permission for us to have our ceremony in the main church. The restoration was almost complete and they were going to open it especially for us, much to the chagrin of some of the members, Louis said, who had wanted to be the first to hold sacraments in the newly decorated building.

Sunday 24th eventually came around, the day before the appointed day, and Sue was due to fly out from London that morning, at least I hoped that's what she was going to do. Louis and I drove down to Lod Airport that afternoon to meet her flight and I stood with some trepidation in the arrivals area waiting for her to appear. There was the usual chaos of untrammelled bickering, quarrelling and general unrestrained clamour which I'd come to learn characterised any such Israeli gathering. It was the one thing I disliked above everything else about this country, but I'm afraid to say that afternoon in my anxiety I joined in the mêlée and pushed my way to the front, where there was a floor to ceiling glass panel allowing visual but silent contact with the baggage hall which is where I stood and waited. Miraculously, in a few minutes Sue appeared among the confusion on the other side of the partition and I managed to attract her attention. I will never forget what she did next. She walked sedately over to the panel and held the palm of her hand up to the glass and I did the same against hers, and she smiled. That was a moment of enormous significance for me. I knew at that instant that I had made the right decision. This calm and lovely girl was tomorrow morning going to be my bride.

It seemed like an age before she finally emerged from among the milling crowd, at which point we grabbed her bags, hurried out of the airport and drove up to Jerusalem at speed. Louis had arranged that Sue would stay at their home in the Old City that night, separately from me of course. I was still staying at the Ritz, and that is where I spent my last unattached evening. I don't remember much about it, but I slept well and when the momentous day dawned, Monday 25th August, I was mentally ready. I showered and dressed in my new suit then went down to the foyer to wait for Louis. As it was a few minutes before the due time, I went over to the leopard-skin bar one last time. Dik the barman was just opening up, and I sat with him for a while nursing a glass of cognac to calm my nerves until the moment came to leave. Louis hailed a taxi and we drove down Salahedin Street and around the famous walls of Sultan Suleiman to the Jaffa Gate, from where we walked to the Patriarchate. Sue and Nura were already waiting upstairs in the office with Father Boutros. Sue was wearing a very elegant full-length, long-sleeved cream dress with an embroidered panel across the bodice; to me she looked absolutely radiant. Around her neck was a silver pendant which Louis had given her in the shape of a Jerusalem cross with an amethyst at its centre.

After Father Boutros had described exactly how the morning would proceed, we walked down stairs from the Patriarchate into the nave of the church. It was the first time I'd seen the interior of the church, which looked most colourful in its freshly painted frescoes. The subject of the paintings was typically Byzantine, yet they were obviously modern in design. The central dome is dominated by the imposing figure of Christ in Majesty, Christ Pantokrator and the apse above the altar features a fresco of the Theotokos, the Virgin and Child. Although the paintings are all in the same traditional positions they occupy in older churches, the names of the accompanying saints are written in Arabic – obviously the language of the community. Sue and I stood before the altar, with Louis and Nura by our side. The only other person in the church was my old student Robin Duckworth. I'd asked him to stay over if he could because I needed a religious sponsor to say that I had never been married before. He was a catholic priest and his word was accepted by the church.

Before the proceedings got underway, I went through the sacrament of re-baptism, which I had agreed to do on the basis that for me Christianity is one faith, indivisible. And after that, the ceremony began. It was to take close to two hours. The service was partly in Greek, which I tried to translate, and partly in Arabic, which Father Boutros translated for us where necessary so we were more or less able to follow what was happening. At the appropriate point we exchanged rings. That was followed by undoubtedly the high point of the morning, the climax of the whole service, the Crowning, a feature which has been at the heart of the Eastern Orthodox and with it the Byzantine marriage ceremony for many, many hundreds of years.

There are two silver crowns which are meant to be a sign of glory and honour, and the two crowns are initially joined, symbolizing unity. Father Boutros placed the crowns on our heads and then changed them one for the other three times as Sue and I walked in great solemnity around the altar, making a circuit three times as well. The whole ancient performance in those hallowed surroundings was profoundly moving.

But finally the service came to an end and much to our joy Sue and I were proclaimed husband and wife. We went into the baptistery and signed the register and were given our marriage certificate, which naturally enough was in Arabic. We thanked those present and walked out into the mid-day sunshine and shadow of the Old City and down to Louis's home where his family had been preparing our wedding breakfast all morning. I shall never forget it. It was laid out for us in an upper room overlooking the Dome of the Rock. In typical Arab style, only Sue and I, Nura, Louis and Father Boutros sat down to the lunch; the rest of the family sat around the walls or busied themselves serving. The meal had all my favourite Arab dishes, the centre-piece of which was *mensaf*, a Palestinian lamb casserole. But there was so much more. Stuffed peppers and baby marrows with a yoghurt sauce, *kibbeh* – torpedoes of minced lamb with bulghur wheat flavoured with cumin and allspice then deep fried – many different kinds of salad dishes, including the usual hummus, baba ganoush and tahini salad; they just kept coming. And in the middle of the table was a bottle of Johnny Walker scotch whisky to make the party go with a swing. When we were full to the brim, we finished the whole thing off with Arabic coffee, flavoured with cardamom. It had been memorable. After a couple of photographs on Louis's balcony it was time to leave.

Louis had absolutely forbidden me to spend the first night of my married life staying at the Ritz. He said that I knew too many people there and as a consequence I would be distracted. So he'd booked a room for us at the Grand Hotel in Ramallah, a few kilometres north of Jerusalem, and he'd organised a taxi to take us there. He said it would be waiting for us at two o'clock. We said our thanks and goodbyes to the family and walked out and up the stepped streets to the Jaffa Gate, looking very noticeable I have to say, with me in a suit and Sue in her wedding dress on such a warm afternoon; many people stopped and stared at us. When we passed outside the gate, we waited. Louis had said we'd recognise the car when we saw it. And so we lingered in the shade of the gate with all the bustle of the Old City going on around us - fully loaded donkeys being driven in and out, and groups of pilgrims looking blankly up at the walls. We stood there for some minutes feeling very visible; a little lad came up and tried to sell us bamboo flutes until he realised we weren't ordinary tourists. Finally our car came. Undeniably there was no mistaking it; it was a large powder-blue Mercedes covered with blobs of cotton wool and balloons. It was fairly obvious who we were too, so we walked over to it and got in. Off we drove looking and sounding really conspicuous as the driver honked his horn all the way from Jerusalem to Ramallah.

In its heyday the Grand Hotel, Ramallah must have been a grand hotel indeed. It was set on a hill above the town and was surrounded by pine-wooded gardens. Under the trees outside there were innumerable metal chairs and tables, but when we arrived they were all empty. In fact the whole hotel was empty. We were the only people staying there. It had once been a fashionable watering hole for families from all over Arabia – from Jordan, Saudi Arabia, Kuwait and the other Gulf States – who would have come here for the cool mountain air and verdant surroundings, but since the 1967 war and the Israeli occupation those customers had dried up completely. No-one came; no-one was able to come any more. It was a sad business. The reception area was eerily quiet and slightly fusty, but there was a receptionist there and when I said who we were she handed us the key. I asked if it was possible to order a bottle of champagne and she enquired whether I would like Israeli sparkling wine or real champagne. I reprimanded her and said it had to be

French champagne; only the best would do on our wedding day, but it turned out that it cost about £30 a bottle, a vast amount in those days. I suppose they didn't have many takers for it anymore.

We went up to our room and a few minutes later a young man appeared with a tray bearing the champagne bottle and two glasses. I should have known what would happen next but I didn't think. He'd never opened a bottle of champagne before, this lad, and after a long struggle during which he flipped the bottle from one hand to the other, he finally popped the cork out so vigorously that a third of the champagne erupted onto the floor. He looked suitably mortified, but we were too happy to scold him and we sent him on his way with a sizeable tip. The rest of the afternoon was our own, the very first of our married life, and we enjoyed it accordingly until the sun started to dip in the west and the shadows to lengthen outside our window. It was time to think about dinner.

There was a restaurant in Ramallah, a very famous Palestinian restaurant called Naoum's which was renowned for its meze. It was said that if the table ordered a bottle of arak at Naoum's, the waiter would over the course of the evening bring a hundred dishes of meze to accompany it. I said to Sue we just had to try this, so we walked downstairs and asked the girl at reception where the restaurant was. It turned out it was only two or three streets away down the hill, so we sauntered down and duly found it. We walked in and were shown to a table. I asked the waiter about the menu, and especially mentioned the plethora of meze dishes I'd been told about. He confirmed that they would do this for us, even though we were only ordering a bottle or two of wine instead of the usual arak. We sat back to await events, and we were not disappointed. Once the bottle of Bethlehem wine had arrived, so the meze started to appear, endless dishes of the most inventive salads and meats you can image – liver, kidneys, steak tartare, lamb kebabs, spiced baby chicken legs, kofte, *kibbeh* – it just went on and on, accompanied by various dips, pickles and piquant sauces and mountains of *khoubiz*, the typical Arabic flat bread. It looked as though it would never stop, until we called a halt and ordered coffee. The waiter told us he'd bring a mixture of Arabic sweets with it – *ma'amoul*, a kind of shortbread with dates, and baklawa with honey.

It was while we were waiting for this to arrive that the girl who had been manning the reception desk at the Grand Hotel came into the restaurant and walked over to us. She said she was terribly sorry but they were about to lock up for the night and go home, and since we were the only guests could we please hurry up and come back to claim our room. It was both heart-breaking and funnily idiosyncratic at the same time, but we didn't want to prolong her anxiety any further so we called for the bill and walked back up the hill. The hotel was in darkness, apart from one or two floodlights which lit up all the empty chairs and tables in the garden, so we stumbled up to our room and went to bed. It was the end of a momentous day, and the start of an even more momentous life.

Next morning, Mr. and Mrs. Price Williams came downstairs. We decided not to stay any longer than we had to at the empty Grand Hotel and so we made our minds up to go back to the Ritz for breakfast. A cab was ordered and we sped back to Jerusalem. We were ecstatically happy. I kissed Sue, but the driver turned around and said we couldn't do that sort of thing in his cab. I was extremely annoyed with him and when we arrived at the Ritz I bounded up the steps and complained to Louis who went out and shouted at the driver, telling him that we had just got married and how dare he spoil our morning. The cab driver was so intimidated he drove off without receiving his fare. I then had a quiet word with Louis and he confirmed the next part of the arrangement was on track. We were about to set off on the first adventure of our married lives – our honeymoon.

CHAPTER TWENTY
# THE ROSE-RED CITY

*It seems no work of Man's creative hand,*
*by labour wrought as wavering fancy planned;*
*But from the rock as if by magic grown,*
*eternal, silent, beautiful, alone!*
*Match me such marvel save in Eastern clime,*
*a rose-red city half as old as time.*
John William Burgon: Petra 1845

Over breakfast at the Ritz I outlined the plans for our honeymoon. We were going to cross over the Jordan River and I was going to show Sue the rock city of Petra, not that I'd seen it myself before, but I had worked on the material from Peter Parr's excavations there in the 1950s so I felt a strong connection with it. In today's world going to Petra from Israel might seem like a simple thing to do. But in 1975 it was in fact technically impossible. The frontier between the Hashemite Kingdom of Jordan and the occupied West Bank was closed to everyone except a few Palestinians who had the misfortune to have family stranded on either side of the border. The main river crossing, just south of Jericho, used to be a fairly straightforward one across the Allenby Bridge which had been built just after the First World War, but in 1967 the Israelis unhelpfully had blown it up. What's more the new subjugating administration had then instantly stripped more than one hundred thousand Palestinians who had fled over the ruins of the bridge to escape the fighting of their right to return to live in their own homes in the West Bank, thereby condemning most of them to immediate and permanent exile in Jordanian refugee camps which had hurriedly been built by the United Nations.

If any members of the families of these unfortunate refugees were still living in the West Bank, and want to visit their dislocated relatives in Jordan they were forced to relinquish their own identity documents at the border before being allowed to cross what was left of the Allenby Bridge. In return they were given a temporary identity card. If they stayed away for more than six months, or they tried to cross more than so many times in a year, their West Bank citizenship was automatically revoked by the occupying Israelis and without any further recourse they, like their relatives, were refused the right to return so that they too were left stranded and stateless on the other side. There was nothing these unfortunate people could do. Under international law what the Israelis were implementing was of course totally illegal but, as with so much else they were doing, that didn't stop them from carrying it out anyway. Although the international community grumbled it largely turned a blind eye to the whole sorry performance, and any United Nations resolutions in favour of the Palestinians were as usual ignored. So, in 1975, it was still only the members of these families, and they alone, that the Israelis would with great reluctance allow to cross over; no-one else.

Now, I'd had all this explained to me by an Israeli police officer by the name of Yusuf who actually worked at the bridge. Yusuf was originally Egyptian. He had come from Cairo and, although he was Jewish, he was very sympathetic to the Palestinian cause. Louis had got to know him well, and it was he who introduced us. We'd had a drink together at the leopard-skin bar just a week before the wedding.

"Listen, if the international community can turn a blind eye to all this, then so can we," he told me. "I know it's completely illegal, but if you want to cross over into Jordan, I can fix it for you. But you'll have to do exactly what I say. You must be at the bridge at precisely eleven o'clock next Tuesday and you'll find me there. Trust me. I'll get you across, OK?"

So that next Tuesday morning on the day after the wedding, when we'd finished breakfast at the Ritz Louis organised a taxi to take us to the bridge. As he beckoned us into the car he reminded us that his uncle, Uncle John, would be waiting to take us up to Amman when we had crossed over to the other side. He'd be bound to recognise us, Louis assured us. With that, we left Jerusalem and drove at great speed down the road to Jericho arriving at the bridge exactly at the appointed hour. Yusuf was waiting for us. In the arid waste-land near the Dead Sea several wooden tables had been set up under a roof of corrugated iron beneath which a few elderly women, their possessions wrapped in bundles, were being interrogated and searched. It was like an oven there, with the sun relentlessly beating down on the sand and the blinding heat rising from the desert floor in vast shimmering waves. Yusuf waved us behind him.

"Go and stand over there, next to that police vehicle. Don't talk to anyone. You're not here, right? I'll tell you in a minute what to do next."

And he turned to answer some query or another from one of his colleagues. The old women standing by the tables were being given a hard time, having to open all their bundles and have them searched and re-searched by a number of armed soldiers. The women had obviously been waiting since dawn, patiently accepting the indignity of it all. They had already handed over all their identity papers in return for the so-called privilege of being able to cross the bridge to see their loved ones. Finally, when they had all been processed, they were ordered towards a dilapidated bus standing at the road-side. Yusuf came over to us.

"When they've all got on, you climb on the bus as well and sit down. Don't talk to anyone, don't say who you are, don't even look at anyone. You'll be fine. I'll see you next Friday. Have a good time."

We did as he said. We got on and walked to the back and sat down. The air on the bus was oppressively hot. The bus started off towards the bridge but in no more than a couple of minutes it stopped again. A soldier with a machine gun climbed on and came up the aisle checking the cards which had been issued to each of the women only a few minutes before. He obviously saw us, but he didn't come up to us. He paid us no attention and then he turned and left. The bus carried on. It soon reached the wrecked spans of the bridge and drove gingerly across. A few minutes later there was a striped barrier across the road. This was Jordan. A Jordanian policeman got on the bus and checked all the cards again, but although he obviously could see we were there he didn't come up to us. It was as though we were invisible. We carried on to the Jordanian border post, where everyone was ordered out. Sue and I were the last to get off. The officer in charge was gesticulating that the women should go into the border post, but when we got off, without saying anything he motioned us to go and stand behind the bus, which we did. After a while, the women came out again and clambered back on the bus. The policeman waved us on as well and the bus set off again and travelled another few hundred yards through yet another barrier to a car park where everyone got off. We had arrived.

As we alighted a man came over to us and announced,

"Hi David, Sue. I'm Louis's Uncle John. Welcome to Jordan. Let's go to my car and I'll drive you up to Amman."

With a certain release of tension, we got in the car and drove up the winding road to the Jordanian capital. At first the country wore the same barren appearance, the same rock desert caste, that it had been on the other side of the river, but as we approached the top of the escarpment, greenery started to appear, first scrubby bushes and then groves of cypress trees. Amman was higher than Jerusalem and caught the last gasp of winter rains from the Mediterranean. The city itself had a similar appearance to East Jerusalem; all the buildings were constructed from attractive honey-coloured limestone blocks. Louis had booked us into the Philadelphia Hotel - 'Philadelphia' was the name by which the Hellenistic rulers knew Amman it, or rather, Ammon, being its more ancient name.

The hotel had the most impressive rear façade of any hotel I've ever stayed in, particularly for me as an archaeologist, I would say. It had been built straight across the orchestra of the huge Roman theatre of Classical Philadelphia. The hotel is no longer there; I think shortly after we stayed there the antiquities people had it pulled down, but at the time it was amazing to sit on the terrace bar at the back sipping a gin sling and looking at the marble seats of the impressive flood-lit Classical auditorium straight in front of us, something which we did on our first evening there. Knowing that we were on our honeymoon, the Nazal brothers who owned the hotel had given us a most comfortable suite and as we changed for dinner I well remember Sue walking towards me across the room and for the first time I felt that she really was my wife.

*   *   *

The next day Uncle John was waiting at the hotel reception at breakfast time with his car outside. We were going to drive down to Petra, which is what I'd promised Sue we would do. The road we were going to take followed what was known in antiquity as 'The Kings Highway', the way the 18th Dynasty pharaohs were rumoured to have campaigned northwards during the Bronze Age. It ran on the west side of the crest of the escarpment at the point where the modern Arab villages were nestling in the mountain folds along the spring line. The first of these was Madaba, an attractive Christian town with quite a number of churches, including the Greek Orthodox Church of St George. The church itself isn't very old, but when they were re-modelling part of it at the end of the nineteenth century they uncovered an extraordinary map, a mosaic map of the Holy Land as it was in Byzantine times, which had decorated the floor of an earlier church. It showed the landscape and its towns right across from the Mediterranean Sea to the centre of what today is Trans-Jordan. It had been made in the middle of the sixth century, and actually included a street plan of Jerusalem, *Hagia Polis* as they called it, the Holy City of Jerusalem.

We had a good look at the whole thing, picking out some of the Greek place-names, while Uncle John spoke to the priest, whom he seemed to know well. As we left, the priest wished us a happy life and rang the bell above the west door for us, allowing himself to be lifted off the ground by the bell rope as he did so.

We continued along the Kings Highway and down through the spectacular gorge of the Wadi Mujib, the ancient River Arnon, and then up the other side to Kerak, a fortified crusader town which was once the headquarters of the Crusader Kingdom of Oultrejourdain. After a while the landscape began to change into a series of wild rock formations as we approached the region around Wadi Musa, the limestone giving way to dramatic outcrops of Nubian sandstone for which Petra was renowned. Petra was the secret capital of the Nabatean Arabs built during the 1st century BC. The Nabateans, who were originally desert nomads, had made a vast fortune from trading in frankincense and myrrh from south Arabia which they particularly sold to Rome and it was that contact with the Roman Empire which had given them a taste for elaborate architecture and opulent funerary monuments. Apparently, in Rome at the time of the Caesars, frankincense was more valuable even than gold. But Petra had been lost to European eyes for many centuries until 1812, when the Cambridge-educated Swiss adventurer, Johann Ludwig Burckhardt, dressed in Muslim robes and styling himself Sheikh Ibrahim Ibn Abdallah, became the first Westerner to set foot in the ancient city. It must have been the defining moment of his life when he rode down the *siq*, the long narrow defile which gives entry into the concealed valley of this incredible Nabatean city and he suddenly saw in the sunlight beyond the deep shadow the imposing facade of the *Khasneh*, the vast rock-cut tomb known as the Treasury.

We arrived at the gateway into the *siq*, the entrance into the hidden city, and Uncle John hired two horses to take us through the ancient site - you could do that in those days - and Sue and I rode with two horse boys down beneath the glowering cliffs of multi-coloured sandstone until twenty minutes later, like Burckhardt, we came face to face with the huge forty metre high quasi-classical pillared rock façade of the Treasury which dwarfs simply everything around it. It's called the Treasury because the pediment is topped by a colossal rock-cut funerary urn which the local Bedouin have always reckoned contains a stash of gold; they continually fire bullets at it in the hope of it breaking and showering them with riches. I didn't know it then but many years later I would come to recognise the heavily damaged central figure in the rotunda beneath the pediment perhaps better than most visitors. When first carved, it had in fact been a sandstone copy of the sculpture of the Praxitales Aphrodite, like the one at Knidos which of course I knew so well, but that's a story for another time.

Sue and I continued our horse ride down the sandy track into the wider outer *siq*, still flanked by beetling cliffs peppered with rock-cut tombs, until we came close to Petra's theatre, also impressively hewn out of the living rock, with tier upon tier of seats cut into the sandstone which made it look just like any other Classical auditorium. Apparently it would have seated seven thousand people. We dismounted to take a closer look and as we were walking I noticed on the sides of the path that the ground was littered with sherds of a very finely made pottery, broken fragments of plates and small shallow bowls which had been painted with elegant floral patterns in dark red; you could see it even on these tiny pieces. This was Nabatean pottery; I recognised it because I'd made drawings of lots of it back at the Institute. I showed it to Sue. I have always found it amazing that these coarse, almost illiterate Bedouin traders from the deserts of Arabia should have been attracted by such sophisticated egg-shell thin earthenware vessels with delicate decorations on them.

Shortly, after the theatre, the centre of Petra opened up in all its magnificence. To our right was a row of gigantic monumental tombs, again cut into the rock, many of similar design to the Treasury, past which we rode on down to the so-called Colonnaded Street, which had been the main thoroughfare of ancient Petra. There's nothing much left of it now. The colonnades have all long since fallen. The middle of the city, the part where the Nabateans actually lived, is in total ruins, having been shivered and shaken to pieces many times by endless violent earthquakes, perhaps the most catastrophic of which was reported in the 4th century AD. On that occasion Petra was so badly devastated that Cyril, the Byzantine Bishop of Jerusalem at the time, reckoned that the city had been utterly destroyed. It's this feature, this juxtaposition between the city proper, now represented by only formless heaps of rubble, and the overwhelming frontage of the tombs, their truly massive façades cut into the cliff faces on either side and thoroughly overpowering the ruined city as they do, which gives Petra its moving and magical quality. Although some of the tomb faces are badly weathered by over two thousand years of exposure to the wind and rain, they can be seen standing to their full height, something you never see in the remains of any normal Classical city. In those cases, where all the block-built monuments and the built-up tomb frontages have fallen down, they have long since been robbed into oblivion. This phenomenon wrongly gives the impression that Petra may have been in some way only a city of the dead, which more recent excavations have clearly demonstrated wasn't the case.

At the lowest point of the city, where the stream which flows through Petra in the rainy season exits through another deep ravine in the opposite wall of cliffs, decorated with yet more tombs, there are the remains of a Roman monumental gateway, beyond which is a building, the only one still free-standing, which is probably a Roman style Nabatean temple. Local Bedouin have named this the *Qasr el Bint Farun*, the 'Palace of Pharaoh's Daughter', based on a bogus story that an Egyptian king, the pharaoh of the Exodus, is said eventually to have settled here with his court after tiring in his pursuit of the Israelites. Nearby was a rest camp owned by the Nazal brothers, the family who owned the Philadelphia Hotel. We stopped there briefly and had a quick lunch before mounting our horses to ride back up through the city and the *siq* and back to the car. The afternoon was wearing on by this time so we took the fast route back to Amman up the Desert Highway, the road that links Amman to Aqaba on the Red Sea, and as the name implies runs through the flat desert land east of the escarpment. We finally reached the Philadelphia again, tired but exultant. It had been an absolutely fascinating day.

On the following day, Thursday, Uncle John had another archaeological treat planned for us – a visit to the Roman site of Jerash, the ancient city of Gerasa. Gerasa, one of the cities of the Decapolis, the ten cities built along the southern border of the Roman province of Syria, is by far the best-preserved Roman site in the Near East. It still has parts of its colonnaded streets intact, as well as a number of monumental arches which sit strategically across them. The whole city had been built of honey-coloured limestone. One of the most impressive features is its colonnaded oval forum which leads into the city, as well as two well-preserved theatres. In the centre of the Classical city stood an enormous sacred area enclosing a temple dedicated to the goddess Artemis, near which have been excavated several Byzantine churches with impressive early mosaics. For Sue and me it was all very romantic, and after this second day we felt we'd seen a fantastic amount in a very short time. We would take back very happy memories of our short stay in Jordan.

The next morning, Friday, was the day we were due to cross the bridge again to get back to Jerusalem. Yusuf had told us to cross as before no later than eleven o'clock, so after breakfast Uncle John drove us back down to the River Jordan and the Allenby Crossing. It was then that we hit a major snag in our travel plans. The Jordanian authorities at the border said it would be impossible for us to cross. At first they gave no reason why this should be, and I found it hard to understand. Surely any difficulty crossing the bridge was exclusively from the Israeli side, but here we weren't dealing with the recalcitrant Israelis. After a lot of remonstrating we were ushered in to see the army major who was in charge of security at the border and it was then we were told the actual reason for the refusal. When we'd crossed into Jordan a few days earlier we hadn't gone into the border post. We'd been told to stay outside behind the bus, you may remember. As a result, we didn't have an entry visa for Jordan in our passports, so how, the major asked us, could we possibly leave? He was a very reasonable man and I argued our case as best I could, pointing out that we had been married in an Arabic service and that were on our honeymoon in his lovely country, even asking him how many British people did he know that would have chosen to spend the first few days of their married life in Jordan. I even mentioned Petra, their key archaeological site, and that I'd worked on the excavated material from there. The major was very sympathetic, but he was also implacable. We could not cross. When I asked him what we should do, he proposed,

"If you want to get back to Jerusalem, I suggest you go to the Ministry of the Interior, get them to give you an entry and exit stamp, and then fly back to London from the Amman Airport and catch a plane back to Israel. That's all I can advise."

On hearing this Uncle John beckoned me over and said quietly that he'd thought of an idea; we should go back to Amman and wait to see if it would work or not. So, with a heavy heart we got into the car again and drove back to the Philadelphia. On the way, Uncle John outlined his idea. The Nazal brothers were apparently very friendly with someone by the name of Said Abu Keraki, who happened to be the present minister of the interior for the kingdom. He felt that between them they may well be able to help us. When we got to the hotel, Uncle John found the two brothers in their office and outlined the problem to them. They said they understood exactly and they would call their friend on the phone and explain the impasse, at which point I should speak to the minister myself and see what could be done. There was only one possible snag, and that was it was Friday, Abu Keraki's day off, and he would be at home, not in his office, but they said they would try to contact him anyway. With that, they dialled his home number and waited. The call was eventually answered and they asked to speak to the minister.

"He's in the shower at the moment. He'll be out in a minute."

There was a long pause. We hung on. After a while someone picked up the phone and answered at the other end. The problem was outlined and the phone handed over to me. An extremely cultured voice said "Hello, can I help you?" and I summarised the problem all over again, this time with four part harmony and descants, in a minor key, of course. I told him how I'd promised to show my new wife Petra, since I'd been involved with the excavations there, I said, and we'd so loved being in Jordan. As I was speaking Uncle John was mouthing something at me about Kerak, apparently the minister's home town, and I quickly added that we'd particularly impressed with Kerak too. The minister thought for a moment, and then he announced that if we would but present ourselves at the border the following morning, he would see to it that we could cross. He thanked us for spending our honeymoon in his country, and then the phone went dead. I hung up and grinned at Uncle John. He'd done it.

Uncle John had to make a phone call to Louis to tell him what was happening, when Louis reminded him that of course Saturday was Yusuf's day off but he said he'd try to get him to the border on the Jericho side at eleven o'clock the next day anyway. I couldn't relax that night, wondering whether or not the stratagem would work, but at half past ten the next morning we presented ourselves at the bridge again and this time there was no hitch at all. Our passports were stamped and we were told to climb onto the bus. Saying our fond farewells and thanks to Uncle John we crossed again over the broken bridge into the West Bank. Yusuf was waiting for us, and bypassing the soldiers and the other police, he ushered us to a waiting taxi which whisked us up to Jerusalem in double quick time. We'd made it. I have often wondered ever after that in what other country in the world could you arrange to speak to the government minister in charge, getting him out of the shower on his day of rest, and persuade him to organise something totally illegal for you?

Nowhere else, I would suggest.

* * *

And with our return to Jerusalem from Jericho, it was all over. The honeymoon was over, the British Western Negev Expedition was over, and for me my time in the Holy Land was over. In a few days we would leave this ancient land once and for all to begin our new married life. I'd come here six years earlier to work at Tell Jemmeh, knowing nothing about the people or the politics of this troubled corner of the globe. I knew its ancient history, about its patriarchs and its arcane languages, and I had known of Jerusalem in the abstract as a heavenly city, a city of transcendent dreams, but I hadn't known of the strife, of the profound hatred and of the deadly confrontation that it currently engendered. Those aspects I gradually learned as I came into contact with them in real time, in today's world.

I did help Louis with his papers, and he did get permission that same year to emigrate to the United States with all his family, where he set up home in Miami, and eventually, thanks to Nura's support, hard work and thrift, he even took up a partnership with his brother Fuad in a hotel at Homestead, Florida, next to the Everglades.

As for Sue and me, we returned to our little house in Putney and in due course told our respective families that we'd got married. Sue's parents were delighted with the news and immediately invited us to stay with them in Swaziland, which we went on to do. And that, I have to tell you, is the beginning of an even more remarkable story (see 'Gazing upon Sheba's Breasts').

Also by David Price Williams
and available from Markosia:

# LOOKING FOR APHRODITE

# GAZING UPON SHEBA'S BREASTS

# THE JOURNEY